Study Wise

A PROGRAM FOR MAXIMIZING YOUR LEARNING POTENTIAL

Lawrence J. Greene

PEARSON
Prentice
Hall

Upper Saddle River, New Jersey
Columbus, Ohio

Library of Congress Cataloging-in-Publication Data

Greene, Lawrence J.
    Study wise : a program for maximizing your learning potential / Lawrence J. Greene.
        p.   cm.
    Includes bibliographical references and index.
    ISBN 0-13-111521-9
    1. Study skills.   I. Title.

LB2395.G73 2004
371.3′028′1—dc21

2003049874

Vice President and Executive Publisher: Jeffery W. Johnston
Senior Acquisitions Editor: Sande Johnson
Assistant Editor: Cecilia Johnson
Editorial Assistant: Erin Anderson
Production Editor: Holcomb Hathaway
Design Coordinator: Diane C. Lorenzo
Cover Designer: Jason Moore
Cover Art: Jason Moore
Production Manager: Pamela D. Bennett
Director of Marketing: Ann Castel Davis
Marketing Manager: Christina Quadhamer
Compositor: Aerocraft Charter Art Service
Printer/Binder: Courier Kendallville, Inc.
Cover Printer: Phoenix Color Corp.

> **DEDICATION**
>
> *For my son, Joshua Ryan Greene*
> *Eight years old and running . . .*
> *everywhere. Your spirit and zest*
> *still enthrall me. I shall always*
> *be thankful for the joy you have*
> *brought into my life.*

Photographs from Corbis Images, Digital Graphics, Digital Vision, EyeWire, and PhotoDisc royalty-free resources.

Pearson Education Ltd.
Pearson Education Australia Pty. Limited
Pearson Education Singapore Pte. Ltd.
Pearson Education North Asia Ltd.
Pearson Education Canada, Ltd.
Pearson Educación de Mexico, S.A. de C.V.
Pearson Education–Japan
Pearson Education Malaysia Pte. Ltd.

10 9 8 7 6 5 4 3 2 1
ISBN 0-13-111521-9

BRIEF CONTENTS

Section Three

APPLYING STRATEGIC INTELLIGENCE   203

Getting What You Want, Need, and Deserve

CONTENTS

Section One

MAXIMIZING YOUR LEARNING POTENTIAL   1

Figuring Out How to Win in School

Section Two

DEVELOPING A SCHOOL SUCCESS SYSTEM   87

Learning How to Study More Productively

Turbocharging Your Reading Comprehension   113

Taking Notes from Textbooks   133

Taking Notes from Lectures   161

Taking Tests   173

Section Three

APPLYING STRATEGIC INTELLIGENCE   203

Getting What You Want, Need, and Deserve

12 Handling the Educational System and Your Finances   259

13 Decisions, Consequences, and Outcomes   279

Being Smart   307

PREFACE

This book has been a labor of love. During the three years that I spent writing it, I was determined not to lose sight of my objectives—namely, to help students derive maximum value from their college experience and to provide accessible, easy-to-learn, and easy-to-use methods for attaining academic and career success.

Whereas some students arrive at college prepared to deal with the formidable challenges that are part and parcel of being in school, other potentially capable students show up without the essential tools. Those who are better prepared have figured out how to learn actively, study effectively, write clearly, think critically, and plan astutely. In contrast, those who are less prepared typically find themselves adrift. These students are at risk academically and vocationally, and one doesn't need a crystal ball to predict the probable consequences. Unless they are methodically taught how to succeed in college, they are likely to tread water and underachieve.

I have designed this book to help college students acquire the basic and advanced study and thinking skills that will allow them to develop their full academic and vocational capabilities. The program provides step-by-step procedures for functioning more productively not only in school, but also in life. Students learn how to study efficiently and effectively, and they learn how to handle real-world challenges, deal with setbacks, solve problems, and avoid miscalculations that could be potentially life altering. In effect, they learn to think strategically, act smart, and study wise.

Two fundamental premises underlie this program. The first is that achievement hinges on deliberately and methodically defining goals, planning carefully, mastering essential skills, being motivated, and working diligently. The second is that conscientious students can easily assimilate a virtually fail-safe system for achieving academically and vocationally. Thirty years of experience teaching thousands of students have convinced me that these premises are valid. I trust that *Study Wise* hits the intended mark. If so, then the students using this book will also hit the mark. A perfect win–win situation!

Acknowledgments

I wish to thank the following reviewers, who offered constructive suggestions regarding how to improve this book: Linda Blair, Pellissippi State Technical Community College; Diane Eisenberg, California State University–Long Beach, Long Beach City College; Carey Harbin, Chabot College; Lewis Gray, Middle Tennessee State University; Kathy Masters, Arkansas State University; Jeanne Nishme, Pasadena City College; Laura Reynolds, Fayetteville Technical Community College; Linda Saumell, University of Miami; Gretchen Starks-Martin, St. Cloud State University; and Elizabeth Stewart, City College of San Francisco.

I would also like to express my sincere appreciation to Senior Acquisitions Editor Sande Johnson and Assistant Editor Cecilia Johnson of Prentice Hall. Their support, patience, professionalism, and steadfastness throughout the process of developing and refining this project were exemplary.

And finally, my eight-year-old son, Joshua, deserves heartfelt words of appreciation for letting me use "his" computer. Those many mornings when he allowed me to work while he turned over all the furniture in the living room and built forts were a blessing. He is clearly destined to become either an architect or a soldier.

Discover the Companion Website Accompanying This Book

THE PRENTICE HALL COMPANION WEBSITE: A VIRTUAL LEARNING ENVIRONMENT

Technology is a constantly growing and changing aspect of our field that is creating a need for content and resources. To address this emerging need, Prentice Hall has developed an online learning environment for students and professors alike—Companion Websites—to support our textbooks.

Companion Website

In creating a Companion Website, our goal is to build on and enhance what the textbook already offers. For this reason, the content for each user-friendly website is organized by chapter and provides the professor and student with a variety of meaningful resources.

For the Professor—

Every Companion Website integrates **Syllabus Manager**™, an online syllabus creation and management utility.

Syllabus Manager™ provides you, the instructor, with an easy, step-by-step process to create and revise syllabi, with direct links into Companion Website and other online content without having to learn HTML.

- Students may logon to your syllabus during any study session. All they need to know is the web address for the Companion Website and the password you've assigned to your syllabus.

- After you have created a syllabus using **Syllabus Manager**™, students may enter the syllabus for their course section from any point in the Companion Website.

- Clicking on a date, the student is shown the list of activities for the assignment. The activities for each assignment are linked directly to actual content, saving time for students.

- Adding assignments consists of clicking on the desired due date, then filling in the details of the assignment—name of the assignment, instructions, and whether or not it is a one-time or repeating assignment.

- In addition, links to other activities can be created easily. If the activity is online, a URL can be entered in the space provided, and it will be linked automatically in the final syllabus.

- Your completed syllabus is hosted on our servers, allowing convenient updates from any computer on the Internet. Changes you make to your syllabus are immediately available to your students at their next logon.

For the Student—

Common Companion Website features for students include:

- **Chapter Objectives** – Outline key concepts from the text.
- **Interactive Self-quizzes** – Complete with automatic grading that provide immediate feedback for students.

   After students submit their answers for the interactive self-quizzes, the Companion Website Results Reporter computes a percentage grade, provides a graphic representation of how many questions were answered correctly and incorrectly, and gives a question-by-question analysis of the quiz. Students are given the option to send their quiz to up to four email addresses (professor, teaching assistant, study partner, etc.).

- **Writing Research Papers Appendix** – Provides hints, steps, and strategies to help take students through the process of writing successful research papers using both library and Internet resources.
- **Reproducible Forms Appendix** – Includes worksheets from the text that can be downloaded and photocopied for students' personal use.
- **Message Board** – Virtual bulletin board to post or respond to questions or comments from a national audience.

To take advantage of the many available resources, please visit the *Study Wise: A Program for Maximizing Your Learning Potential* Companion Website at

www.prenhall.com/greene

INTRODUCTION

No one has to tell you that being in college isn't a walk in the park. Having to study, do homework, memorize information, take tests, do research, and write papers can be rough. This is true whether you've recently graduated from high school or whether you've been out in the real world working, earning a living, and perhaps supporting a family. Meeting your academic obligations can be a monumental challenge, and you can count on having to make many personal sacrifices if you want to do well in school.

The decision to go to college is often motivated by the hard facts of life: You realize that you must learn new skills to get a job, keep your job, or advance your career. Some students who enroll in school are motivated by an even more compelling reason: They are unemployed, or marginally employed, and they discover that they cannot find a rewarding job that has a future without acquiring specialized and marketable talents.

It's also possible that you've chosen to go to college because you have "unfinished business." You may have decided to get a job after graduating high school because you wanted to earn money right away. At the time, buying a car, getting your own apartment, and being independent were your priorities. Perhaps you found high school frustrating. If you struggled academically, you may have felt inadequate and demoralized. These negative school experiences may have caused you to conclude that you weren't smart and that going to college was not a realistic option. Instead, you decided to go to work and earn an income. You may have taken a job as a salesperson, a clerk, a telemarketer, a receptionist, or an apprentice electrician or plumber.

Your perspective is probably very different now. You realize that having a car, an apartment, and independence are not as fulfilling as you fantasized when you were 16 or 17. You discovered that a car means monthly payments, an apartment means rent that is due on the first of the month, and independence means bills that pile up on your desk. If you own a house, you face mortgage payments, property taxes, and repair and upkeep costs. You are confronted with a constant need for more money to meet your obligations, and you realize that the only way to get out of the hole is to increase your income. To do so, you must be able to sell your skills to an employer who is willing to pay top dollar. This is, of course, easier said than done. You now recognize that your career options are severely limited without salable skills, a degree, and self-confidence.

Whatever your reasons for going to school, you want to get value returned on your investment. Your time is valuable, and the money you spend for tuition is undoubtedly in short supply. You're making major sacrifices, and when you finally arrive at the end of the academic production line, you want to possess talents that can open doors to more pay and greater job satisfaction. At the same time, you're not naive. You realize that you face major challenges: paying tuition, commuting to class, giving up your free time to study, handling the obligations of the course work, taking exams, and juggling your schedule so that you can meet your other non-academic responsibilities. You want to get the job done as quickly and painlessly as possible. You want to get on with your life and reap the benefits of your efforts.

Many factors can make school especially stressful and unpleasant. If you have a history of academic difficulties in high school, you may have trouble understanding or recalling what you read in textbooks. You may not know how to identify important information when you study. You may have problems taking tests. You may not be able to take good notes in class or from textbooks. You may have trouble setting goals, establishing priorities, getting organized, solving problems, planning projects, or managing your time effectively.

If you're wrestling with any of these issues, you can breathe a sigh of relief. The program you are about to begin offers practical, easy-to-use methods for succeeding in college and for making your academic life easier, more productive, and more rewarding. The program systematically teaches you the "nuts and bolts" of school and life success. Once you master these methods, your grades and self-confidence cannot help but improve. You'll be able to learn more productively. You'll discover that *you can win the study game if you learn how to play the game effectively.* You'll also discover that *you can handle the challenges and obstacles you face in the arena outside of school.*

This comparison of studying productively and handling life's challenges effectively with playing a game is deliberate. Think about basketball or tennis. Before you can become a good player, you must learn the rules. You need a good coach. You have to practice and drill the fundamentals, and when you compete, you must have an effective game plan. But even this is not enough. You have to add three additional components: *You must define your objectives, focus on attaining your defined goals, and work your tail off!*

This book will be your coach. It will provide you with the skills and the practice you need to succeed in school. The program, however, is not a magical potion. **You must provide the effort and motivation.**

How the Program Works

This book is divided into three sections:

Section One   Maximizing Your Learning Potential: Figuring Out How to Win in School

Section Two   Developing a School Success System: Learning How to Study More Productively

Section Three   Applying Strategic Intelligence: Getting What You Want, Need, and Deserve

In Section One, you'll learn how create order and efficiency in your life and how to use your natural talents. Specifically, you will learn how to:

- identify and capitalize on your preferred learning modality
- identify and capitalize on your own distinctive type of intelligence
- record assignments accurately and efficiently
- manage time
- solve problems and deal with challenges
- get organized
- create a study environment that is conducive to learning

In Section Two, you'll learn how to handle your academic obligations. Specifically, you will learn to:

- think strategically
- read with better comprehension
- think critically
- identify important information
- take effective lecture and textbook notes
- memorize key data
- prepare for tests
- anticipate the questions that are likely to be asked on tests
- write powerful essays

In Section Three, you'll learn how to achieve your goals in school and in life. Specifically, you will learn how to:

- establish short- and long-term goals
- develop priorities
- develop an effective study plan
- handle the educational system
- deal with your finances
- anticipate potential consequences
- make difficult decisions
- use good judgment

If you are prepared to work diligently, you can master every one of the skills listed by the time you complete this program. Equipped with these capabilities, you will become a *power player in the study game.*

Being in school doesn't have to be unbearably stressful or frustrating. By learning how to *think strategically and study wisely,* you can overcome challenges, achieve academically, and expand your career options. This program will show you how!

Taking a Look in the Mirror: A Self-Assessment

Whenever you begin a new regimen, it makes sense to establish a baseline or starting point. If you begin a diet or exercise program, you should weigh yourself or record data about your current endurance (e.g., how many push-ups or barbell repetitions you can perform, amount of weight you can bench press, and how far you can jog or swim). You might even want to photograph yourself before you start the program and then photograph yourself at various stages of the training. This initial baseline information allows you to gauge your improvement as you proceed through the program.

The same procedure can be useful with this study enhancement program. Before you learn the methods in the book, take a few minutes to evaluate yourself and your past and current academic and study skills strengths and weaknesses. Your responses to the following questions and statements not only establish a baseline, they also provide you with insight into your current study habits, attitudes, and academic *modus operandi* (i.e., way of doing things). After you finish the program, you can, if you wish, complete this self-assessment again, and you will able to compare your initial responses with your subsequent responses.

PART 1 Performance Inventory

Evaluate your current capabilities and academic skills. Base your assessment on your performance in high school or, if you have already taken college courses, on your performance in these courses.

	Usually	Sometimes	Rarely
1. I understand what I read in my textbooks.	○	○	○
2. I can study and concentrate intensively for 30 minutes at a time.	○	○	○
3. I can recall information I read in textbooks.	○	○	○
4. I recall the information I hear in lectures.	○	○	○
5. I understand written instructions.	○	○	○
6. I'm motivated to do well in school.	○	○	○
7. I'm well-organized.	○	○	○
8. I'm in the habit of establishing short-term goals (e.g., get a B on the next English test).	○	○	○
9. I establish long-term goals (e.g., earn an A.A. degree in computer science within two years).	○	○	○
10. I have clearly defined career objectives.	○	○	○
11. I can develop effective strategies for attaining my personal goals.	○	○	○
12. I am in the habit of establishing priorities.	○	○	○
13. I bounce back from setbacks.	○	○	○
14. I learn from my mistakes and don't repeat them.	○	○	○
15. I have an effective system for recording assignments.	○	○	○
16. I plan ahead.			
17. I manage my time effectively.	○	○	○
18. I make up a schedule and keep to it.	○	○	○
19. I intentionally limit distractions when I study.	○	○	○
20. I can identify important information when studying.	○	○	○

	Usually	Sometimes	Rarely
21. I'm committed to spending sufficient time studying so that I can get good grades.	○	○	○
22. I can recall key information when I take a test.	○	○	○
23. I am confident and calm when taking tests.	○	○	○
24. I know how to take good notes in class.	○	○	○
25. I know how to take good notes from textbooks.	○	○	○
26. I can figure out what my instructors are likely to ask on tests.	○	○	○
27. I'm in the habit of carefully checking over my work to find errors.	○	○	○
28. I have confidence in my academic skills.	○	○	○
29. I see myself as being capable and successful in school.	○	○	○

Interpreting your responses: If you've marked "rarely" for more than three statements or if the majority of your responses are "sometimes," you will undoubtedly benefit from this program. During the next months, you're going to acquire a range of powerful study, thinking, planning, and organizational tools. To pinpoint your strengths and weaknesses, it is necessary for you to evaluate your current skills with even greater precision. As previously explained, this information will serve as a baseline to help you gauge your improvement.

PART 2 Academic History

Provide the following information about your performance. If you have just returned to school and haven't received any grades, enter the grades you received during your last year of school, assuming you can remember them.

Subject: _____	Grade: _____
Subject: _____	Grade: _____
Subject: _____	Grade: _____
Subject: _____	Grade: _____
Subject: _____	Grade: _____
Subject: _____	Grade: _____

How do you rate your previous high school or college academic performance?

1	2	3	4	5	6	7	8	9	10
poor				fair				good	

How pleased are you with your previous high school or college academic performance?

1	2	3	4	5	6	7	8	9	10
not pleased			somewhat pleased				very pleased		

PART 3 Self-Appraisal

In this section, assess your current attitudes and performance. This self-assessment provides information about how you currently perceive yourself.

How do you evaluate yourself in the following areas?

Overall ability:

Overall effort in school:

Your attitude about school:

Overall quality of school work:

Overall quality of homework (e.g., reports, lab notebooks):

Quality of your planning skills (scheduling time to complete work):

Your performance in the workplace (if you have or have had a job):

Your problem-solving skills:

Your ability to handle crises:

Your ability to handle disappointments, setbacks, and failures:

Your potential to be successful in school:

poor   average   good

Your potential to be successful in life:

poor   average   good

Your overall self-confidence:

poor   average   good

Your self-respect:

poor   average   good

PART 4 Personal Objectives

Indicate your personal goals for this study skills–life skills course.
Check the areas in which you want to enhance your capabilities:

- ○ Using vocabulary effectively
- ○ Memorizing information
- ○ Identifying important information
- ○ Understanding information in textbooks
- ○ Understanding information in class (e.g., lectures, discussions)
- ○ Completing homework within a reasonable amount of time
- ○ Writing papers and reports
- ○ Studying for tests
- ○ Organizing schoolwork
- ○ Budgeting time
- ○ Planning ahead
- ○ Improving concentration
- ○ Taking notes in class
- ○ Taking notes from textbooks
- ○ Participating effectively in class discussions
- ○ Handling anxiety
- ○ Figuring out what is likely to be asked on a test
- ○ Improving analytical thinking
- ○ Developing problem-solving skills
- ○ Improving performance on multiple-choice and short-answer tests
- ○ Improving performance on essay tests
- ○ Being motivated
- ○ Improving academic self-confidence
- ○ Improving grades

List the specific target grades you want to receive in the next semester (be realistic!):

Subject: _____   Grade: _____

Subject: _____   Grade: _____

Subject: _____   Grade: _____

Subject: _____   Grade: _____

Subject: _____   Grade: _____

Subject: _____   Grade: _____

PART 5 Your *Modus Operandi* (Way of Doing Things)

If are currently attending school, please answer the following questions. If you have just started school, use your last semester in school as a reference point.

YES NO

○ ○ Do you bring home the materials you need to do your homework?

○ ○ Do you write down your assignments every day?

○ ○ Do you study while listening to music or watching TV?

○ ○ Do you study with a lot of interruptions?

○ ○ Do you have a written weekly study schedule that you follow?

○ ○ Do you forget to do or hand in important assignments?

○ ○ Do you submit late assignments?

○ ○ Do you carefully proofread your work?

○ ○ Do you analyze the types of tests your instructors give and the types of questions they ask on tests?

○ ○ Do you become overwhelmed by difficult challenges and complex assignments?

○ ○ Do you procrastinate?

○ ○ Do you make an effort to do your best work in school?

○ ○ Do you believe you're doing enough studying?

○ ○ Are you satisfied with your current study skills?

How much time do you spend doing homework on a typical school night?

_____

Do you believe you are spending adequate time studying?

○ yes   ○ no   ○ not sure

Describe how you react when you experience a failure or setback.

_____

_____

_____

_____

_____

_____

Describe how you react when you make a mistake.

_____

_____

_____

_____

_____

_____

Summing Up

As initially stated, the objective for this self-assessment is to help you acquire insights into your present *modus operandi* (i.e., behavior, attitudes, and style). These insights will allow you to define areas in which you want to make improvement.

For the time being, put aside any anxieties you might have about your schoolwork. You're about to learn a broad range of powerful thinking and study skills, and you'll have repeated opportunities to practice and master these skills. If you're willing to work and apply the methods, your academic performance in college and your self-confidence should improve significantly.

Let's get started.

ONE

Maximizing Your Learning Potential

FIGURING OUT HOW TO WIN IN SCHOOL

LEARNING STYLES AND MULTIPLE INTELLIGENCES

OBJECTIVES

- Identifying your dominant learning style
- Linking learning styles and career choices
- Using your natural and preferred learning modality to improve school performance
- Understanding and using your distinctive intelligence

Using Your Natural Talents

Rebecca was feeling the general anxiety that she often experienced when faced with an important exam. She had never liked science when she was in high school, and now she was confronted with having to prepare for what was certain to be a very difficult college earth science midterm. To make matters worse, her instructor had a reputation for giving really tricky tests.

As an art major, Rebecca felt intimidated by the demands of a science class. There were so many concepts to understand and details to memorize, and the required labs seemed unbearable. Who wants to spend hours in a lab studying rocks and outcroppings when you could be in a studio painting? Despite her obvious preference for art classes, Rebecca was keenly aware that she needed this course to fulfill the general science requirements for her degree.

After graduating, Rebecca's goal was to get a job in a first-class art gallery. She wanted to find an apartment and make one room into a small studio where she could paint in her free time. She planned on working for a few years to earn some money, and then she wanted to continue her education at the state university, earning a B.F.A. (a bachelor's degree in fine art), a master's degree in art education, and a high school teaching credential. This plan would allow her to teach, have a good income, and continue to paint.

The immediate challenge Rebecca faced was to get a decent grade on the upcoming midterm. Her plan was simple: She would use her natural visual skills to help her understand and recall the information.

When she had difficulty with a course in high school, Rebecca's guidance counselor recommended that she complete a learning styles inventory. The inventory indicated that Rebecca's preferred learning modalities were visual and tactile–kinesthetic and that she had a natural talent for remembering formulas, definitions, and facts if she creatively represented information in diagrams, drawings, and charts. By using her hand to draw (**a tactile–kinesthetic procedure**) and her eyes to recall (**a visual procedure**), she could capitalize on these natural talents. This method worked wonderfully in high school, and although she hadn't enjoyed her science, math, and government classes, she never received a grade lower than a B–. To her utter amazement, she even received an A– in a biology course her junior year.

Armed with this insight about her preferred learning style and natural strengths and encouraged by her positive experiences using the visual and tactile–kinesthetic modalities to prepare for tests in high school, Rebecca was confident that she could use the same strategy in college. There was more to learn, of course, but her system would make it much easier for her to understand and remember the information.

As she reviewed the six textbook chapters covered by the midterm, she used colored felt markers and a large pad of paper to draw diagrams and artistic representations of the data. She carefully labeled her diagrams and wrote terms and definitions in different colors. Proceeding through each chapter, she carefully studied the photos, tables, and graphs in her book, and she drew her own graphics to highlight and explain the important facts and concepts used in the textbook and in her notes. She then closed her eyes and "saw" in her mind the diagrams and the facts and concepts. It was as if she had imprinted the information on a roll of film. Despite the "dryness" of the information, she found that she could recall the data when she quizzed herself.

Rebecca was certain that she could pass the earth science exam and perhaps even get a B–. She was wrong. When the exam was returned, her grade was 84. She had gotten a solid B.

zooming in on the issues

Analyzing One Student's Study Strategy

A detailed examination of a problem or challenge can produce important insights. Your lens (i.e., your eyes and your mind) zooms in and reveals details that affect the outcome.

Given Rebecca's insight into her natural learning strengths, rate her study plan for the midterm.

1	2	3	4	5	6	7	8	9	10

not smart   fairly smart   very smart

Why did you make this assessment? _____

_____

_____

Evaluate Rebecca in the following areas:

Her motivation.

1	2	3	4	5	6	7	8	9	10

poor   fair   excellent

Her attitude.

1	2	3	4	5	6	7	8	9	10

poor   fair   excellent

Her effort.

1	2	3	4	5	6	7	8	9	10

poor   fair   excellent

Rebecca has developed a very specific plan for her life (or at least for the next six or seven years). Taking into consideration her interests and talents, evaluate the wisdom of her life plan.

1	2	3	4	5	6	7	8	9	10

not smart   fairly smart   very smart

Why did you make this assessment? _____

_____

_____

Drawing a Conclusion from the Evidence

In this program, you will use the "case method" to examine key issues and master analytical-thinking procedures. Developed and refined at the Harvard Business School, this instructional method is now regularly used at the finest universities to train students in a wide range of academic disciplines, including law and medicine.

By methodically analyzing a particular situation or "case," you learn how to:

- identify important information
- evaluate decisions
- solve problems
- arrive at conclusions
- develop strategies
- make valid generalizations
- apply insights
- avoid predicaments

The case method requires that you learn how to apply *inductive reasoning*. This type of reasoning differs from the other common form of logical thinking, called *deductive reasoning*. Let's take a few moments to differentiate these two types of logic.

DEDUCTIVE REASONING

Deductive method: *A reasoning procedure in which a statement is corroborated (supported) by facts and data.* The position is sustained by reasoning from the general (the stated position) to the specific (supporting evidence). The method is best visualized as a triangle—the position statement represents the point of the triangle and the supporting data are stacked in descending layers below and form the base.

If an automotive engineer contends that *"heavy cars are significantly safer than light cars,"* she is expected to back up this statement with supporting research data and concrete facts. For example, the supporting evidence might include a study of head-on collisions that occurred in 1999: 11,000 fatalities or serious injuries resulted when the vehicles weighed less than 2,000 pounds, and 8,500 fatalities or serious injuries resulted when the vehicles weighed more than 2,000 pounds. Without this corroborating evidence, the engineer's statement about the greater risks associated with lighter cars lacks credibility and is subject to challenge. The process of backing up a position (or a point) with corroborating evidence is an example of the **deductive method** of reasoning.

INDUCTIVE REASONING

When information in the form of facts and data is presented and a conclusion is drawn from this information, the reasoning process is described as the **inductive method** of reasoning. Using this method, the automotive engineer who wants to substantiate her argument about car safety presents relevant facts and statistics that document the enhanced safety of the heavier models in head-on collisions. Based on the facts she presents, she then reaches a logical and ideally irrefutable conclusion; namely, that *"heavy cars are safer than light cars."* (Methods for applying deductive and inductive reasoning when writing essays are described in Chapter 7.)

Position statement

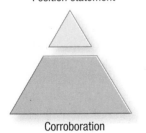

Corroboration

APPLYING THE INDUCTIVE METHOD

After reading about the challenge that Rebecca faced (i.e., the "case") and her way of handling this challenge, you should be able to draw a conclusion from the information presented in the story. For example, you know that Rebecca's high school counselor helped her identify her learning strengths and preferences, and you know that Rebecca capitalized on this information to improve her grades. You also know that Rebecca is planning to use these insights about her preferences when she studies for the earth science midterm.

It's time to draw a conclusion from the evidence. Using the *inductive method*, express in a well-crafted sentence what you have concluded. *Remember:* You are summarizing the **point** of the story *that is represented by the inverted tip of the triangle.*

The point of Rebecca's story: _____

_____

_____

_____

_____

Inductive method: *A reasoning procedure in which a conclusion is derived from presented data.* The position is sustained by reasoning from the specific (i.e., the facts) to the general (i.e., the logical conclusion). This method might be visualized as an inverted triangle with presented information stacked in descending layers that lead to the point.

Information

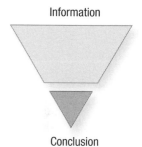

Conclusion

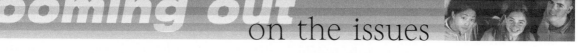

zooming out on the issues

Different Learning Styles and Preferences

Zoom lenses can zoom in on details, but they are also capable of other functions. They can zoom out and reveal the larger picture. By examining issues from afar, you have a broader perspective, and you can often make valid generalizations about how the parts of the picture blend together and form the whole. A close-up (or tight shot) of a flower might reveal the veins and pollen on the petals of the flower. A long-range perspective showing all of the flowers on a hillside might disclose the stunning designs produced by the entire field of flowers. The sum of the parts—that is, the colors, shapes, and shadows of the individual flowers—melds into a broad landscape. Both perspectives—the zoomed-in close-up and zoomed-out long-range view—can produce key insights.

After analyzing the introductory case study, you should realize that students do not all learn in the same way. Students who think smart identify and capitalize on their natural learning strengths. Rebecca is a case in point. She is a pragmatist (someone who is realistic, logical, and practical). Once she discovered how she learned best, she deliberately used this insight to her advantage, especially when studying material that did not particularly interest her.

The differences in the way people learn can usually be traced to inborn abilities and natural aptitudes and talents. **Tactile learners** learn best by handling materials and using their hands to perform concrete procedures. They prefer to build a model of something rather than study a picture or read a description in a book. **Kinesthetic learners** learn best through body movement and physical activities. They prefer to practice plays on the basketball court rather than study them on a chalkboard. Other students, who are both tactile and kinesthetic, learn best by combining hands-on experience with movement. For example, most car mechanics are **tactile–kinesthetic learners** who learn about how engines work and how to fix them by using their hands. They may only require one experience with disassembling and reassembling an engine to understand how the pieces fit together. By reaching under, inside, and around the motor, they can "feel" whether a part is worn, missing, broken, or improperly seated. Of course, mechanics must also use their eyes to inspect parts, scan diagnostic equipment, and study diagrams, but many of their skills are acquired through hands-on trial and error learning.

The same principle of using natural talent applies in athletics. Gifted basketball players are **visual, kinesthetic,** and **tactile learners.** Their eyes scan the other players on offense and defense and tell them when to pass, surge toward the basket for a lay-up, shoot a jump shot, reach in and steal the ball, or block a shot. A kinesthetic sense within their bodies tells them how to jump, twist, and contort in order to execute the play, and their hands use a tactile ability to control the ball as they dribble, shoot, or reach in for a steal.

Professional musicians are typically **auditory, visual,** and **kinesthetic learners.** Usually, they need to hear a joke or the words and melody to a song only once to remember the material. Many musicians can also see the musical notes in their mind (a visual ability), and they of course use tactile–kinesthetic talents to play their instruments.

Most professional writers are **combined auditory** and **visual learners.** They can sense when a sentence should be revised by the way the words sound when read silently or recited aloud. They can also sense when the cadence and rhythm of a paragraph are "off," and they can perceive when their writing is unclear or labored. They can also recognize when their writing should be revised by the way the words and sentences *look* on the page.

Students who identify their learning strengths and learning preferences and who use their natural abilities are operating pragmatically and strategically. Recognizing that they must *see* information to understand and remember it, smart-thinking *visual learners* write down key data and read it over several times. They watch a class demonstration intently and imprint the procedures and steps in their mind, in much the same way a camcorder records visual images. Before hooking up a new computer, they carefully read the instructions and examine the illustrations. (If they also have natural *kinesthetic abilities,* they draw diagrams and pictures to help them understand and remember information, as Rebecca did in the introductory case study.)

Smart-thinking *auditory learners* recognize that they must *hear* information in order to understand and remember it. They recite information aloud and listen carefully to what is being said in class, in much the same way as a CD burner imprints auditory information on a disk. They benefit from class discussions, and they like to hear directions as opposed to reading or seeing them. As they assemble a stereo system, rather than read the instructions themselves, they may ask a friend to read them aloud as they work.

Smart-thinking *tactile–kinesthetic learners* realize that they must *touch, hold,* and *feel* in order to understand and recall information. Preferring to work with concrete materials they can handle, they tangibly represent what they are learning whenever possible (as Rebecca did in the case study). In a chemistry class, they might manipulate a three-dimensional model of a nucleus surrounded by revolving electrons to comprehend the principles. In an anatomy class, they use

Primary Learning Modalities

Visual learners. These individuals prefer to get everything down on paper so they can visually "digest" what they've recorded. They prefer to assimilate information through their eyes—it's easier for them to understand and recall what they read in their notes and textbooks than what they hear.

Auditory learners. These individuals prefer to listen and not be distracted by having to write down information. They would rather assimilate data through their ears because it's easier to understand and recall what they hear.

Kinesthetic learners. These individuals learn best through movement and by involving themselves in meaningful physical activities. They prefer to learn by doing instead of reading about it or hearing directions.

Tactile learners. These individuals learn best through feel and touch and by manipulating objects and parts. It's easier for them to understand and recall through hands-on contact.

Experiential learners. These individuals learn best by doing something and observing and assessing how things turn out. It's easier for them to understand and recall what they've directly experienced through personal trial and error as opposed to reading a book or listening to a lecture. Mechanics, inventors, gardeners, and designers are primary examples of this type of learner. Experiential learners require practice and hands-on application in order to achieve mastery.

Olfactory–gustatory learners. These individuals learn best by smell and taste (e.g., chefs, bakers, tea tasters, wine connoisseurs, perfume developers). They prefer to deal with aromas and flavors, and they can better understand, recall, and analyze information experienced through taste and smell.

their hands to feel the way the bones of a skeleton are connected. They may also build a bookcase by touch, without looking at the instructions.

Learning Modalities and Academic Achievement

Two of the key characteristics that distinguish achieving students from underachieving students are their ability to figure out how to capitalize on their natural strengths and their ability to compensate successfully for their deficits and limitations. Rather than resign themselves to having a poor visual memory when they have to assimilate written material from their textbooks and notes, these students deliberately develop practical compensatory techniques that allow them to derive maximum benefit from their study time. They not only take advantage of their dominant learning strengths, but they also strategically tailor their study methods to the demands of the academic content. If they are required to memorize many facts *written* in a textbook, and if visual memory is not their learning strength, they devise a practical and effective alternative method for getting the job done. For example, a student who prefers to assimilate information using the auditory modality may have to learn 20 formulas for a final chemistry exam. Recognizing her learning preference, she may use her auditory memory and repeatedly recite the information aloud. At the same time, she may realize that using this auditory strategy exclusively is insufficient, and she may conclude that to learn the formulas, she also has to use visual memory methods (*Please note:* Specific techniques for improving visual memory skills are examined in Chapter 9). The same principle applies in sports. A professional baseball player may be an excellent power hitter, but may only be a mediocre fielder. He may prefer batting to fielding, but he realizes that he must improve his fielding to avoid being used exclusively as a "pinch hitter" and spending most of his time sitting on the bench.

Some students have no difficulty using multiple modalities when studying. Often described as "natural students," they use whatever works best in each academic situation, and they find it relatively easy to understand and recall what they see, hear, and learn from hands-on (tactile–kinesthetic) experiences. Most students, however, have one or perhaps two dominant learning modalities. Those who think smart intentionally develop *alternative learning strategies* that they use when a particular learning situation demands.

USING WHAT WORKS

Successful students are prepared to use the learning modality that is best suited to the specific material that they are studying. For example, a smart olfactory–gustatory learner enrolled in a culinary program realizes that he must also be able to *read* a recipe and *visualize* the presentation of the food.

A smart criminal justice major may be a visual learner, but she understands that she must be able to assimilate auditory information in class and during discussions. She must also be able to *hear* whether the essay she is writing *sounds good* when she reads it to herself.

A learning strategy that works when studying certain material may prove disastrous when studying other material. Unless an auditory learner also possesses tactile–kinesthetic learning abilities, it would probably be ill-advised for her to plan on becoming an auto mechanic. Nor would it be advisable for a tactile–kinesthetic learner to major in French or English unless he also possesses decent auditory and visual learning abilities. Smart students recognize the facts of life and do everything possible to "stack the deck" by utilizing their natural talents.

Certain learning situations may require using modalities that may not be natural or preferred. For example, you may be an auditory learner who is preparing for a final chemistry exam. You may do everything possible to capitalize on the auditory modality when studying (e.g., reciting key information aloud, using a cassette recorder, and giving oral "lectures" about the material to an imaginary class). Despite these efforts, you may still have to memorize a great deal of visual information such as chemical symbols, definitions, and facts from your textbook and class notes. To get a good grade on the exam, you may conclude that you must also acquire techniques for using the visual modality. This type of strategic thinking can make the difference between a good grade and a mediocre or poor grade.

Before beginning the academic components of this program, take a few moments to identify your own preferred learning style and learning modality or modalities. The statements found in the following inventory will help you uncover how you learn best, and this insight will permit you to derive maximum benefit from your study time.

Identifying Your Preferred and/or Dominant Learning Modality Inventory

	Yes	No	Generally	Not Sure
1. I learn most effectively by reading material in textbooks, textbook notes, and lecture notes.	○	○	○	○
2. I can recall and understand information best when I see it.	○	○	○	○
3. A visual presentation, such as a science experiment in class, helps me assimilate and master what's being taught.	○	○	○	○
4. I can recall data more easily when it is represented in diagrams, graphs, charts, and pictures.	○	○	○	○
5. Visually represented information stimulates my interest, motivation, and active involvement in what I am learning.	○	○	○	○
6. I learn most effectively by listening to lectures, audiotapes, and verbal explanations.	○	○	○	○
7. I can recall and understand information best when I hear it.	○	○	○	○
8. Class discussions help me assimilate and master what's being taught.	○	○	○	○
9. I can remember jokes and the words in songs when I hear them.	○	○	○	○
10. Information that I listen to stimulates my interest, motivation, and active involvement in what I am learning.	○	○	○	○
11. I learn most effectively when activities are physical.	○	○	○	○
12. I can recall and understand information best when I am moving around concrete materials.	○	○	○	○
13. Doing an experiment in a lab, drawing a picture, plotting a graph, or building a model to represent information helps me comprehend what's being taught.	○	○	○	○
14. I can learn the steps to a dance or the moves on the court or the playing field quickly if I practice them once.	○	○	○	○
15. Physical activities stimulate my interest, motivation, and active involvement in what I am learning.	○	○	○	○
16. I learn most effectively when I am touching, holding, or manipulating what I have to learn.	○	○	○	○
17. I can construct something without instructions.	○	○	○	○
18. I can understand and recall how things work through hands-on experience.	○	○	○	○
19. I enjoy mechanical projects, and I can disassemble and reassemble objects with little difficulty.	○	○	○	○
20. Hands-on activities stimulate my interest, motivation, and active involvement in what I am learning.	○	○	○	○
21. I prefer to learn through trial and error.	○	○	○	○
22. I learn best by figuring out how to do something on my own.	○	○	○	○
23. I prefer not to follow formal instructions.	○	○	○	○
24. If I make a mistake, I learn from the mistake and make appropriate adjustments so that I can get it right the next time.	○	○	○	○
25. I prefer to work independently, at my own pace, and without supervision.	○	○	○	○

INTERPRETING THE SURVEY

Statements 1–5: These statements relate to visual learning. If you have responded primarily "Yes" or "Generally," your learning preference is most likely visual.

Statements 6–10: These statements relate to auditory learning. If you have responded primarily "Yes" or "Generally," your learning preference is most likely auditory.

Statements 11–15: These statements relate to kinesthetic learning. If you have responded primarily "Yes" or "Generally," your learning preference is most likely kinesthetic.

Statements 16–20: These statements relate to tactile learning. If you have responded primarily "Yes" or "Generally," your learning preference is most likely tactile.

Statements 21–25: These statements relate to experiential learning. If you have responded primarily "Yes" or "Generally," your learning preference is most likely experiential.

- Based on your responses to the survey statements, indicate your primary preferred (or most natural) learning modality: _____

- Five primary learning modalities are described. Prioritize the modalities in the order of your personal preference. Begin with the most preferred and descend to the least preferred.

  1. _____   4. _____

  2. _____   5. _____

  3. _____

- If specific material requires you to combine modalities to master the content and derive maximum benefit from your study time, what would be your *preferred personal combination?*
  - ○ visual–auditory
  - ○ visual–tactile
  - ○ visual–kinesthetic
  - ○ auditory–visual
  - ○ auditory–tactile
  - ○ auditory–kinesthetic
  - ○ tactile–kinesthetic

Just as students have different preferred learning styles, instructors have preferred *teaching styles.* Many instructors unconsciously teach the way they learn best. Some lecture. Others emphasize class discussions and small cooperative learning groups. Others incorporate demonstrations and experiments. If an instructor is visually oriented and stresses graphs, diagrams, and many facts that you are expected to include in your class notes and assimilate from your textbook, you must adjust your learning strategy accordingly. Of course, you can and should devise creative ways to capitalize on your own preferred learning modality, but you must also figure out a strategy for learning visually loaded content. This may require that you deliberately improve your visual memory skills. Successful students accommodate themselves to the realities of the situation.

UTILIZING MULTIPLE LEARNING MODALITIES

Engineering. A person with a natural mechanical aptitude who is studying to be a mechanical engineer would probably master the course content very differently from a student who is studying Spanish. A mechanical or electrical engineering student relies on the *visual modality* to *see* how an engine is constructed in a diagram. He also uses this modality when studying notes and textbooks. If he is working with materials in a shop or lab, he uses the *kinesthetic–tactile* or *tactile modality—feeling* how the parts fit together. As he listens to a lecture or a description, he avails himself of the *auditory modality.* He also learns using the *experiential modality* when he *practices* disassembling and assembling equipment in the shop. Although the electrical engineer is using four overlapping learning modalities, his natural learning modality preference might be visual or kinesthetic–tactile. His unconscious choice of words often reveals his preference. If he is fixing a car, he might say, "This spring-loaded shaft *feels* (if he is a kinesthetic–tactile learner) or *looks* (if he is a visual learner) like it's inserted and seated properly." He might also remark, "According to the diagram, this part *looks* like it's assembled correctly." Although listening to verbal instructions and explanations may be challenging, he must be able to assimilate verbal information and function in the auditory modality to succeed in school.

Foreign languages. A successful student majoring in Spanish may be a natural visual learner and may rely primarily on this modality to learn the conjugations, grammar, vocabulary, and idioms printed in her textbook. She might write information on index cards and reread the material until she masters it. At the same time, she also recognizes the value of using the auditory modality to assimilate proper pronunciation, idiomatic constructions, conjugations, vocabulary, and dialogues. Although using her natural learning talents and preferred learning modality (i.e., visual) clearly makes sense, she realizes that auditory learning is beneficial when mastering specific skills. If she is clever, she learns how to use this modality to the greatest advantage. She might listen to audiotapes and recite vocabulary, dialogues, idiomatic expressions, and conjugations aloud, using the auditory modality to "record" the material. She may practice speaking Spanish with other students or native speakers, again capitalizing on the auditory modality. Using multiple modalities is the hallmark of strategic thinking and learning.

Sciences/history. A successful biology student, learning biology phyla (classifications), who is a *visual learner* might write the phyla on index cards and read them over and over, taking advantage of her learning modality preference. If she's primarily an *auditory learner*, she will recite the phyla aloud or record them on a cassette recorder and play them back while she's eating, commuting, or even sleeping. As previously mentioned, a supplemental learning method that the auditory learner might use involves delivering a biology lecture to an imaginary class. She will visualize herself presenting the material and hear herself verbalizing the content. *This visualizing–verbalizing procedure can be a powerful reinforcement for learning and a major confidence builder.* The student might further reinforce mastery of the material by using *both* the auditory and visual modalities. She could recite the phyla aloud *and* write them on index cards. She might also decide to study with a classmate. During these sessions, they could recite and write the phyla (thus, capitalizing on the auditory, visual, and tactile–kinesthetic modalities). By prompting and quizzing each other, they further enhance and reinforce mastery.

Careers That Integrate Overlapping Learning Modalities

Surgeon: visual, kinesthetic–tactile, auditory, experiential*

Graphic artist: visual, kinesthetic–tactile, experiential

Musician: auditory, visual, experiential

Electrician: visual, kinesthetic–tactile, experiential

Lawyer: visual, auditory, experiential

Psychologist: visual, auditory, experiential

Photographer: visual, kinesthetic–tactile, experiential

Chef: kinesthetic–tactile, olfactory, experiential

Contractor: kinesthetic–tactile, visual, experiential

Sculptor: kinesthetic–tactile, visual, experiential

Teacher: visual, auditory, kinesthetic–tactile, experiential

Dancer: kinesthetic–tactile, visual, auditory, experiential

Engineer: visual, auditory, kinesthetic–tactile, experiential

Pilot: visual, auditory, kinesthetic–tactile, experiential

Choose three of the occupations listed and briefly explain why the described learning modalities are likely to be involved in becoming competent in the field.

CAREER	REASONS FOR USING THE DESCRIBED LEARNING MODALITIES
_____	_____
	_____
	_____
	_____
	_____
_____	_____
	_____
	_____
	_____
	_____
_____	_____
	_____
	_____
	_____

---

* Experiential learning is vital to acquiring the skills associated with all of these vocations and is a key component in virtually all skill mastery.

ADDITIONAL CLUES ABOUT YOUR PREFERRED LEARNING MODALITY

After completing the Preferred Learning Modality Inventory and reviewing the material, you should have a better understanding of how you learn best. If you're not sure, other clues can be very revealing about your learning style.

Another practical way to identify how you learn best is to *monitor the vocabulary you use to express yourself.* For example, if you tend to say, "It *feels* right," this often signals that you are primarily a *tactile learner.* If you tend to say, "I *hear* you" or "It *sounds* right," this often signals that you're primarily an *auditory learner.* If you tend to say, "I *see* what you mean" or "It *looks* right," this often signals that you're primarily a *visual* learner.

You can also confirm your preferred modality and learning strengths by objectively observing your learning *modus operandi.* If your inclination is to reach out and manipulate a model of a skeletal hand in a physiology class, you can reasonably conclude that you are probably a *kinesthetic–tactile learner.* If your inclination is to look closely and inspect the model, you can reasonably conclude that you are probably a *visual learner.* If your inclination is to listen closely to what the instructor is describing, you are probably an *auditory learner.* These learning preferences will manifest themselves in specific, identifiable learning strengths.

Possibility #1: You're a visual learner. As a visual learner, you have a great advantage when it comes to recalling data written in textbooks and notes because you can remember the written material with relative ease. This talent is especially useful in courses such as history that often emphasize the recall of many facts. Because you can *"see"* the correct spelling of words in your mind, you are also probably a good speller. Most likely, you can catch many misspelled words because "the word just doesn't *look* right." You can also probably recall telephone numbers written in an appointment book and information that you read in a newspaper or on a billboard. You can use your visual skills to imprint and retrieve the information in diagrams and graphs.

Possibility #2: You're an auditory learner. As an auditory learner, you do well in conversation-oriented foreign language classes because you can recall and assimilate spoken dialogues, idiomatic expressions, vocabulary, and verb conjugations. You have a natural facility for comprehending and remembering verbal information and for integrating this information into your own communication. You enjoy class discussions. You recall data best by "recording" mental "sound tapes" that contain vocalized and subvocalized (whispered) word pictures, oral instructions, and verbal explanations. You tend to remember the words to songs and the content of radio interviews. You also probably have good oral communication skills and use your auditory skills when you write. When a sentence or a paragraph doesn't *sound* right, you edit and revise the material until the problem is fixed. You prefer to master course content by vocalizing or subvocalizing the data. If you are strategic, you also deliberately develop your visual memory skills to use in courses that require the mastery of a great deal of visually loaded information such as science or math formulas and historical dates.

Possibility #3: You're a kinesthetic–tactile learner. As a kinesthetic–tactile learner, you have an advantage when a course emphasizes the handling of concrete materials. Dissections in a biology lab, experiments in a chemistry or physics lab, hands-on applications in a technology or mechanics course, and classification activities in an earth science or geology course represent content that favors the kinesthetic–tactile learner. You try to translate information into concrete terms whenever possible. For example, you might create two- and three-dimensional models of what you are being asked to learn. Although intentionally making information as concrete as possible is clearly a well-conceived learning strategy, you must also develop skills in other learning modalities if you are going to be successful in most academic programs.

Possibility #4: You're an experiential learner. All learning is enhanced by application and experiential opportunities. As an experiential learner, you seek out hands-on opportunities. You tend to thrive in physical science, technology, and mechanical engineering classes that involve working in a lab or sitting (or standing) at a workbench. You attempt to discover or invent practical applications for written or spoken information. For example, you do experiments to help you understand, associate, and recall the concepts involved in a principle of physics. At the same time, you realize that to succeed academically, you must be prepared to use other learning modalities when appropriate. The experiential learner who wants to be an engineer must also be able to understand, recall, and apply textbook and class lecture information.

(*Please note:* Because the *olfactory–gustatory learning modality* has highly specialized vocational applications that are more relevant to a trade school curriculum than an academic curriculum, this modality is not examined in this section.)

POWERHOUSE THINKING

Steps for Maximizing Your Learning Effectiveness

- Identify what you must learn to get a good grade in each course and create a practical plan to achieve this objective.
- Identify your preferred learning modality and intentionally capitalize on your natural abilities and preferences.
- Identify material that can best be learned using another modality (e.g., the visual modality for memorizing formulas).
- Compensate for your deficits by learning and utilizing innovative and effective alternative study methods.
- Make tactical adjustments in your study procedures if they aren't producing positive payoffs.

The more you understand about your personal learning "fingerprint," the more likely you will be able to use this information to improve your academic performance. Keep your preferred learning style in mind as you begin the academic components of this program. Be creative in capitalizing on your strengths and structure opportunities to profit from deliberately using your natural talents.

Multiple Intelligences

Your ability to recognize, understand, and capitalize on your dominant or preferred learning modality clearly plays a key role in maximizing your learning potential. Understanding your own intelligence plays an equally important role in deriving full benefit from your college education. This insight can also help you select a career that takes full advantage of your natural abilities.

A Harvard professor named Howard Gardner recognized the inherent limitations of the traditional definitions of intelligence. In his critically acclaimed book *Frames of Mind*, he contends that there are different types of intelligence that are not assessed by standard IQ tests. Using the term *multiple intelligences* to describe this expanded definition of intelligence, he has identified eight major areas in which intelligence may express itself.

Verbal–linguistic intelligence.   Students who possess this type of intelligence have highly developed auditory and verbal communication skills. They rely on spoken language to help them comprehend and retain information. Thinking in words rather than pictures, these students imprint verbally communicated data in their mind. Preferring to listen and talk about issues, they do well in courses that have class discussions, verbal presentations by students, cooperative study groups, debates, and writing assignments. Because of their natural linguistic abilities, they generally delight in recounting stories, telling jokes, and expressing their insights and conclusions. Students who recognize and capitalize on their verbal–linguistic intelligence are likely to gravitate to careers in the following areas: journalism, TV and radio news and commentary, writing, law, acting, teaching, and politics.

Visual–spatial intelligence.   Students who possess this type of intelligence form graphic mental images (i.e., pictures) and use these images to imprint, comprehend, and retain information. They can *see* in their mind what they are learning and prefer to learn by looking at books, charts, demonstrations, videos, maps, and movies. They do better in courses in which they are expected to recall data written in their textbooks and notes. Students who recognize and capitalize on their visual–spatial intelligence are likely to gravitate to careers in the following areas: engineering, mechanics, interior design, graphic arts, fine art, sculpture, and architecture.

Logical–mathematical intelligence.   Students who possess this type of intelligence feel most comfortable and most capable when they are in situations in which can apply logic and reason. When confronted with a problem, they are more rational than emotional. They enjoy solving problems, doing puzzles, and figuring out "brain teasers." Possessing a natural facility for using numbers, they think conceptually and are adept at perceiving and using number patterns. They have a facility for linking pieces of information so that they can better comprehend the totality of what they are learning. They enjoy classifying and categorizing data, working with abstractions, doing mathematical calculations, and applying reason and logic. Acutely aware of and intrigued by the phenomena that occur around them (e.g., the El Niño weather phenomena), they enjoy doing experiments that help them understand the dynamics of these events and the underlying concepts that are responsible for them. They like to ask questions so that they can see how the components fit together to form a whole. Students who recognize and capitalize on their logical–mathematical intelligence often gravitate to careers in the following areas: mathematics, engineering, geology, astronomy, theoretical science, applied physical science, scientific research, teaching, medicine, computer hardware development, computer software development and/or programming, and accountancy.

Interpersonal intelligence.   Students who possess this type of intelligence are very comfortable relating to others. They are empathetic, able to perceive issues from the other person's vantage point, and concerned about how the other person thinks and feels. They are good at establishing relationships, organizing events, mobilizing people to work toward a common goal, resolving conflicts, building trust, maintaining group harmony, and encouraging cooperation. They can typically communicate using both verbal and nonverbal language (e.g., gestures, facial expressions). Students who recognize and capitalize on their interpersonal intelligence often gravitate to careers in the following areas: sales, marketing, human resource development, management, advertising, psychology and counseling, and politics.

Intrapersonal intelligence.   Students who possess this type of intelligence are introspective and aware of their innermost feelings. They are highly contemplative, intent on acquiring insights about themselves and others, and motivated to understand the dynamics of their relationships. Students who recognize and capitalize on their intrapersonal intelligence often gravitate to careers in the following areas: psychology and counseling, literature, religion, philosophy, writing, and university teaching.

Body–kinesthetic intelligence.   Students who possess this type of intelligence are especially talented in using their body. They can control their movements (as in gymnastics, dancing, karate, ice skating, or basketball) and can manipulate objects with great dexterity (a football, baseball, or hockey stick). Expressing themselves and their abilities through movement, they excel in physical pursuits. They use movement, body language, and their interaction with the surrounding environment to process and imprint information such as complex football or basketball plays, dance steps, and gymnastic routines. Students who recognize and capitalize on their body–kinesthetic intelligence often gravitate to careers in the following areas: dance, acting, martial arts, art, athletics, choreography, and coaching.

Music–rhythmic intelligence.   Students who possess this type of intelligence have a natural talent for performing or creating music. They relate to rhythm, lyrics, melodies, and tonal patterns. They delight in singing, playing musical instruments, performing on stage, composing music, being part of a band, and rehearsing. Adept at recalling melodies, the words to songs, and the notes in musical scores, they think in musical patterns and respond primarily to sounds. Those who recognize and capitalize on this type of intelligence often gravitate to the following careers: singer, composer, musician, band or orchestra member, disc jockey, record producer, and music impresario (someone who assembles and promotes talented musicians).

Naturalist intelligence.   Students who possess this type of intelligence have a talent for dealing with issues related to the world of nature. They are attuned to what is happening environmentally and are interested in the biological, chemical, ecological, and physical principles and phenomena that affect forests, oceans, jungles, seasonal cycles, animal reproduction, natural resource preservation and management, food chains, and species survival. They enjoy working with wildlife and being outdoors. Those who recognize and capitalize on this type of intelligence often gravitate to careers in the following fields: botany, biology, oceanography, conservation, zoology, ecology, exploration, animal husbandry, veterinary medicine, zoo management, and forestry.

As you can see, the different types of intelligence that Gardner describes and the preferred learning modalities are directly linked phenomena. A visual learner is likely to possess better than average visual–spatial intelligence, and an auditory learner is likely to possess better than average verbal–linguistic intelligence. A tactile learner is likely to possess better than average body–kinesthetic intelligence. By deliberately taking the time to identify your learning strengths, natural aptitudes and talents, and preferred or dominant learning modality or modalities, you can gain a significant advantage in school. Applying these insights about your natural intelligence and your natural and preferred learning style will help you maximize your performance, not only in school but also in your chosen career. Students who think and act strategically make certain that they take full advantage of all the natural talents with which they have been blessed.

For Your Information

Each human brain is endowed with distinct strengths and weaknesses that are genetically imprinted and environmentally shaped. These unique characteristics can be powerful resources if channeled and used effectively. Therefore, it is critically important for you to identify, understand, and capitalize on your strengths and to compensate successfully for your weaknesses. This is the essence of thinking smart.

Just as you are likely to have preferences about colors or food, you are also likely to have preferences about how to learn most effectively. Some students intuitively figure out their most effective learning style and use their natural talents, preferences, and dominant learning modalities when they study. Other students are unaware of their natural abilities and, as a consequence, struggle with virtually every academic challenge they face in school.

To achieve in college, you must be prepared to apply your preferences, talents, and distinctive intellectual gifts. Identifying and capitalizing on your natural abilities will turbocharge your learning capacity and play a key role in your becoming a better student.

MANAGING TIME, RECORDING ASSIGNMENTS, AND SOLVING PROBLEMS

OBJECTIVES

- Developing a personalized time-management system
- Creating a study schedule
- Developing an effective method for recording assignments
- Recognizing the importance of recording assignments consistently and accurately
- Learning to handle problems, challenges, and setbacks
- Understanding the role that strategic intelligence plays in the achievement equation

Winning the Battle with the Clock

Diego realized that if he didn't learn how to manage his time more effectively, he might not get his degree. Taking 12 units and working 25 hours a week at an auto parts store would be a challenge for anyone. For Diego, it was the equivalent of climbing Mt. Everest.

Diego's wife continually complained about his disorganization and procrastination. He hated to admit it, but he realized that Gloria was right. To meet his school, job, and family obligations, Diego realized that he had to improve his time-management skills.

Ever since he was a kid, Diego had preferred to put off the unpleasant chores until the very last minute. Now, as an adult, mowing the lawn, installing winter storm windows, washing the car, fixing torn screens, and painting the house were at the top of his "I'll do it tomorrow" list. Schoolwork was also high on the same "put it off for as long as possible" list.

To survive the next two years and complete his degree, Diego decided he had to create a study schedule and discipline himself to keep to the schedule. As he was not by nature an organized person, he knew that this would be difficult. After thinking about the challenge, Diego concluded that making a study schedule was similar to deciding to work out at the gym. You developed a personal training procedure, and you stuck to it no matter what. Once you started to skip workouts or short-cut the repetitions, you were doomed. Despite his tendency to procrastinate, Diego was determined to turn things around. He had to. There was too much riding on him getting his degree. His promotion to store manager and ultimately to regional manager hung in the balance.

After his first day of classes, Diego studied the syllabus for each course. He made a list of his specific academic responsibilities, realizing that he might have to make changes as the semester progressed. He then made another list of his family and job-related obligations.

To get a sense of how much studying he would have to do, he scanned his course textbooks. The required reading seemed overwhelming, especially because he still had many of the same reading problems he had struggled with in high school. Forcing this unpleasant thought out of his mind, Diego wrote down when reports, papers, weekly quizzes, unit exams, midterms, and final exams were scheduled. As he looked at what lay ahead, he felt his stomach churning. Distasteful memories from high school came flooding back. Meeting deadlines had always been stressful, and in the past, he had dealt with the problem by simply disregarding the deadlines. He was aware that if he resorted to this behavior in college, his goose was cooked.

After glancing again at the list of assignments, reports, tests, and exams, Diego felt even more depressed. He was tempted to chuck the whole idea of getting an A.A. degree. Trying to organize the endless responsibilities staring him in the face seemed impossible.

Later that evening he discussed his concerns with his wife, and she urged him to talk with his academic advisor. Realizing that Gloria's advice made sense, Diego decided to call and make an appointment the next morning. If he didn't get help, he was certain he would drown. He was sacrificing a great deal to be in school, and he was determined to complete the program successfully. The degree was his ticket to the promotion, and the promotion coupled with the override for store sales could conceivably double his current monthly income.

zooming in on the issues

Changing Old Habits

Diego made *three* key decisions. *Underline* each decision. Then, list and evaluate the decisions. (Clue: Look for the word "decided.") *List only his decisions.*
Don't list what he actually did, yet.

Decision 1: _____

_____

Evaluate this decision.

1	2	3	4	5	6	7	8	9	10

not smart   fairly smart   very smart

Decision 2: _____

_____

Evaluate this decision.

1	2	3	4	5	6	7	8	9	10

not smart   fairly smart   very smart

Decision 3: _____

_____

Evaluate this decision.

1	2	3	4	5	6	7	8	9	10

not smart   fairly smart   very smart

Now, identify the five specific steps Diego actually took to handle his
predicament. Underline each step twice, then evaluate it. (*Note:* There may
be two steps described in one sentence.)

Step 1: _____

_____

Evaluate this step.

1	2	3	4	5	6	7	8	9	10

not smart   fairly smart   very smart

Step 2: _____

_____

Evaluate this step.

1	2	3	4	5	6	7	8	9	10

not smart   fairly smart   very smart

Step 3: _____

_____

Evaluate this step.

1	2	3	4	5	6	7	8	9	10

not smart   fairly smart   very smart

Step 4: _____

_____

Evaluate this step.

1	2	3	4	5	6	7	8	9	10

not smart   fairly smart   very smart

Step 5: _____

_____

Evaluate this step.

1	2	3	4	5	6	7	8	9	10

not smart   fairly smart   very smart

If Diego decided _not_ to ask his advisor for help with setting up a study schedule and study plan, you could predict some likely consequences, based on the description of his _modus operandi._ Make three predictions about the potential effects of a choice to "go it alone," and indicate whether you believe your predictions are _possible_ or _probable._

1. _____

_____

○ possible   ○ probable

2. _____

_____

○ possible   ○ probable

3. _____

_____

○ possible   ○ probable

Drawing a Conclusion from the Evidence

Having examined Diego's dilemma, what specific conclusion can you draw from the information presented in the story? Using the _inductive method,_ express in a well-crafted sentence what you have concluded. _Remember:_ you are summarizing the **point** of the story (the inverted tip of the triangle).

The point of Diego's story:

_____

_____

_____

_____

POWERHOUSE THINKING

Four Keys to Effective Scheduling and Time Management

- Specify your academic goals and obligations.
- Create a study schedule that will allow you to attain your goals.
- Adhere to your schedule despite temptations to do otherwise.
- Evaluate the effectiveness of your schedule periodically and make adjustments if appropriate.

zooming out on the issues

Scheduling Study Time

The ability to manage time is vital to developing productive study habits. Being over-scheduled and feeling stressed is the bane of college life, and Diego's advisor had undoubtedly counseled many students who were struggling with time-management problems.

A way to avoid becoming overwhelmed and discouraged by the challenge of handling multiple responsibilities is to react constructively. This proactive behavior is described as **coming from cause** (i.e., taking responsibility for handling challenges and predicaments). This behavior is diametrically opposed to **coming from effect** (i.e., reacting ineffectually to negative events).

Students who _come from cause_ are easily recognizable. They are focused, efficient, and self-confident. They get the job done with a minimum amount of wheel-spinning and fish-tailing. Students who _come from effect_ are also recognizable. They are scattered, nonproductive, and continually in crisis mode.

Strategic students are intent on coming from cause. They want to be actively in charge of their own destiny. Nonstrategic students are willing to assume a passive role in determining what happens to them in school and in life.

The _Seven-Step Time-Management Method_ described next is designed to help you take charge of your academic obligations. It provides you with a practical template for creating a personalized schedule that will permit you to work more efficiently and effectively.

If you maintain your schedule and work out the kinks, you'll discover that you can complete your assignments with less stress. You'll probably also discover that you actually have more free time! Keeping to your schedule even when it's inconvenient or requires a sacrifice is vital if you're going to make your schedule work. For example, some friends may ask you to go to a movie with them. If you have homework to do, you may have to say "no." If you decide to join them, you may have to adjust your schedule the next evening and study until midnight to catch up and complete your assignments. Having an overview of your obligations and a clear sense of your priorities makes these choices less stressful. You can see at a glance what your responsibilities, time requirements, and time constraints are. This information is invaluable as you wrestle with choices and temptations.

Schedules require self-discipline and a willingness to suspend immediate gratification and focus on long-term payoffs. You must realize that your goals (e.g., getting your degree) are more important than going out with friends. Students who think strategically, establish personal goals and priorities, periodically review their goals, plan carefully, and keep to their schedules are far more likely to do well in college than those who float through life in a cerebral haze.

Maintaining a schedule is similar to beginning a serious athletic training program. You establish your objectives. You figure out how much time you want to devote to training. If you're serious about the program, you'll maintain your schedule and go to the gym or do your daily run even when you're tempted to skip a session. This consistency and discipline provide the structure you need to attain your objective. Reminding yourself about your goals and priorities makes the tough decisions easier. You can say to a friend, "I can't get together with you today because every Tuesday afternoon I go to the gym and work out." A study schedule serves the same purpose. You'll be able to say to your wife, husband, children, significant other, or friends, "I'm sorry, but I can't go to the beach on Saturday afternoon because that's when I have to study for my biology midterm."

Seven-Step Time-Management Method

Step 1. Using the following form, list all academic subjects and the approximate amount of daily time required to complete the assigned work.

ACADEMIC OBLIGATIONS
Approximate projected daily time required to do a first-rate job.

MY COURSES	AMOUNT OF STUDY TIME REQUIRED
Total Weekly Study Time	

You may not know precisely how much daily study time is required in each of your courses, especially if the semester is about to begin or has just begun. Talk with other students (choose successful, serious students!) who have taken the same courses and ask them how much time they spent studying each night or each week. Also, ask the instructor how much time students are expected to spend studying and doing assignments. *Many instructors advise a 2:1 study rule: This means two hours of study for each hour in class.*

Be prepared to make adjustments in your time projections as the semester progresses. You may discover you can do a first-rate job and complete the work in less time than you anticipated, or you may discover that you need additional study time. (Students returning to school may initially require more time and effort to get back into the "swing" of studying. Those with reading, comprehension, math, vocabulary, or writing deficits should be prepared to do more homework.)

Step 2. **Write down the time periods during which you can realistically study and do homework** (for example: between 8:45 P.M. and 11:00 P.M.).

Monday: _____

Tuesday: _____

Wednesday: _____

Thursday: _____

Friday: _____

Saturday: _____

Sunday: _____

Step 3. **Use colored felt-tip pens or pencils to create a code, or write the appropriate words to indicate on your Monday through Friday schedule the different ways in which you use your time each day** (see sample schedule below). In this book, words are used to indicate how time blocks are utilized. For example, if you're working while attending school, you may be at work between 8:30 A.M. and 4:00 P.M. and arrive home at 4:30 P.M. You may eat dinner between 5:30 P.M. and 6:00 P.M. and attend school from 7:00 P.M. to 9:00 P.M. three nights a week. You may study from 4:00 P.M. to 5:30 P.M. and from 9:30 P.M. to 11:00 P.M. every evening during the school week. Refer to Diego's modeled schedule (see Figure 2.1) as a guide. Use colors or words to indicate how you plan to use the time units in the schedule on page 29. The result is a visual representation of your personal weekly time-management plan. If you have any free time, indicate this with a different color.

Step 4. **Follow the same procedure (Step 3) and complete a weekend time-management schedule.** Most students who work while attending school do the bulk of their studying during the weekend. To complete their schoolwork and fulfill their obligations, they must develop first-rate planning and time-management skills.

| FIGURE 2.1 | Diego's weekly schedule* |

TIME	MON	TUES	WED	THURS	FRI
7:00 A.M.–7:15 A.M.	Breakfast	Breakfast	Breakfast	Breakfast	Breakfast
7:15–8:00	Commute	Commute	Commute	Commute	Commute
8:00–2:00 P.M.	Work	Work	Work	Work	Work
2:00–2:45	Commute	Commute	Commute	Commute	Commute
3:00–3:55	Study	Study	Study	Study	Study
4:00–6:00	Biology	Spanish	Biology	Spanish	Study
6:10–6:50	Dinner	Dinner	Dinner	Dinner	Dinner
7:00–9:00	English	Library	English	Bio. Lab	Study
9:00–9:30	Commute	Commute	Commute	Commute	Free
9:45–11:00	Study	Study	Study	Study	Free

* *Note:* This schedule does not reflect weekend study time.

Step 5. Keep to your schedule for two weeks. Note whether you are fulfilling your academic obligations with less stress and anxiety and if you are working more productively.

Figure 2.1 shows Diego's schedule after completing the first five steps of the scheduling method.

Instead of using words, you may prefer to use colored markers to indicate blocks of time. In this case, you need a code that explains the meaning of each color. For instance, blue could designate time spent at your job. Red might designate study time, and green might designate commute time.

At first glance, it may appear that this scheduling procedure requires a great deal of extra effort, but the time you spend developing a personal time-management system will ultimately save you time, stress, and anxiety. The process is akin to learning a new computer program. It requires extra work at first, but once you master the procedure, the payoffs more than justify the initial "investment."

When you have completed your study schedule, photocopy it. Put one copy in a plastic sleeve and insert it in your binder. Tape the second copy on the wall near your desk at home. You may also want to purchase a month-at-a-glance calendar to record key events, obligations, and deadlines. Put this calendar in a plastic sleeve and insert it in your binder next to your weekly schedule. Tape a duplicate copy to a wall in your study area at home. Make it a daily ritual to consult your schedule and use it as a guide when you study.

My Weekly Study Schedule

TIME	MON	TUES	WED	THURS	FRI

My Weekend Study Schedule

TIME	SAT	SUN

Step 6. Record your grades in every subject (e.g., quizzes, exams, homework assignments, reports). Put this recording form in your binder next to your schedule. Do this for the two-week trial before making any major adjustments in your schedule. The recording process allows you to track your performance and fine-tune your schedule. For example, if your English grade doesn't improve or goes down, you will have to schedule more time for writing, editing, and proofreading. (Specific techniques for improving your grades are presented in subsequent chapters.) Figure 2.2 will allow you to record your grades efficiently and systematically.

Step 7. After the initial two-week experiment, critically evaluate your schedule and make appropriate adjustments. You may have to increase your scheduled study time in a particular subject and reduce it in another. Thereafter, periodically reassess your schedule and fine-tune it when conditions change. Obviously, you'll have to make up a new schedule if your work or class hours change. You'll also have to make up a new schedule at the end of each semester to reflect changes in your homework and studying responsibilities.

FIGURE 2.2 *Two-week grade-tracking experiment.*

COURSE:

HOMEWORK:

Date						
Grade						

QUIZZES/TESTS/EXAMS/PAPERS:

Date						
Grade						

COURSE:

HOMEWORK:

Date						
Grade						

QUIZZES/TESTS/EXAMS/PAPERS:

Date						
Grade						

COURSE:

HOMEWORK:

Date						
Grade						

QUIZZES/TESTS/EXAMS/PAPERS:

Date						
Grade						

COURSE:

HOMEWORK:

Date						
Grade						

QUIZZES/TESTS/EXAMS/PAPERS:

Date						
Grade						

Personal contract.   **FIGURE 2.3**

Date: _____

Dear Me:

Recognizing the need for good time management and planning, I, _____,
voluntarily agree to maintain my study schedule during a two-week trial period. If after this trial, I
conclude that my schedule should be adjusted, I'll do so. Once these changes are made, I agree
to maintain the revised schedule for a minimum of four weeks. If I'm pleased with the results and
both my study efficiency and grades improve, I'll continue to use the schedule for the remainder
of the semester. If necessary, I'll make further adjustments in my schedule every four weeks.

Your name: _____

Witness (optional): _____   *(husband, wife, classmate, friend)*

A STUDY SCHEDULE CONTRACT

The temptation to "let things slide" for a day can be appealing when you
have demanding obligations and a demanding schedule. Just as running five
miles every other day or keeping a New Year's resolution to begin a diet can
be challenging, so is the prospect of having to study for three hours. You may
"cheat" one day and discover that "cheating" the next day is much easier.
Then, you may begin to avoid your responsibilities on a regular basis, and
finally, you may simply abandon the commitment.

A powerful incentive for resisting the temptation to let things slide is to
sign a personal "contract" with yourself (see Figure 2.3). This contract testifies
in very concrete terms that you've made a commitment. It serves as a tangible reminder that maintaining your study schedule is important to you. It
also underscores that you've established important personal goals and that
you consciously realize that this schedule will help you attain these goals.

If you conclude that the procedure of drawing up a contract works for
you and decide to sign it, tape the contract on the wall near your desk and
place a copy in your binder. If you're tempted to let things slide, take a
minute to review it.

STUDY BREAKS

The amount of time a student can study intensively and productively varies from
person to person. Many factors play a role in your study formula, including:

- the intensity of your goal orientation (e.g., "I'm determined to get my
  degree in June!")

- your interest in what you are studying (e.g., "I really enjoy my programming course" versus "I find this material is so boring, but I must force myself to do the work because I need this course to get my degree.")
- your reaction to the difficulty of the material (e.g., "I hate doing these physics problems because I can't understand them.")
- your sense of urgency (e.g., "I've got a midterm tomorrow!")
- your capacity to discipline yourself and concentrate (e.g., "I know I can learn these irregular conjugations if I stay focused for 45 minutes.")
- your intellectual stamina (e.g., "My mind just shuts down after 20 minutes of intense studying, and I must take a break.")

Everyone should take occasional study breaks, but a pattern of frequent interruptions usually undermines concentration and productivity. Getting up every 10 minutes to go to the kitchen for a snack, call a friend, watch TV, or play with the dog is a distraction that cannot help but reduce study effectiveness.

A Recommended Formula for Study Breaks

Study intensively for at least 30 minutes before taking a 5-minute break.

Students who think strategically realize that they study better when they concentrate intensely with no distractions for reasonable blocks of time. They discipline themselves, work diligently, and sustain their concentration before taking time out to "recharge their batteries."

You may be able, or may prefer, to work for longer periods before taking a break. This formula is intended only as a general guideline. If you can study for longer periods (35 to 60 minutes) without an interruption, by all means do so. If you have difficulty working for 25 minutes at a stretch, you might want to create a mental training program to increase your study stamina. The program might be similar to an athletic training program designed to build up your endurance for jogging, doing aerobics, or doing weight training at the gym. At the beginning, set a kitchen timer to buzz after 12 minutes of studying. Concentrate and study intensely for 12 minutes and then take a short break. Each day, add two minutes to the study intervals before taking a break. If you follow this plan, you will build your mental endurance, and in approximately one week, you should be able to study for 25 minutes without interruption. You may decide to continue using the kitchen timer method until you reach your ultimate goal—perhaps to study for 35 minutes at a stretch without a break.

Just as you can train your body and enhance your physical stamina and efficiency, so, too, can you train your brain and enhance your mental stamina and efficiency. The requirements for developing your full range of mental abilities and talents include desire, effort, practice, strategic thinking, and commitment.

What Was That Assignment?

Kerri had the sinking feeling she was forgetting to do something important, but when she went through her mental checklist, she couldn't remember what it was. She had completed her math problems, and she had studied for the quiz. She had also organized her research notes and index cards for the computer science report that is due next week. Still, a voice inside her head told her there was another assignment. The voice kept saying "biology."

Kerri tried to recall what her biology instructor had written on the board at the end of class the previous day. She could remember that there would be a test, and she remembered the assigned chapter. She was almost certain that he had written something else on the chalkboard, but her brain wouldn't cooperate. She was angry with herself. This wasn't like her. Usually, she could remember assignments without writing them down. Sure, she forgot things from time to time, but by and large, she got by.

Kerri looked at the clock. It was already 11:15 P.M. Although she was tempted to call Candice to find out what she had forgotten, she knew her friend had an 8:00 A.M. class and would probably be asleep. Candice certainly would not appreciate a call at 11:15. Oh, well. Kerri closed her books and stuffed everything into her book bag. The voice, however, wouldn't be quiet. She was troubled, and she had a difficult time falling asleep.

In school the next day, Kerri discovered that the voice in her head had been right. Her biology lab book was due, and she hadn't written up her last two experiments. If she handed in the lab book late, her grades on the two experiments would be lowered. Kerri was furious with herself. Her B in the class was now in serious jeopardy, and she knew it was her fault.

zooming in on the issues

Forgetting the Essentials

Based on the information in the story, evaluate Kerri's overall academic diligence.

1	2	3	4	5	6	7	8	9	10
poor				fair					excellent

Why did you make this evaluation?

_____

_____

Kerri had developed a "style" for recording assignments. How would you rate this style?

1	2	3	4	5	6	7	8	9	10
ineffective			relatively effective					very effective	

Why did you make this evaluation?

_____

_____

List the potential consequences of Kerri's "in her head" homework recording system.

Potential consequence 1: _____

_____

　○ possible　　○ probable

Evaluate the likely impact of this consequence on Kerri's grades.

1	2	3	4	5	6	7	8	9	10

low　　　　　　　　　　moderate　　　　　　　　　significant

Potential consequence 2: _____

_____

　○ possible　　○ probable

Evaluate the likely impact of this consequence on Kerri's grades.

1	2	3	4	5	6	7	8	9	10

low　　　　　　　　　　moderate　　　　　　　　　significant

Potential consequence 3: _____

_____

　○ possible　　○ probable

Evaluate the likely impact of this consequence on Kerri's grades.

1	2	3	4	5	6	7	8	9	10

low　　　　　　　　　　moderate　　　　　　　　　significant

Drawing a Conclusion from the Evidence

Having zoomed in on Kerri's dilemma, what specific conclusion can you draw from the information presented in the story? Using the *inductive method*, express in a well-crafted sentence what you have concluded. *Remember:* you are summarizing the **point** of the story (the inverted tip of the triangle).

The point of Kerri's story: _____

_____

_____

_____

_____

_____

_____

_____

_____

_____

zooming out on the issues

Shortcuts That Don't Work

We've zoomed in on Kerri's situation. Now, let's zoom out and take a long-range view of her situation and the academic implications. Rather than write down her assignments, Kerri chose to rely exclusively on her memory. This time, she discovered that her normally reliable memory failed her. Perhaps she was too lazy to write down her assignments or too confident about her ability to recall details.

It's possible that Kerri had acquired bad habits in high school and believed she could get by using the same procedure. She was smart enough to recognize, however, that the shortcuts that may have worked in high school could produce serious negative consequences in college.

Kerri had concrete evidence that she had to make a fundamental change in her method of recording assignments. By relying exclusively on her auditory memory, she was putting herself at risk—she would undoubtedly experience additional memory lapses and calamities.

Successful students who think strategically analyze their miscalculations and setbacks. (A comprehensive examination of strategic intelligence and its applications appears later in this chapter.) *They learn from negative experiences and make every effort to avoid making the same mistakes. They don't have to be repeatedly bopped over the head in order to realize that they must make tactical adjustments in their* modus operandi *(way of doing things).*

If you do not have or do not consistently use a good system to record your assignments, you are bound to overlook important details. These forgotten details can make the difference between a good grade and a marginal grade. You are likely to forget deadlines, specific page references, and explicit directions about how to do a project or an assignment. Most instructors take a dim view of students who fail to follow explicit directions and will not accept excuses, no matter how creative these excuses are.

POWERHOUSE THINKING

Basic Requirements for Productive Studying

- Know what your assignments are in every course.
- Record when the assignments are due.
- Record key details and the instructor's explicit directions.
- Make note of your instructor's hints, clues, and suggestions.

A FAIL-SAFE ASSIGNMENT RECORDING SYSTEM

Look at the sample homework assignment in Figure 2.4. Assume that today is Monday, and you're in the fourth week of the semester.

| FIGURE 2.4 | *Sample homework assignment summary.* |

CRIMINAL JUSTICE:

D. Wed.

Rd Ch 3

Ans ques Ch 2/U. 1 & 2 p. 42

Q Fri U. 1 & 2

Rpt d 10/21—See h/o specifics

BIOLOGY:

D. Wed.

Rvw Ch 1

L principles evolution

Rd Ch 2 p. 23–48

Ans ques 1, 3, 5, 7 on p. 48

Und all tech terms—df. in parentheses

T Ch 1 Fri.

MATH:

D. Wed.

p 13, prob 1–12

p 17, prob 1–8

s.w. (not just answers)

Q 10/5

ENGLISH:

D. Tues.

Rd sonnets p. 19–28

H/i essay: Shakespeare's craft 10/3

D. Thurs.

Oral explication: Sonnet CXVI

Key: Ans. = answer; Ch = chapter; D. = due; Df. = define; h/i = hand-in; h/o = handout; L. = learn; rd. = read; Q. = quiz; p. = page; ques. = questions; rpt. = report; rvw = review; s.w. = show work; prob = problems; U. = unit; und. = underline (See list of additional abbreviations on page 41.)

As you can see, certain assignments are due in two days. Tests and quizzes are scheduled for Friday, and a Criminal Justice report is due 10/21. The instructors in two courses have given explicit directions about how they want the assigned questions answered—disregarding these directions will undoubtedly result in a lower grade for the assignment. Submitting late or incomplete work will produce the same consequence.

Not every instructor writes assignments on the chalkboard. Some announce in class what the assignments are and when quizzes, tests, exams, and reports are scheduled. Others may hand out a sheet with the assignments for the week, month, or semester. Following verbal instructions can be particularly challenging for visual learners who prefer written instructions. These students must train themselves to listen intently when instructors announce assignments verbally, and it would be wise for them to verify oral assignments with a classmate.

To see how the *Study Wise* Assignment Recording System works, examine Figure 2.5, Sample Assignment Sheet. Figures 2.6 and 2.7 offer additional practice assignment sheets.

Note that a typical homework assignment has been recorded on the Sample Assignment Sheet as a model. Using this as a guide, transfer the assignments in Figure 2.4 (Criminal Justice, Biology, and Math) onto Figure 2.6, Practice Assignment Sheet I. (If you're already using an assignment recording system that you like, use it to record the assignment. You may

Sample assignment sheet.   **FIGURE 2.5**

WEEK OF:	10/1

SUBJECTS	MONDAY	TUESDAY	WEDNESDAY	THURSDAY	FRIDAY
MATH	P 93 PROB 1–10 P 96 PROB 1–8 SW Q 10/4				
CRIMINAL JUSTICE	RD P 156–165 ANS QUES. 1–5 P 166 COMP SEN/SKP LNE CH T FRI 10/7				
BIOLOGY	RD P 87–109 KNOW DEF. 10 WRDS P 105 RPT D MON. 10/10				
ENGLISH	ANLYZE POEM DH LAWRENCE P 130 D. Wed. ESSAY D 10/23				
TESTS, QUIZZES & PAPERS	C.J. RPT 10/21 BIO. RPT. 10/10 M . Q WED 10/7 ENG. ESSAY 10/9 CJ T 10/27				

| FIGURE 2.6 | *Practice assignment sheet I.* |

WEEK OF:

SUBJECTS	MONDAY	TUESDAY	WEDNESDAY	THURSDAY	FRIDAY
_____					
_____					
_____					
_____					
_____					
TESTS, QUIZZES & PAPERS					

want to experiment with the format used in this book. Many different types of assignment organizers are available at college bookstores. Whatever format you select, make sure to include all the key information.) Whenever possible, use abbreviations so that you can fit the assignment into the space provided. Some common abbreviations can be found on page 41. As you use these abbreviations, they'll become "second nature." The process is akin to learning to type. With practice, you no longer have to think about where the keys are. You can also make up your own abbreviations, but be certain that you understand them! (A list of abbreviations that can be used when taking notes from textbooks and lectures is found on page 139.)

Mastery: More Practice Recording Assignments

Using Figure 2.5 as a guide, record the following on Figure 2.7, Practice Assignment Sheet II.

ENGLISH:
D. Wed. 11/1
Q Identifying grammar/syntax mistakes
D. Fri. 11/3 run-ons/tense
sub/verb agreement
D. Mon. 11/6 Essay—500 wrds.
deductive format
Title: "Writing Skills: Rediscovering
a Lost Art"

PHYSICS:
D. Wed. 11/1
Rd p. 26–33
Prob 1–9 on p. 34
Rd p 35–43
Prob 1–9 on p. 44
Lab Notebook Exp. #3
D. Mon. 11/6
Q Unit 1 ch 3—know symbols

MATH:
D. Wed. 11/1
st prob 1–15 p. 43
D. Fri. 11/3
st prob 1–15
D. Mon. 11/6
prob 1–9 on p. 50
D. Wed. 11/8
Rv Ques.
1,3,5,7,9 on p. 52
E Ch 3

GOVERNMENT:
D. Wed. 11/1
Rd p 114–142
Ans ques 1–7 on p. 156
D. Fri. 11/3
Rd p 143–155
Ans ques 8–16 on p. 157
D. Mon. 11/6
Q Ch 4
D. Wed. 11/8
5 p essay: "Did Checks &
Balances Work during Watergate?"

CONSISTENCY: MAKING THE ASSIGNMENT RECORDING SYSTEM WORK

Use the Study Wise Assignment Recording System (or your own system) for the next two weeks. Be consistent and discipline yourself to write down the important information and details for each of your courses. After this two-week experiment, you may want to modify the recording system, or you may want to incorporate components from several different systems to develop your own personal, individualized recording method. The key is to develop a method that works for you.

FIGURE 2.7   *Practice assignment sheet II.*

WEEK OF:

SUBJECTS	MONDAY	TUESDAY	WEDNESDAY	THURSDAY	FRIDAY
_____					
_____					
_____					
_____					
_____					
TESTS, QUIZZES & PAPERS					

Helpful Assignment Recording Abbreviations

ans	= answer	F	= final exam	org	= organize	rvw	= review
ch	= chapter	f/d	= final draft	p	= page	rw	= rewrite
cmb	= combine	fin	= finish	prac	= practice	sec	= section
comp	= complete	form	= formula	prob	= problem	sk	= skip
corr	= correct	h/w	= homework	prfrd	= proofread	st	= study
d	= due	h/i	= hand in	Q	= quiz	sw	= show work
df	= define	h/o	= handout	ques	= question	syl	= syllabus
disc	= discuss	imp	= important	rd	= read	T	= test
E	= exam	inc	= include	r/d	= rough draft	U	= unit
ess	= essay	incrp	= incorporate	rp	= repeat	und	= underline
ex	= example	L	= learn	r/r	= reread	w	= with
exer	= exercise	m/t	= midterm	rprt	= report	wr	= written
exp	= explain	o/b	= open book	rvs	= revise	w/o	= without
ext	= extra	or	= oral				

Remember to write down any clues your instructors provide regarding upcoming quizzes, tests, and exams. Omitting key instructions could lead to disaster—you might study the wrong material, do the wrong problems, omit key information, or fail to meet a deadline.

Each assignment sheet has room for one week's assignments. To use the Study Wise Assignment Recording System, you'll have to make extra photocopies of the assignment sheet. Punch holes in the sheets and insert them in a section in your notebook labeled "Assignments."

At first, using an assignment sheet may seem like extra work, but once you get into the habit of carefully recording your assignments every day, you'll automatically do so without even thinking about it. You'll discover that the procedure actually saves time. You'll no longer have to call classmates to find out the assignment, and your anxiety level will decrease. When you go to class, you will feel secure that you have completed everything that's due. Recording your assignments "religiously" will become a key study skills resource that makes your academic life easier and less stressful and your efforts more productive.

Problems: A Hard Fact of Life

iego, the student who struggled with managing time in the introductory case study, and Kerri, the student in the second case study who didn't record assignments, confronted problems that were caused by their own actions. Diego created a plan to handle his time-management problem. This solution required improved planning and self-discipline. Kerri took responsibility for the consequence that derived from not recording her biology assignment, but it was uncertain from the information in the story that she was committed to modifying her behavior.

Both stories underscore a basic fact of life: Everyone can expect to confront problems and challenges in school and in life. They "go with the territory." In fact, being able to solve problems represents a key portion of what life is about. People who can handle predicaments and neutralize obstacles resourcefully are far more likely to be successful in school and in their careers than those who fall apart in a crisis and respond ineffectively or irrationally.

The more responsibilities you have—academic and financial obligations, kids, family, aging parents, demanding bosses—the more problems and challenges you are likely to face. At times, these problems may appear to be so overwhelming that you conclude that they cannot be solved. This can lead to frustration, demoralization, evasion of responsibility, and, in extreme cases, to potential emotional or physical immobilization.

One particularly ineffectual way to deal with problems is to deny they exist. This may be convenient in the short term, but you usually have to pay a heavy price down the road. The person with a serious drinking or gambling problem is clearly on a collision course with reality. Unless the problem is confronted and resolved, this person is all but certain to crash into a wall.

Kerri's problem, of course, is less severe than an alcohol or gambling problem, but it is a problem that could have serious academic consequences. Her experience with forgetting to write up her biology lab report is not likely to be an isolated incident. Kerri will undoubtedly suffer other missteps because she doesn't consistently record her assignments.

There is a powerful method for identifying and solving problems that Kerri could use if she wants to do something constructive about her proclivity to "wing it" when assignments are given. The method is called **DIBS.**

DIBS: THE SMART WAY TO SOLVE PROBLEMS

DIBS has four steps:

D = Define the problem accurately (pinpoint the problem precisely).

I = Investigate what is causing the problem.

B = Brainstorm solutions to the problem (as many as possible).

S = Select an idea to try out as a possible solution, and if it doesn't work, select another.

As you can see, the word **DIBS** is an acronym formed from the first letter of each step in the procedure. It is important to note that the first step in the procedure—*defining the problem accurately*—can be quite challenging. There is a tendency to describe the *symptoms of the problem* and *not pinpoint the actual problem.* For example, let's say you discover that you do not have enough money to purchase some important software that you need to do a project. You might be tempted to define your problem as:

1. The monthly check from my parents is late.

2. I spent too much money on socializing this month.

3. My brother never repaid the money he owes me.

4. Fixing my car used up all of my available funds.

5. I just can't seem to make ends meet each month.

All of these statements may be perfectly true, but they do not define the problem. Rather, the statements represent the *causes* or the *symptoms* of the problem. The actual problem is: **I don't have enough money to buy the software I need.** Once you have accurately defined the problem, you can begin to investigate the reasons for the problem and brainstorm solutions that might include:

- borrowing money

- working more hours at your part-time job

- selling some old textbooks

- selling your concert tickets

Let's look at another example of confusing the actual problem with the causes of the problem. Let's say you are upset with an instructor who's assigning a great deal of homework. You may define the problem as "My instructor is unfair and gives too much homework." Although this may be true, it is not an accurate definition of your problem. What you have written might be contributing to the situation, but blaming the instructor doesn't help solve the problem. It is far more effective to define the problem as "I'm having trouble completing all of the work that my instructor assigns." Now that you have accurately defined the problem, you can examine the causes of the problem (perhaps an "unfair" instructor), and you can begin to brainstorm practical solutions (e.g., talking to the instructor, taking a speed-reading course, organizing your time better, or taking fewer credits).

Now, let's see how Kerri could use DIBS to solve her homework recording problem. Start by trying to define her problem.

1. DEFINE the problem: _____

_____

Please note: It is possible to see problems from different perspectives. If you personally "own" a problem, you are likely to be more emotionally entwined than if you are analyzing someone else's problem. Clearly, your perspective or vantage point will influence how you define a problem. As you analyze and define Kerri's predicament, be as objective as you can (i.e., focus on actual facts rather than subjective feelings). Your goal in this exercise is to interpret her situation rationally and logically.

As stated earlier, defining a problem accurately can be difficult because of the tendency to confuse the symptoms of the problem with the actual problem. For example, you might be tempted to define Kerri's problem as follows: *Kerri acquired bad habits in high school about recording assignments.* This is true, but it is actually one of the possible *causes* of the problem.

Let's look at a partial application of DIBS in solving Kerri's problem. Following are two plausible definitions of Kerri's problem. You may come up with other equally valid definitions.

1. **Define the problem.** Here are two options for defining Kerri's problem:

   Problem: *Kerri doesn't want to take the time to record her*

   assignments

   Problem: *Kerri is getting lower grades because she is not*

   recording her assignments.

2. **Investigate the causes of the problem**—list as many reasons as you can that could explain why Kerri is not methodically recording her assignments.

   Reason 1: *Kerri acquired bad habits in high school.*

   Reason 2: *Kerri was able to get by in high school by using her auditory*

   memory skills for her assignments.

   See if you can come up with two other reasons.

   Reason 1: _____

   Reason 2: _____

3. **Brainstorm** some reasonable solutions to the problem.

   Solution 1: _____

   Solution 2: _____

4. **Select** the most reasonable solution to the problem to try—#_____.

   Important: The solution you select must be specific enough to solve the problem that you've defined. For example, you may have selected the solution "Learn abbreviations to streamline the recording procedure." This solution might work if you defined the problem in narrow terms—"Kerri doesn't want to take the time to record her assignments." If you defined the problem in broader terms—"Kerri resists recording her assignments"—then learning abbreviations is not a sufficient solution. To solve this broader problem, you might propose: "Kerri has to have a good homework recording system and a daily checklist where she indicates that she has recorded the assignment for each course." *Remember:* You must gear your brainstormed solutions to your definition of the problem.

   It is also possible that the brainstormed solution you select may not work. In this case, you have to select another of the solutions to try. If none work, then you must go back to the drawing board and brainstorm additional ideas. This trial and error procedure is vastly superior to becoming discouraged and concluding, "I'll never be able to solve this problem." Sometimes, problems aren't solved until the fourth or fifth try, and it may even take 10 tries to resolve a difficult dilemma. If solving the problem is important to you, then you must hang in until you find the key.

POWERHOUSE THINKING

Key Principles of Successful Problem Solving

- Define the problem accurately and precisely.
- Do not confuse the symptoms of the problem with the actual problem.
- Make certain that your solutions address the defined problem.
- If your selected solution doesn't work, try another solution until you find one that does work.

Practicing DIBS

To practice using DIBS, examine the following situations and accurately define each problem. (*Hint*: It is useful to use an "I" message such as "I am having difficulty.")

1. Money is tight. I haven't had any accidents or moving violations, but my automobile insurance rates have been increased by 25 percent.

   Define the problem: _____

   _____

   An accurate and precise definition of this problem is:

   I'm having problems paying the new insurance premiums for

   my car.

2. My boss is hassling me and assigning a great deal of overtime. I may not be able to complete my degree this June as planned.

   Define the problem: _____

   _____

3. My roommates (or my kids) are making too much noise, and I can't concentrate when I do my homework.

   Define the problem: _____

   _____

Let's examine problem #2 and *investigate* plausible causal factors. Write down possible reasons that might explain why the situation developed. For example, one plausible cause might be that the office is understaffed.

Define the problem: My boss is assigning so much overtime that I may not be able to complete my degree in June.

Investigate:

Possible hypothetical causes for the problem include:

Investigate: My supervisor is on maternity leave.

The salespeople are writing up too many orders for us to handle.

The computer system is antiquated and we need new and more efficient software.

The office is highly disorganized.

Some of my coworkers are not carrying their load.

I have not clearly explained my academic obligations to my boss.

My boss is often unreasonable in her demands.

Now, brainstorm some reasonable solutions to this problem.

Brainstorm:

An example of a reasonable brainstormed solution is:

Brainstorm: I could explain my situation to my boss, communicate my desire to graduate in June, and ask if she could give someone else the overtime.

The DIBS solution to problem #3 might be:

D: I can't study when my roommates are making noise.

I: My roommates are not as serious as I am about school.

I have a problem concentrating and filtering out distractions.

Because of my learning problems, I have to work harder than other students.

Our house is not ideal for studying because the walls are thin.

My room is right next to the living room.

B: I could study in the library.

I could buy earplugs or ear protectors.

I could try to exchange my room for one further away from the living room.

I could sit down and discuss the problem with my roommates and ask them to agree to specific periods of quiet time.

S: I'll buy earplugs to filter out the noise.

Your investigation and brainstormed solutions may be very different than those modeled here. This is perfectly OK! What matters is that you *accurately analyze and define* the problem, *objectively investigate* the causes, and *brainstorm* logical and practical solutions that could resolve the problem. If the solution you initially select doesn't work, go back to your list and select another that might prove more effective.

Additional Practice Using DIBS

Now use DIBS to solve the following problems. Remember, DIBS means:

D = **D**efine the problem accurately (pinpoint the problem precisely).

I = **I**nvestigate what is causing the problem.

B = **B**rainstorm solutions to the problem (as many as possible).

S = **S**elect an idea to try out as a possible solution, and if it doesn't work, select another.

1. Your best friend wants to borrow your car. You believe that he is a reckless driver, and you know that he has had two accidents in the last year.

D: _____

_____

I: _____

_____

B: _____

_____

S: _____

_____

2. Your husband (wife, boyfriend, girlfriend, friend) wants you to go to a party on Saturday night. You know the people who will be at the party, and you find them very boring.

D: _____

_____

I: _____

_____

B: _____

_____

S: _____

_____

3. Your instructor is upset with you because you sometimes fall asleep in his class. You're working 8 hours a day at your job, and you're taking 10 credits at the same time.

D: _____

_____

I: _____

_____

B: _____

_____

S: _____

_____

MASTERY: MAKING DIBS WORK WHEN YOU NEED IT

No matter how much natural talent you may have in a particular area, you must be willing to practice if you are to perfect your talent. This principle—"practice and diligence make perfect"—applies to acquiring virtually any new capability, be it in the area of foreign languages, karate, gymnastics, accounting, woodworking, skiing, expository writing, dance, or computer repair. Serious athletes must practice their moves over and over again until they have them down pat. Surgeons must repeatedly practice the skills they were taught during their training, and actors must repeatedly rehearse their lines. This principle also applies to developing first-rate analytical-thinking and study skills.

This program provides you with many opportunities to practice each specific skill so that you can fully assimilate it. As you become increasingly proficient, you will discover that you are using the methods automatically.

Like a well-trained basketball player, you will be in the right place at the right time on the court. You will execute the play flawlessly, and the ball will not even hit the rim as it swooshes through the net.

The following exercise is designed to enhance your analytical problem-solving skills. Use DIBS to solve at least four of the problems—the more you practice, the easier it will be for you to apply DIBS in all areas of your life:

- Your boss asks you to work overtime on Saturday. You had already promised your friends that you would go with them to the beach.

- Your psychology instructor introduces a new concept that you find very confusing. You are insecure about your skills and a bit intimidated by the instructor.

- You have to take two final exams and turn in a term paper on the same day.

- You're getting poor grades in English because your essays have too many grammatical errors.

- They've just installed a new computer system at work. You're having a great deal of difficulty using the system, and you sense your boss is getting upset with you.

- You're in danger of getting a D in a math course.

- You want a letter of recommendation from your history instructor, but you are concerned that she doesn't know you well enough to write the letter.

You will be provided with many other opportunities to practice DIBS. By the time you complete the program, you will be an expert at solving problems and handling challenges.

Strategic Intelligence

Throughout this book, you will be repeatedly asked to solve real-world problems, handle challenges, and develop strategies for attaining your personal objectives in school and in life. The goal of the exercises is help you develop your **strategic intelligence.** Your instructors went through a similar training process when they were in college and graduate school. They were systematically taught by their professors to:

- observe
- analyze
- draw conclusions from the evidence
- evaluate
- question
- critique
- apply
- associate
- communicate their insight and knowledge

Over two thousand years ago, the great Greek philosopher–teachers—Socrates and Plato—developed and applied a systematic instructional process

Strategic intelligence: the ability to make your life work and attain your personal goals by thinking, planning, and acting rationally, logically, and tactically.

of asking their students penetrating questions in order to arrive at, or confirm, an underlying truth. The ultimate goal of this mental training procedure was to enhance students' self-knowledge. Referred to as the *Socratic method*, the process of analyzing issues by employing logic and reason later formed the foundation for the famous *case method* that is used as an instructional tool at many of the finest graduate schools.

The human mind, no matter how *inherently* capable it may be, must be trained if its potential is to be maximized. You are in enrolled in college to acquire this intellectual training. Yes, you undoubtedly have very pragmatic reasons for pursuing your education: You want to acquire skills and knowledge to help you find a rewarding job and advance your career. Despite your practical reasons for being in school, developing and honing your analytical-thinking skills is a primary objective for becoming educated. You will use analytical thinking throughout your life, and the many benefits that will accrue from developing your mental powers will motivate you to acquire new skills and knowledge long after you complete your formal schooling.

Your goal is to achieve maximum mental efficiency. In some respects, the process is akin to fine-tuning the engine of an expensive sports car. The motor may be *potentially capable* of generating more than 300 horsepower and *potentially capable* of running exquisitely, but unless the timing and fuel injectors are adjusted and the spark plugs are cleaned, a Ferrari or Lamborghini will run like an old clunker. Instead of whining like ten thousand excited hornets as it rolls along a curving road, your flawlessly engineered car will cough, chug, and, perhaps, even stall.

This program will function as your mechanic. It will show you how to generate maximum mental horsepower and torque. Once you begin to think and study more efficiently and effectively, your strategic and critical intelligence will automatically engage. Your ability to handle problems will become a powerful personal resource. Clear thinking will not only help you get out of jams, it will also help you avoid jams and attain the payoffs you desire in life.

APPLICATIONS OF STRATEGIC INTELLIGENCE:

- establishing goals
- developing a workable plan for getting from point A to point B
- calculating the odds
- understanding and utilizing the principles of cause and effect
- anticipating potential problems
- bouncing back from setbacks and defeats
- solving problems and neutralizing obstacles
- learning from past experience and applying this data to current situations
- avoiding the repetition of mistakes
- focusing intellectual and physical energy on achieving defined goals
- figuring out practical tactics for surviving and prevailing in a highly competitive world

QUESTIONS THAT INDICATE YOU ARE THINKING STRATEGICALLY

- What are my objectives?
- What possible problems may I encounter?

- How can I get the job done successfully and efficiently?
- How can I avoid mistakes?
- What can I learn from my past mistakes?
- How can I increase my chances of success?
- What are my available resources for attaining my objective?
- How do I use my strengths and minimize my weaknesses?

Strategic intelligence is a form of *applied intelligence* (AI). This type of practical intelligence (also referred to as "street smarts") is responsive to systematic training. You can learn how to develop and apply your AI productively in much the same way that you can learn to use a tennis racket or a golf club more productively.

Examples of applied strategic intelligence can be found in all walks of life. The smart basketball player who is shooting poorly asks his coach for help and feedback. With the coach's guidance, he carefully analyzes what he's doing wrong, makes adjustments, and doggedly "works his way out" of his slump. The smart executive who suffers a business setback uses the same tactics. She consults with people who are knowledgeable about the challenges she is facing, and she uses the data derived from the negative experience to make sure that her next business venture turns out differently. The smart general whose troops are struggling to gain the upper hand on the battlefield carefully analyzes the enemy's tactics and his own tactics. He then adjusts his strategy and tactics so that his forces can prevail.

A core theme is repeatedly emphasized in this program: To attain your goals and prevail in school and in life, you must deliberately and methodically develop your strategic or applied intelligence. This theme is woven into the fabric of this book, and you will be provided with many opportunities to develop this vital capability. (*Critical thinking* is another type of applied intelligence. In Chapter 5, critical intelligence is carefully examined in the context of questioning premises, searching for underlying meaning, comprehending course content, identifying important information, and studying for tests.)

For Your Information

TIME MANAGEMENT

Academic achievement demands the capacity to self-regulate. Students must complete their work, plan ahead, and meet deadlines. To do so, they must be prepared to create a study schedule that allows them to manage their time efficiently. The red-flag behaviors and attitudes that signal ineffective time management include:

- procrastination
- missed deadlines
- incomplete assignments
- disorganization
- poor planning
- resistance to studying and doing homework
- inadequate motivation and effort

- irresponsibility
- excessive stress due to feeling overwhelmed and scattered
- repeated excuses for marginal performance

Some students have difficulty managing time because of poor judgment. They typically act impulsively, surround themselves with distractions, and fail to recognize the fundamental cause and effect principle that links focused effort, efficient scheduling, and academic success.

Students who study irresponsibly or ineffectively often justify their behavior with the following rationalizations:

- "This course is so boring."
- "The instructor is an idiot."
- "I see no value in learning what I'm being taught."
- "Why bother to study hard? I'll do poorly no matter how hard I try."
- "I guess that I forgot to do that assignment."
- "The instructor didn't tell us that there was a quiz."
- "I tried to check over my work, but I ran out of time."
- "I'm not worried. I'll get all the work done."
- "I had too many things to do."

Students resorting to these rationalizations are clearly unwilling to take responsibility for the negative consequences of their own decisions, behaviors, and attitudes. By blaming others, making excuses, and denying responsibility, they delude themselves that nothing is wrong. The illusion, of course, shatters when they get their grades.

RECORDING ASSIGNMENTS

Some students do not work up to their full potential for a very basic reason: They don't record their assignments accurately and completely. Because they do not remember what work is due and when it's due, they often submit incomplete or late homework that does not conform to their instructors' explicit instructions. Some of these students are too lazy to record their assignments. Some have not learned an effective system for writing down essential information. Some may delude themselves that they can remember the important details without having to record them. Others appear unconcerned about meeting deadlines or following their instructors' directions. This cavalier attitude about their academic responsibilities clearly puts them on a collision course with the grading system.

The potential repercussions of failing to record assignments properly are predictable. The consequences include:

- failure to conform to explicit instructions
- missed deadlines
- incomplete assignments
- inadequate preparation for tests
- lower grades

Students who think strategically realize that school is easier, stress is reduced, and grades are improved when they establish a pattern of working and studying productively. These students may not be "naturally" organized, but they recognize that the payoff for efficient work more than justifies the extra effort and self-discipline. They also realize that the minor time investment required to record assignments accurately is inconsequential if this investment produces a higher G.P.A.

HANDLING PROBLEMS

Problems are an inevitable part of the human condition, and we must all deal with them. When problems appear monumental and insurmountable, one can easily become discouraged and overwhelmed. The likelihood of feeling powerless significantly increases when you do not know how to define a problem accurately, identify the underlying causes, and devise practical and logical solutions. Students who don't understand *why* things are going wrong are like cars slipping on an icy road and fishtailing from side to side. The lack of forward momentum produces frustration, demoralization, and diminished self-confidence.

Many students who believe they cannot solve their problems unconsciously try to protect themselves from feeling incompetent by latching onto defensive and counterproductive attitudes and behaviors. Those observing from the outside may conclude that these defense mechanisms (e.g., procrastination, irresponsibility, poor motivation, and lack of effort) are *causing* the predicament when, in most cases, the behaviors are actually *symptoms* of underlying issues that have not been adequately addressed and resolved. The underlying issues may include poor academic skills, learning disabilities, attention deficit disorder, inadequate time management, deficient study skills, and chronic disorganization.

Effective problem-solving skills and clear, rational thinking are powerful tools that can help you avoid stress-producing situations and save you a great deal of stress and grief. Mastering DIBS gives you a powerful problem-solving resource. You will be able to use your applied strategic intelligence to analyze life's imbroglios, find logical solutions, and prevail over the obstacles that might otherwise limit your success in school and in life.

GETTING ORGANIZED

OBJECTIVES

- Creating order in your study environment
- Evaluating your organizational skills
- Developing practical and effective organizational methods

The Effects of Chaos

Jonathan was exhausted when he pulled his pickup truck into the carport at 10:20 P.M. He had left for work at 7:15 A.M., and the awful stop-and-go morning commute now seemed like a distant memory. As he removed his key from the ignition, he sighed. The day was a blur: 8 hours of working the cash register and packing groceries into plastic sacks, 20 minutes to wolf down a fast-food burger and fries, and 3 solid hours of accounting and English classes.

In the kitchen, Jonathan made himself a turkey and cheese sandwich and began brewing coffee. He would have to study for at least an hour before going to bed. At moments like this, he asked himself if he was crazy to take eight units and work full-time. Forcing the negative thoughts from his mind, he focused instead on his goals: Finish his A.A. degree, transfer to a four-year college, earn a B.A. in accounting, start his own business, and be his own boss. Jonathan wanted to earn a good living by using his head, not his back. One thing was certain: He didn't want to be a grocery clerk for the rest of his life.

The salary Jonathan was earning at the supermarket was very good. The union contract provided excellent medical and dental benefits, time and a half for over-time, and job security. Because he was working full-time and living with his parents, he was doing fine financially. But the work didn't give him any satisfaction, and he knew he was determined to do something more rewarding with his life.

Jonathan went into his bedroom, sat down at his desk, and turned on his desk lamp. Papers were strewn all over the room. Piles of homework assignments littered his desk, and books were scattered on the floor. Pushing aside some of the papers and books, he tried to make room for his notebook and accounting textbook. He then began to search for the assignment he had begun the previous evening. It had to be somewhere! In frustration, he dumped a pile of papers on the floor, got down on his knees, and furiously began to search through the mess. The more frustrated he became, the angrier he became. After 15 minutes, he found the assignment under one of the books on the floor. At that moment, Jonathan made a promise to himself. He would take three hours during the weekend to organize his desk and his room.

It was now almost eleven o'clock, and Jonathan didn't have time to waste looking for lost assignments. He had more than an hour of home-work to do before he went to bed, and he would have to be up at 6:15 the next morning if he was going to get to work on time.

When Jonathan was finally about to begin the accounting assignment, he pan-icked when he realized that he had simply written down "Chapter 3, p. 22." He hadn't recorded the actual problems that had been assigned. He also couldn't find his calculator. By this time, he was so upset and angry at himself that he knew it would be impossible to get any productive work done that evening. He'd have to do the problems tomorrow and hand them in late. This would be the sixth time he had submitted a late assignment, and the semester was only three weeks old. Each time he missed a deadline, his grade was lowered.

"Enough is enough! This is crazy. I'm wasting too much time looking for things," he thought angrily. "I'm going to organize this mess on Saturday, even if it takes all day. I've got to get some order in my life, or I'll drown."

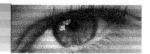

zooming in *on the issues*

Drowning in Clutter

Carefully reread the case study and underline as many specific descriptions of Jonathan's study environment as you can find. List six of the most significant descriptions here.

1. _____

2. _____

3. _____

4. _____

5. _____

6. _____

Evaluate Jonathan's organizational skills.

1	2	3	4	5	6	7	8	9	10

poor   fair   excellent

Evaluate Jonathan's study procedures.

1	2	3	4	5	6	7	8	9	10

poor   fair   excellent

Make some predictions about the potential consequences of Jonathan's current *modus operandi.*

His grades:

1	2	3	4	5	6	7	8	9	10

poor   fair   excellent

His stress and anxiety level:

1	2	3	4	5	6	7	8	9	10

low   average   high

Based on the description in the case study, estimate the average amount of additional time Jonathan has to spend on his homework each evening as a direct result of his chronic disorganization. _____

Assume that you're Jonathan's friend. He describes his situation and asks you for advice about how to get more organized. What *specific* recommendations would you make to help him work more efficiently?

1. _____

2. _____

3. _____

4. _____

5. _____

6. _____

Drawing a Conclusion from the Evidence

Having read about Jonathan's *modus operandi*, what specific conclusion can you draw from the information presented in the story? Using the *inductive method*, express in a well-crafted sentence what you have concluded. *Remember:* You are summarizing the **point** of the story.

The point of Jonathan's story:

_____

_____

_____

_____

Using DIBS

Let's say that you conclude that simply giving your disorganized friend advice about how to create more order in his life is not going to work. You decide that it would be more effective to apply the DIBS method. Pretend that Jonathan is sitting next to you at a desk, and you show him how to use DIBS to solve the problem. Remember to use "I" messages (e.g., "I am having difficulty with too many distractions when I study").

As you recall, DIBS consists of four steps:

D = Define the problem accurately.

I = Investigate what is causing the problem.

B = Brainstorm solutions to the problem.

S = Select an idea to try out as a possible solution.

Define the problem:

_____

Investigate what is causing the problem:

_____

_____

_____

Brainstorm solutions to the problem:

_____

_____

_____

Select a solution to try out:

_____

Ideally, this problem-solving process will help Jonathan realize that specific and deliberate steps must be taken to get organized. These steps might include creating a filing system; adding shelves used exclusively to store school-related materials; allocating desk drawers to hold pencils, paper, and pens; and developing a system for organizing his binder.

zooming out on the issues

Having the Tools

No surgeon begins an operation without the necessary scalpels, scissors, clamps, and retractors. And no mechanic begins to overhaul an engine without the necessary diagnostic equipment and tools. The same organizational principles apply to effective studying. To do the job properly, you must have immediate access to your books, assignments, paper, pencils, and pens. You may also need access to a computer. Without these essential tools, you are at a severe disadvantage, and you can anticipate two predictable repercussions: undermined performance and lower grades.

Becoming more organized may initially require extra time and effort, but you'll soon discover that your increased efficiency actually reduces your workload. Because you don't have to waste precious time and effort searching for what you need, your stress level decreases, and your homework is easier to manage and complete. You can now focus on getting your work done efficiently, leaving more free time to do things you enjoy.

If you suspect that you might be disorganized and working inefficiently, take a few moments to complete the following *Organizational Inventory*. It will indicate whether you should be concerned about organization.

Organizational Inventory

YES   NO

○   ○   I have divided my notebook (using labeled tabs) into a section for each course.

○   ○   I place all class and textbook notes in the designated sections of my notebook.

○   ○   I use a drawer or drawers to store school-related materials.

○   ○   I place completed homework assignments, graded tests, course syllabi, and other materials in folders (or large envelopes) that are labeled for each subject.

○   ○   I make copies (or backup disks) of important materials.

○   ○   I keep a copy of my study schedule in my notebook and it is accessible where I do my homework.

○   ○   I write all of my assignments on an assignment sheet.

○   ○   I keep my assignment sheet in my notebook.

○   ○   I have a month-at-a-glance calendar for listing all of my monthly obligations and appointments.

YES NO

○ ○   I prioritize my academic and personal obligations.

○ ○   I make checklists of tasks I have to complete and check off those that I've done.

○ ○   I plan ahead and budget the necessary time to complete projects and assignments.

○ ○   I make certain that I have the supplies I need to complete my assignments (e.g., textbooks, dictionary, calculator, paper, ruler, pens, pencils, paper).

○ ○   I have a designated area at home where I can study and keep school-related materials.

○ ○   I have a backpack or book bag in which I keep all of the materials I have to take to and from school.

○ ○   I have the phone numbers of classmates I can call if I need help or information.

○ ○   I can usually access the materials I need to complete my assignments quickly and without having to search for them.

A "no" answer to any of the listed statements may signal an organizational problem. If you conclude that disorganization is causing you to waste time and work ineffectually, it makes sense to develop some simple and practical procedures to create more order in your life.

There are five key payoffs for having the tools and materials you need to get the job done properly. These include:

1. greater efficiency
2. more productivity
3. enhanced performance
4. reduced stress
5. more free time

A Method for Getting Organized

Organizational skills can be significantly improved by using basic checklists that spell out the important details and responsibilities that are requisite to studying efficiently. The methodical process of checking off what has to be done helps you plan ahead and use your time effectively. The procedures also help you avoid counterproductive crises, frustration, stress, and anxiety.

The checklist procedure is a vital requisite in many fields. A pilot systematically completes a preflight checklist before taking off. An assistant lighting director on a movie set makes certain the necessary equipment is packed in the truck. A surgical scrub nurse in an operating room uses a similar methodical written or mental checklist procedure. They all realize that something essential may be forgotten or overlooked if they bypass this systematic process, and under some circumstances, the consequences could be disastrous.

The repercussions for not having what you need to get the job done can be equally disastrous for a student. You may fail to put important software back where it belongs and then waste 20 precious minutes looking for it, or you may forget to take with you to the library the previously completed notes necessary for writing your report. Because of this oversight, you have to go home, get the notes, and return to the library, causing a loss of valuable library time.

With sufficient practice, you can become so familiar with your personal organizational checklists that you can do the procedure automatically. Of course, you may prefer to continue using a manual system and insert the checklists in your binder, or you may want to input them into your laptop or hand-held organizer.

If you are having difficulty with organization, make use of the following three-part *Study Materials Checklist.* Once organization becomes an ingrained habit and you can mentally run through the process of ensuring that you have everything necessary to do your work, you can abandon the formal system. (Feel free to modify this checklist so that it meets your individual needs.)

Study Materials Checklist

BRING HOME FROM SCHOOL:	MON.	TUES.	WED.	THURS.	FRI.
Notebooks	○	○	○	○	○
Textbooks	○	○	○	○	○
Assignment sheet	○	○	○	○	○
Graded tests and reports	○	○	○	○	○
Corrected homework assignments	○	○	○	○	○
Lab books	○	○	○	○	○
Laptop	○	○	○	○	○
Relevant hard copy	○	○	○	○	○
Calculator	○	○	○	○	○
Calendar	○	○	○	○	○

BRING TO SCHOOL FROM HOME:	MON.	TUES.	WED.	THURS.	FRI.
Notebooks	○	○	○	○	○
Textbooks	○	○	○	○	○
Assignment sheet	○	○	○	○	○
Completed homework	○	○	○	○	○
Graded tests and reports	○	○	○	○	○
Corrected homework assignments	○	○	○	○	○
Lab books	○	○	○	○	○
Laptop	○	○	○	○	○
Relevant hard copy	○	○	○	○	○
Calculator	○	○	○	○	○
Pencils, pens, paper, subject dividers	○	○	○	○	○
Calendar	○	○	○	○	○
Small stapler	○	○	○	○	○
Folders	○	○	○	○	○
Plastic sleeves	○	○	○	○	○

MATERIALS NEEDED AT HOME:	MON.	TUES.	WED.	THURS.	FRI.
Dictionary	○	○	○	○	○
Thesaurus	○	○	○	○	○
Calculator	○	○	○	○	○
Pencils, pens, paper	○	○	○	○	○
Ruler, protractor, etc.	○	○	○	○	○
Organized filing system	○	○	○	○	○
Good lighting	○	○	○	○	○
Three-hole punch	○	○	○	○	○
Stapler	○	○	○	○	○
Sticky notes	○	○	○	○	○
Plastic sleeves	○	○	○	○	○
Folders	○	○	○	○	○
_____	○	○	○	○	○
_____	○	○	○	○	○

Your initial reaction to using these checklists may be negative. Going through a methodical checklist procedure may simply seem like too much extra work. You must make a value judgment and decide whether the procedure will help you become more organized and efficient. There's no need to complete the checklists if you are naturally organized and do not have problems keeping track of and accessing the materials necessary to do your work successfully. However, if you're spending valuable study time looking for things, using organizational checklists can make your life in school much easier and less stressful.

You may want to experiment with using the system for a week. Keep track to see whether you are spending less time searching for things. If the checklist procedure appears to be working for you, continue using it (either on paper or mentally) until you have made good organization an entrenched habit.

ORGANIZING YOUR BINDER

Keeping your notebook organized can be a major time-saver. You can put your finger on what you need instantly: assignments, class notes, study notes, work-in-progress, completed assignments, and graded tests and reports.

Below are 10 commonsense steps for getting your binder organized. (If your notebook is *already* well organized, feel free to disregard the following section.)

1. Buy or make dividers for each of your courses.

2. Label each subject.

3. Label a section COMPLETED/CORRECTED ASSIGNMENTS.

4. Label a section ASSIGNMENTS TO TURN IN.

5. Label a section MISCELLANEOUS.

6. Place all school materials you want to keep (e.g., quizzes, tests, reports, course syllabi, reading lists, notes) in the appropriate subject category.

7. Put dates on all materials and place them in the appropriate section in chronological order.

8. Tape your study schedule (the one you created in Chapter 2) on the inside front cover of your notebook.

9. Put another copy of your study schedule in a plastic sleeve and insert it in the front of your notebook.

10. Punch holes in any papers you want to keep that do not have holes. You might want to use reinforcements for important papers so that you don't lose them.

Having a well-organized binder gives you immediate access to everything you need and saves a great deal of time and a great many headaches. Searching for books and papers can be frustrating, stressful, demoralizing, and infuriating, especially when you have homework due the next day and it's 10:30 P.M. Students who think strategically want to get their homework done quickly and efficiently and with the minimum of grief.

Which Study Environment Is Likely to Produce Better Grades?

WHAT'S WRONG IN THIS PICTURE?

Identify as many conditions in the picture as you can that might interfere with effective studying.

_____

_____

_____

_____

_____

Predict the likely outcomes of a student studying in this environment. Circle your prediction.

Productivity:	Excellent	Good	Average	Poor
Concentration:	Excellent	Good	Average	Poor
Comprehension:	Excellent	Good	Average	Poor
Recall:	Excellent	Good	Average	Poor
Quality of academic work:	Excellent	Good	Average	Poor
Grades:	Excellent	Good	Average	Poor

WHAT'S RIGHT IN THIS PICTURE?

Describe all of the details that you see in this illustration that would enhance effective studying.

_____

_____

_____

_____

Predict the likely outcomes of a student studying in this environment. Circle your prediction.

Productivity:	Excellent	Good	Average	Poor
Concentration:	Excellent	Good	Average	Poor
Comprehension:	Excellent	Good	Average	Poor
Recall:	Excellent	Good	Average	Poor
Quality of academic work:	Excellent	Good	Average	Poor
Grades:	Excellent	Good	Average	Poor

ORGANIZING YOUR STUDY AREA

Smart students realize that they must create a practical filing and storage system for school-related materials. Here are some simple guidelines to help you develop a personalized organizational system for your at-home study area. (Refer to Chapter 4 for additional suggestions.)

1. Place those books you periodically refer to (e.g., dictionaries, thesaurus, reference books) on shelves near your desk or table.
2. Set up a hanging file into which you can place file folders.
3. Label the file folders according to content or course title.
4. Have a filing cabinet or a filing box for labeled files.
5. Put materials (e.g., graded tests, essays, projects) in the appropriate files and don't let them accumulate elsewhere.
6. Keep personal records (e.g., tax receipts, checkbook, credit card statements) separate from school-related materials.
7. Tape your study schedule to the wall near your desk.
8. Have a specific and accessible place for pencils, pens, ruler, highlighters, etc.
9. When appropriate, make backup copies of important materials.
10. Designate (and label) specific drawers or shelves for the exclusive storage of school materials.

POWERHOUSE THINKING

Key Principles for Improving Organization

- Identify specific materials and procedures that facilitate studying and doing homework.
- Create and consistently use either manual or mental checklists to verify that you have the necessary study materials at home and in school.
- Designate specific areas on your desk and in your binder for important materials (e.g., previous tests, returned assignments, due assignments).

ORGANIZING YOUR COMPUTER FILES

Computers are very "organization-friendly." Papers, reports, lecture notes, and textbook notes can easily be labeled and placed in files that you can place on your desktop for easy access. Identify each file with the course name (e.g., Chemistry II, English 104). If you've taken notes in your geology course and have to review them, all you have to do is click on the file to open it and find the specific material. You can then either review the material on the screen or print out a hard copy. Always remember to label your files accurately, identify precisely the specific documents in your files, and back up your work on a floppy disk, zip drive, or CD.

Your computer will create much of the organization necessary to study productively. It indicates the date each file or document was created and revised. It makes an alphabetized list of each file's contents, and it allows you to move files and transfer documents. Your computer also allows you to download and file important material from the Internet and from research sources such as CD-ROM encyclopedias.

In many respects your computer is a "personal organization tool." This tool is dedicated to helping you find, access, and process the information you need to study successfully. Strategic students deliberately take full advantage of its built-in organizational capabilities.

For Your Information

Good organizational skills, effective study skills, and strategic thinking go hand in hand. Successful students plan ahead, carefully record their assignments, and make certain that they have the required tools to get the job done efficiently. They make sure that they take their assignment sheet, course syllabi, textbooks, and notebooks home and that they have access to their previous tests, essays, and reports. They also have on hand the mundane material necessary to do their work: pencils, pens, paper, dictionary, typewriter or computer, software, calculator, and so on. When they go to class, they have a system for verifying that they have all of the essential materials. Their organizational procedures are both deliberate and methodical.

Students who are chronically disorganized operate very differently. They characteristically forget to bring home the books and other materials required to complete their assignments. Their study areas are in chaos. Their binders are a mess. Their assignment sheets are incomplete and contain inaccurate information—if they bother to have an assignment sheet at all. They don't know what work is due or when it's due. Their disorganization produces two predictable consequences: a great deal of wasted time and a great deal of unnecessary stress. Despite these negative repercussions, they may be oblivious to, or may simply deny, the obvious cause-and-effect link between their counterproductive attitudes and habits and their chronic anxiety.

Ironically, those students with the greatest need to change their *modus operandi* are usually the most resistant to change. Associating suggestions about how to become better organized with nagging, they insist on doing it "their way." Unfortunately, their way is usually inefficient and anxiety-producing, not only for them, but also for those with whom they interact.

Improved organization will make your life in school and outside of school more efficient and productive. As you intentionally reduce the disorder in your study environment, you'll discover that your performance will improve. There's also another important payoff for becoming more organized: You will have more time for your non–school-related interests and pursuits.

CREATING A STUDY SANCTUARY

OBJECTIVES

- Learning methods for handling difficult dilemmas, compromising productively, and reaching accord
- Exploring the impact of a positive study environment
- Learning methods to improve concentration

Finding Peace and Quiet

When Amanda and Jackson burst into the room for the third time, Lisa knew she had to get stern. "You kids can't keep coming in here and bothering me! Go back downstairs and finish your homework. When you're done, you can watch TV. I have my own homework to do, and I've got a math midterm tomorrow. You must leave me alone. You can't come into my room again unless it's an emergency!"

Realizing she was neglecting her children, Lisa felt a pang of guilt. With great discipline, she drove the feelings from her mind and turned her attention back to her math textbook. She hadn't taken a math class since high school, and she was extremely frustrated as she tried to solve the problems. Algebra II was proving to be a nightmare. Lisa knew that the same types of problems she was struggling to solve would be on the midterm, and she felt a sense of desperation. Refusing to allow panic to overwhelm her, she forced her mind to focus as she plodded through each problem.

After finally completing the review problems, Lisa scanned her previous tests and quizzes. She carefully noted the problems she had missed and highlighted her mistakes with a yellow marker. When she couldn't figure out why an answer was wrong, she referred to the solved examples in her textbook. She was determined to make certain that she understood the principles and procedures.

When she finished her math review, Lisa sighed and rubbed her eyes. Before she could go to bed, she had to complete an English essay that was due tomorrow. She had written the first draft, but she still had to edit, revise, retype, and carefully proofread the essay to find typos, grammar mistakes, and spelling errors.

While she was editing, the phone rang. Lisa decided not to answer it. The machine would take the message, and she could call back during a study break, assuming she had time for one. When Amanda burst through the door again to complain that Jackson was teasing her, Lisa put her hand up and pointed to the door. Getting the message, Amanda pouted, turned, and marched out of the room. Lisa knew her children wanted her to spend more time with them. Working eight hours a day and taking six units was putting a terrible strain on everyone. She hated having to be tough with her kids. She felt awful about not spending as much time as she should with them, but she was determined to complete her A.A. degree. If she didn't, she would never get a better job, never be able to afford the house in the suburbs she desperately wanted for her family, and never be able to send her children to decent schools. It was a question of priorities and sacrifices. She had to keep reminding herself that, in the long run, her family would be much better off when she completed her degree. She was convinced that she would be able to look back and say that the sacrifices were worth it. Right now, however, trying to juggle all of the balls she had thrown in the air had become a never-ending nightmare.

zooming in on the issues

Environmental Control

Go back through the story and underline and number each of Lisa's study-related actions.

Evaluate Lisa's motivation.

1	2	3	4	5	6	7	8	9	10
poor				fair					excellent

Why did you reach this conclusion? _____

_____

_____

How would you evaluate Lisa's effort?

1	2	3	4	5	6	7	8	9	10
poor				fair					excellent

Why did you reach this conclusion? _____

_____

_____

Predict Lisa's grades.

1	2	3	4	5	6	7	8	9	10
poor				fair					excellent

Why did you make this prediction? _____

_____

_____

Predict the likelihood of Lisa completing her degree.

1	2	3	4	5	6	7	8	9	10
poor				fair					excellent

Why did you reach this conclusion? _____

_____

_____

Predict the likelihood of Lisa balancing her family and school responsibilities.

1	2	3	4	5	6	7	8	9	10
not likely				fairly likely					very likely

Why did you reach this conclusion? _____

_____

_____

Predict the likelihood of Lisa's children being emotionally damaged by her decision to return to school and limit the time she spends with them.

1	2	3	4	5	6	7	8	9	10

unlikely   fairly likely   very likely

Why did you reach this conclusion? _____

_____

_____

Evaluate the overall effectiveness of Lisa's methods for handling the challenges she faces.

1	2	3	4	5	6	7	8	9	10

poor   fair   excellent

Are there any perfect solutions to the predicament Lisa faces?

○ yes   ○ no   ○ not sure

If you were confronted with a similar predicament, would you handle the situation in the same way?

○ yes   ○ no   ○ not sure

What would you do differently?

1. _____

2. _____

3. _____

4. _____

5. _____

6. _____

Do you think that these modifications would significantly alter the outcome?

○ yes   ○ no   ○ not sure

Do you believe the "guilt factor" (i.e., feeling remorse about being stern and denying her children as much time with her as they want) could be a determining factor in whether or not Lisa attains her objective?

○ yes   ○ no   ○ not sure

If so, how significant might this guilt factor be?

1	2	3	4	5	6	7	8	9	10

not at all   moderately   extremely

Do you believe that certain problems, such as the one Lisa confronts, are essentially unsolvable and that under certain circumstances, the best we can do is jury-rig a solution that allows us to survive?

   ○ yes   ○ no   ○ not sure

Drawing a Conclusion from the Evidence

Having read about Lisa's predicament, what specific conclusion can you draw from the information presented in the story? Using the *inductive method*, express in a well-crafted sentence what you have concluded. *Remember:* you are summarizing the **point** of the story.

The point of Lisa's story: _____

_____

_____

_____

_____

_____

zooming out
on the issues

Juggling Conflicting Responsibilities

Sometimes, a thorny problem may not lend itself to a complete or immediate solution. The problem may be complex and may involve other people who have their own needs and agendas. There may also be core conditions that you cannot significantly alter. For example, you may be the primary caregiver for a parent or a child with a chronic illness or disability. Or you may have a chronic illness or disability and have to accept this condition as a fact of life. Certainly, you may be able to apply analytical problem-solving skills to handle elements of the dilemma more effectively, but you may, nonetheless, continue to confront formidable challenges. In these circumstances, the most logical objective may be to learn how to cope with the situation as successfully as possible.

    Lisa's situation was a case in point. She was a committed and conscientious single parent who wanted to provide a better life for herself and her family, and to attain her goals she was willing to make monumental personal sacrifices. At the same time, she recognized that her children had legitimate age-appropriate emotional and physical needs and that she was obligated to meet these needs as best she could. Lisa's situation was constantly in flux—every day she was forced to confront major challenges as she struggled to juggle her school and family responsibilities. Certainly, she needed to establish rules and guidelines for her children, but these solutions could not be simplistic or inflexible. When appropriate, she had to be willing to make expedient compromises and reasonable accommodations.

    If you are faced with a complex problem that does not lend itself to a complete or immediate solution, describe the circumstances in the space provided. Include how you have dealt with the predicament and how you might experiment with altering your current strategy. If the situation is highly personal, feel free to write your response on a separate sheet of paper. You are under no obligation to share what you have written during a class discussion. It's your option.

Coping with a "No-Easy-Solution" Dilemma

_____

_____

_____

_____

_____

_____

_____

_____

_____

_____

Compromising: Creating a Win–Win Strategy

Lisa found herself in a battle with her children as she tried to carve out time to do her schoolwork. Somehow, she had to strike a balance between her children's legitimate needs to interact with her, and her own legitimate needs to pursue her education and provide a better life for her family.

In an athletic competition, one person or one team strives to win the game or the race. The overriding objective is to establish superiority and vanquish the opponent. No serious competitive athlete intentionally aims for a tie or a draw.

Despite what many famous basketball and football coaches contend, the principles that fuel an athletic competition seldom apply in the real world—the "winner-take-all" mentality is rarely an effective strategy for interacting successfully with other people. Many conflicts are best resolved by deliberately orchestrating a _draw_ in which everyone wins something. Lisa's situation is a perfect example of a conflict that can be resolved by applying this _shared-win principle_. Lisa is not at war with her college or with her children, although on particularly bad days, it may appear so. To attain her goal, she has to figure out how to deal with the challenges and mini-crises attendant to being a single parent of two children and a student.

Many problems can be best handled through compromise, reasonable accommodations, and negotiation. The goal is for those involved to reach accord by deliberately working together to attain mutually shared objectives.

REACHING ACCORD MODEL

Step 1: Specify mutually shared interests.

Step 2: Establish mutually appealing benefits.

Step 3: Determine mutually acceptable tactics for attaining goals.

This negotiated settlement procedure is central to handling labor disputes, international disagreements, and family conflicts successfully. The alternative is to go to "war," and although this extreme action may sometimes be necessary, wars are invariably brutal.

In a me-against-you scenario, a balanced analytical approach to problem resolution plays no role. The objective is simply to prevail at all costs, and there three possible outcomes.

COMPETITOR/ADVERSARY MODEL

■ **I Win—You Lose**

■ **You Win—I Lose**

■ **We Both Lose** (e.g., both teams get eliminated from the playoffs or all of the soldiers on the battlefield are killed)

I Lose ▲ You Lose

The desired outcome in the *negotiated settlement/reaching accord model* is very different.

IDEAL OUTCOME FOR THE REACHING ACCORD MODEL

■ **Everybody Wins** (this is referred to as *"Win–Win"*)

I Win ▲ You Win

Applying the Win–Win Strategy

Describe how Lisa might create a *win–win* situation for herself and her children that permits her to cope successfully with the academic and family challenges she faces. For ideas, refer to your responses to "What would you do differently?" on page 70.

WHAT LISA MIGHT OFFER:

_____

_____

_____

_____

_____

WHAT LISA MIGHT ASK IN RETURN:

_____

_____

_____

_____

_____

Let's assume Lisa uses this win–win model. Predict the likelihood that she can balance her family and school responsibilities.

1	2	3	4	5	6	7	8	9	10
unlikely				fairly likely					very likely

Why did you reach this conclusion? _____

_____

_____

POWERHOUSE THINKING

Key Principles for Creating a Win–Win Context

- Seek mutually shared interests.
- Define mutually beneficial payoffs.
- Agree on mutually acceptable tactics.

Mastery: Practice Creating a Win-Win Context

Resolve the following predicaments by intentionally producing a win–win situation. Write down as many ideas as possible for meeting your needs and the other person's needs.

- Both you and your roommate have dates on Saturday night. Each of you wants the other to "disappear" so that you can cook a romantic dinner for your date and have some privacy.

WHAT I COULD OFFER: **WHAT I WOULD ASK IN RETURN:**

_____   _____

_____   _____

_____   _____

- Your significant other believes you are prioritizing your schoolwork over the relationship, and he or she is upset that you are not spending sufficient alone time together.

WHAT I COULD OFFER: **WHAT I WOULD ASK IN RETURN:**

_____   _____

_____   _____

_____   _____

- You resent that your chemistry lab partner is not carrying his or her weight and is too dependent on you to do the experiments.

WHAT I COULD OFFER:

_____

_____

_____

WHAT I WOULD ASK IN RETURN:

_____

_____

_____

■ You want to spend your bonus check on a vacation, and your significant other wants to invest the money.

WHAT I COULD OFFER:

_____

_____

_____

WHAT I WOULD ASK IN RETURN:

_____

_____

_____

Operating at Peak Performance

Everyone must learn how to handle simultaneously multiple tasks that demand varying degrees of attention. For example, you may be talking with a friend on the phone, and someone in the room may ask you a question that requires an immediate response. You may have to adjust your side view mirror while driving on the freeway. You may be chatting with a friend while changing the oil in your car. You may have to study and focus despite occasional intrusions by your roommates. This ability to "juggle" multiple tasks while remaining focused on the primary task is an especially vital resource in an era of high-tech distractions.

The capacity to shift effortlessly from task to task varies from person to person. Some people have relatively little difficulty handling a transition that requires *centering* (focusing on a task), *de-centering* (focusing temporarily on something else), and *re-centering* (returning to the original task after the distraction has been addressed). Others find these transitions disconcerting.

In certain situations, having too many things going on simultaneously can significantly undermine the concentration, productivity, and test performance of even the most conscientious students. However comfortable you may be with juggling multiple tasks, your mental efficiency is likely to be negatively affected when your children or roommates are yelling as you are discussing with a classmate how to solve a complex calculus problem.

FORTRESSES, ISLANDS, AND CAVES

Some students are convinced that they can study effectively with the TV or stereo playing. Perhaps they can. Having grown up in a world where pulsating music and background noise are everyday occurrences, these students may have become habituated to environmental stimuli—they are likely to argue vehemently that they *must* have the stereo or TV on in order to study.

Most students will acknowledge that there are times when they must eliminate noise and distractions so that they can concentrate and study intensely. Imagine struggling to solve a complex chemistry problem and your neighbor turns on a noisy leaf blower. The noise may be so upsetting and intrusive that you find it impossible to concentrate. Nor would you want to study for a final exam while your neighbors are having a loud party and setting off fireworks. The reasons are obvious: The distractions are likely to undermine the focused concentration requisite to performing at peak efficiency and getting a good grade on the exam.

If you examine the *modus operandi* of most successful students, you are likely to discover that they study in a controlled environment where distractions are intentionally limited and where they can focus intensely and exclusively on the task at hand. You might visualize this controlled environment as a *study island*, a *study fortress*, or a *study cave*. While sitting at your desk, you might pretend that you are on an island or inside a fortress or cave. You have access to everything you need to do your work. You have the necessary study materials: textbooks; assignment sheet; study schedule; previous tests and papers; binder; paper, pens, and pencils; and dictionary. Your refuge is organized, quiet, and protected. The area is off-limits to others unless there's an emergency. The phone is hooked up to an answering machine with the volume turned down. When you've finished studying, you can put your things away, leave the fortress, and reenter the real world.

Using DIBS

Let's imagine that you look at the illustration of the "study zoo" on page 63 and conclude that your own study environment at home looks similar. You realize that the distractions are negatively affecting your grades, and you decide that you must deal with the issue. Use DIBS to solve the problem. Remember to use "I" statements (e.g., "I am surrounded by too many distractions when I study").

Define: _____

Investigate: _____

_____

_____

Brainstorm: _____

_____

_____

Select: _____

_____

Ideally, the solution that you select is specific enough to make a difference. Perhaps your solution is to turn off the TV or loud music when you are studying. Perhaps your solution is to turn the ringer off on the phone and to let your answering machine or voice mail handle the calls. Maybe your solution is to make sure that your children (or roommates) don't disturb you when you are studying. *Remember:* If the first solution you select doesn't work, go back and select another solution to try.

Experiment: Improving Your Study Environment

You may want to try an experiment to help determine if you can improve your grades by intentionally controlling distractions in your study environment. Do the experiment for two weeks, and make a sincere effort to do the best possible job of studying. If you note an improvement in your academic performance, continue limiting distractions when you study.

Step 1. List the specific modifications that you could make in your study environment to produce better organization, reduce distractions, enhance concentration, and improve study efficiency. Indicate how effective you believe making each modification would be in improving your school work and how likely you are to implement this alteration in your study *modus operandi*.

Modification #1: _____

_____

Predict the effectiveness of this study environment modification.

1	2	3	4	5	6	7	8	9	10
none				marginal					significant

Indicate the likelihood of you actually doing this.

1	2	3	4	5	6	7	8	9	10
unlikely				fairly likely					very likely

Modification #2: _____

_____

Predict the effectiveness of this study environment modification.

1	2	3	4	5	6	7	8	9	10
none				marginal					significant

Indicate the likelihood of you actually doing this.

1	2	3	4	5	6	7	8	9	10
unlikely				fairly likely					very likely

Modification #3: _____

_____

Predict the effectiveness of this study environment modification.

1	2	3	4	5	6	7	8	9	10
none				marginal					significant

Indicate the likelihood of you actually doing this.

1	2	3	4	5	6	7	8	9	10
unlikely				fairly likely					very likely

Modification #4: _____

_____

Predict the effectiveness of this study environment modification.

1	2	3	4	5	6	7	8	9	10

none   marginal   significant

Indicate the likelihood of you actually doing this.

1	2	3	4	5	6	7	8	9	10

unlikely   fairly likely   very likely

Modification #5: _____

_____

Predict the effectiveness of this study environment modification.

1	2	3	4	5	6	7	8	9	10

none   marginal   significant

Indicate the likelihood of you actually doing this.

1	2	3	4	5	6	7	8	9	10

unlikely   fairly likely   very likely

Modification #6: _____

_____

Predict the effectiveness of this study environment modification.

1	2	3	4	5	6	7	8	9	10

none   marginal   significant

Indicate the likelihood of you actually doing this.

1	2	3	4	5	6	7	8	9	10

unlikely   fairly likely   very likely

Modification #7: _____

_____

Predict the effectiveness of this study environment modification.

1	2	3	4	5	6	7	8	9	10

none   marginal   significant

Indicate the likelihood of you actually doing this.

1	2	3	4	5	6	7	8	9	10

unlikely   fairly likely   very likely

Step 2. During the next two weeks, implement the study environment modifications you developed. To evaluate the effects of these ideas, you must make your best effort during the experiment. Keep track of your grades on homework, papers, and tests in each subject on the form provided. (*Please note:* This same grade-tracking system is also used in an experiment in Chapter 2.) If you find that regulating your study environment and reducing distractions improves your grades, it makes sense to continue doing so. If you like to listen to music when studying and are resistant to turning off your stereo, you might consider listening only under certain study conditions, such as when you are doing less intellectually demanding work. You might also consider experimenting with reducing the volume.

TWO-WEEK GRADE-TRACKING STUDY ENVIRONMENT EXPERIMENT

COURSE:

HOMEWORK:

Date					
Grade					

QUIZZES/TESTS/EXAMS/PAPERS:

Date					
Grade					

COURSE:

HOMEWORK:

Date					
Grade					

QUIZZES/TESTS/EXAMS/PAPERS:

Date					
Grade					

COURSE:

HOMEWORK:

Date					
Grade					

QUIZZES/TESTS/EXAMS/PAPERS:

Date					
Grade					

COURSE:

HOMEWORK:

Date					
Grade					

QUIZZES/TESTS/EXAMS/PAPERS:

Date					
Grade					

Graphing Your Progress

You may prefer to track your performance using a graph. The advantage of this method is that it summarizes on one page your grades in all subjects, allowing you to gauge your improvement with a quick glance. Figure 4.1 has sample graphs for homework grades and test grades. If you prefer this method, you can use these graphs to plot your progress. You can insert one copy in your binder and tape a second copy on the wall near your desk. Blank graphs are also provided in Figure 4.2, and you have permission to photocopy them.

FIGURE 4.1 *Sample performance tracking graphs.*

HOMEWORK GRADES

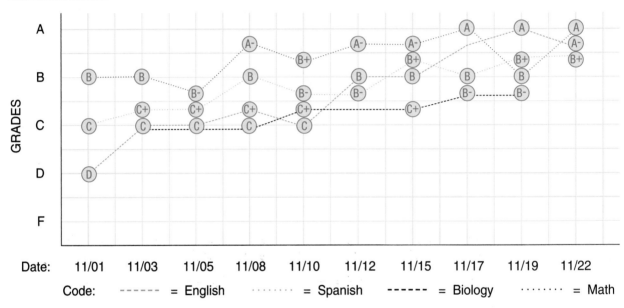

TEST GRADES

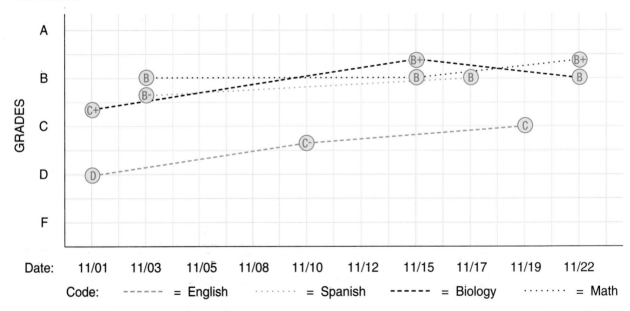

Performance tracking graphs.   **FIGURE 4.2**

HOMEWORK GRADES

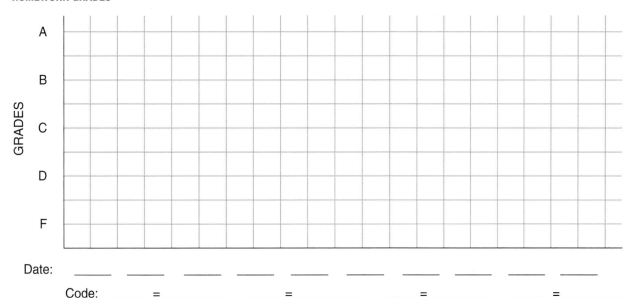

Date: _____

Code: ____ = _____   ____ = _____   ____ = _____   ____ = _____

TEST GRADES

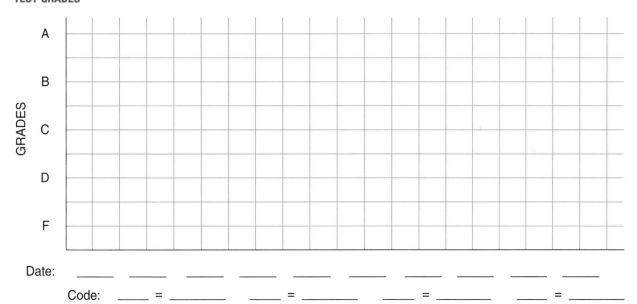

Date: _____

Code: ____ = _____   ____ = _____   ____ = _____   ____ = _____

Assessing Distractibility

ven the most conscientious student can sometimes become distracted. External stimuli can be difficult to filter out. When these stimuli are intrusive, they obviously interfere with concentration and productivity.

Internal emotional factors can also infringe on concentration and study efficiency. A student who has just fallen in love, or who has just fallen out of love, is likely to have more difficulty paying attention and staying on task than the student who is on an even emotional keel.

Handling distractions can be significantly more challenging for students with chronic focusing problems. These students may become "hyper" and may begin wandering aimlessly around the room, scanning TV channels, or playing with the dog. Some students become stressed and distracted when the work is difficult and they feel overwhelmed and discouraged. As a coping mechanism, they may head for the kitchen or start surfing the Internet. Certain students are vulnerable to distractions after a few minutes of intense work. They may be listening to a lecture or studying in the library and become absorbed by unrelated thoughts. As they are working on a page of math problems, they may begin thinking about what movie they want to see on Saturday night or where they plan to watch the Sunday football games. Other students simply drift off. They may become sleepy and may even fall asleep in class or while doing homework.

Past negative associations with academics can also affect a student's mental endurance and capacity to sustain focus. Students who were repeatedly criticized as children for inattentiveness may be quite defensive about their proclivities. They may justify their distractibility by consciously or unconsciously rationalizing that the material is boring or irrelevant and doesn't merit diligence.

The first step in enhancing your capacity to concentrate for sustained periods of time is to identify potentially distracting external and internal stimuli and to gauge your typical reactions to these stimuli. Be conscious of your own distinctive response patterns. For example, you may react to difficult material by tuning out and daydreaming or by tapping your pencil, drawing cartoons, and fidgeting. You may begin to leaf through a magazine, take excessive study breaks, make unnecessary telephone calls, or glance at the clock every few seconds. You may start looking out the window or doodling in your notebook. You may get up every few minutes and wander aimlessly around the room, or you may wander into the kitchen and search through the refrigerator.

Distractibility Inventory

Evaluate your current behavior patterns.

	Yes	No	Sometimes
1. I have difficulty sustaining my concentration when doing homework and studying.	○	○	○
2. I have difficulty sustaining my concentration in class.	○	○	○
3. Difficult material causes me to "shut down" mentally.	○	○	○
4. I can only concentrate for sustained periods of time when I am doing something I enjoy.	○	○	○
5. I allow my attention to wander when I am doing work that requires intensely focused effort.	○	○	○
6. I have many easily accessible "playthings" in my study environment and I use them to entertain myself when doing homework.	○	○	○

	Yes	No	Sometimes
7. When I feel overwhelmed by challenging assignments, I look for any excuse to escape from doing the work.	○	○	○
8. When I feel academically frustrated and discouraged, my mind wanders and I begin to daydream and procrastinate.	○	○	○
9. When my stress level rises, I turn on the TV, pick up a magazine, call a friend, go on-line, or play a video game.	○	○	○
10. I need to take a study break every few minutes.	○	○	○
11. I rationalize and defend my inattentiveness.	○	○	○
12. I spend additional hours each week doing homework because of my distractibility.	○	○	○
13. My learning efficiency is negatively affected when I am distracted.	○	○	○
14. My grades are negatively affected by my distractibility.	○	○	○

Interpreting the inventory. A pattern of "yes" responses to the statements in the inventory should be interpreted as a red flag. (Chronic distractibility and inattentiveness could signal attention deficit hyperactivity disorder. If you believe that you may have this condition, talk with your academic advisor. An evaluation may be advisable.) These behaviors suggest that your inattentiveness is having a negative impact on your academic performance. A pattern of "sometimes" responses should be interpreted as a yellow flag indicating the need for vigilance and appropriate adjustments in your study *modus operandi*. Of course, every student occasionally becomes distracted, but recurring patterns can pose major obstacles to school success. Once you identify your behavior patterns, you have several options. You may decide that you must admonish yourself when you become inattentive. You may say, "Stop! I'm in charge here, and I can control my thoughts and actions." Or you may conclude that you must reduce your anxiety so that you can calm down and begin to focus on the task at hand.

PRACTICAL TECHNIQUES FOR ENHANCING CONCENTRATION

The following procedures can be used individually or in combination. Experiment until you find the method or mix of methods that works best for you.

Breathing. When you become aware that that your anxiety, stress, inattentiveness, or activity level is rising, close your eyes for a few seconds. Breathe slowly and deeply and feel your lungs and chest expand. (*Do this no more than three times or you may hyperventilate and become dizzy.*) Feel your body relax. Then, calmly direct yourself to refocus your attention on your work.

Focusing. Focus on a spot on your body (e.g., knee or big toe) or on a wall. Deliberately direct all of your thoughts and feelings to that spot for two minutes. Feel the stress and distractibility begin to flow slowly and gently from your body. Feel your body relax. Then, calmly direct yourself to refocus your attention on your work.

Visualizing. Form a mental picture of doing your work calmly and effectively. Visualize yourself in your study cave or study fortress concentrating efficiently and filtering out distractions. See yourself confidently completing assignments or remaining attentive in class. Put details in your mental picture: your books, your desk, or the instructor standing in front of the class. Tell yourself that *you are in control of your mind.* Remind yourself that the *responsible you,* and not that inattentive part of your brain, is "calling the shots." Form a mental image and see yourself as being calm, competent, and efficient. Remind yourself that you want to get good grades and complete your academic program successfully. See yourself looking at your grades and feeling proud and gratified. Then, visualize yourself in a cap and gown receiving your diploma at graduation. This mental imaging procedure requires no more than a few minutes. Once you have completed the process, intentionally refocus your attention on the task at hand. Pat yourself on the back when you've successfully refocused! With practice, the procedure will become easier, and you will be in control when you have to be in control.

SELF-DIRECTED BEHAVIOR MODIFICATION

Some students respond best to procedures that are highly concrete. They discipline themselves most effectively by keeping meticulous track of their actions and working to improve their "score." In a sense, this procedure is akin to a daily training regimen checklist that an athlete might use. Each day, the athlete might work toward augmenting her endurance by increasing the length of her workouts in the gym. A tennis player might improve the power and efficiency of his tennis serve by working to increase the velocity and top spin, and a competitive runner might use specific training equipment to enhance her ability to get off the starting block more quickly. Over time, methodical practice and meticulous record keeping will produce minor daily improvements that, in turn, generate a significant cumulative improvement.

If you work best by establishing and checking off specific daily goals, consider using the following *Self-Regulation Checklist.* Experiment to see whether the checklist helps you concentrate. You may also combine the checklist with the other techniques described earlier.

Self-Regulation Checklist

Code: 1 = poor   2 = average   3 = good   4 = excellent

	MON.	TUES.	WED.	THURS.	FRI.	WEEKEND
1. I disciplined myself to pay attention in class.	○	○	○	○	○	○
2. I disciplined myself to pay attention while studying.	○	○	○	○	○	○
3. I disciplined myself to calm down when I became distracted or hyperactive.	○	○	○	○	○	○
4. I disciplined myself to complete my assignments.	○	○	○	○	○	○

	MON.	TUES.	WED.	THURS.	FRI.	WEEKEND
5. I disciplined myself to look for errors in my work.	○	○	○	○	○	○
6. I disciplined myself to submit my work on time.	○	○	○	○	○	○
7. I disciplined myself to follow instructions.	○	○	○	○	○	○
8. I disciplined myself to study without taking excessive study breaks.	○	○	○	○	○	○
9. I disciplined myself to relax when I became anxious or hyperactive.	○	○	○	○	○	○
10. I disciplined myself not to play with objects in my study environment.	○	○	○	○	○	○

If your responses to the statements indicate that you are having difficulty in specific areas (e.g., relaxing when taking tests), your goal is to eliminate these deficits or, at least, compensate successfully for them. Continue using the checklist until you attain your goal and are able to focus more effectively when doing homework and studying.

POWERHOUSE THINKING

Key Principles for Improving Your Concentration

- Intentionally create an impenetrable study fortress.
- Identify and reduce distractions and interruptions.
- Designate blocks of uninterrupted study time.
- Apply breathing, anatomical spot focusing, visualizing, or self-initiated behavior modification techniques.

For Your Information

Some students believe they can concentrate and study productively while watching TV or listening to loud music. They also believe that repeated interruptions to make and receive phone calls, surf the Internet, and wander into the kitchen do not have any effect on the quality of their studying.

Students who are convinced that they can work productively despite repeated distractions and interruptions may be deluding themselves. They may not realize (or they may be intent on denying) that their learning efficiency is being undermined by their maladaptive study behaviors, and they may be unwilling to examine the evidence objectively (e.g., marginal grades and negative comments from instructors about the quality of their work).

They may be unwilling to admit that if they deliberately reduce distractions, sustain their focus, and become more organized, they could significantly improve their school performance.

Students who cannot stay on track, focus, filter out distractions, be organized, inhibit their impulses, and control their body are rarely able to function in school at a level commensurate with their full potential. Those with chronic concentration problems may have attention deficit hyperactivity disorder (ADHD). Scientists have pinpointed a brain anomaly that could explain ADHD. Research indicates that the brain of hyperactive adults uses 8 percent less glucose (the brain's main source of energy) than normal. The finding suggests that hyperactivity results when specific regions of the brain that control attention, motor coordination, handwriting, and inhibited responses are not functioning properly. This research, in tandem with previous research that found that approximately 30 percent of all children with ADHD have at least one parent with ADHD, confirms that hyperactivity is genetically and/or biologically based (*New England Journal of Medicine*, November, 1990). The following behaviors are often associated with ADHD:

- impulsiveness
- distractibility
- disorganization
- inattentiveness
- disregard of details
- improperly recorded assignments
- missed deadlines
- poor time management
- sloppy work
- inaccuracies
- poor planning

Concentration deficits can be especially problematic when students are required to do work they find uninteresting or difficult. Challenging, repetitive, or "boring" academic tasks that require sustained effort, attention to details, and extended self-discipline can produce stress, procrastination, and avoidance behaviors (e.g., playing with objects in the environment, frequent interruptions). Many students, however, have *selective* concentration problems. They may be able to focus for five hours at a stretch while rebuilding a car engine or working in the garden, but they may struggle to pay attention for more than a few minutes when doing math problems or reading a chemistry textbook.

Ironically, those students who have the greatest need to discipline themselves, concentrate, and work efficiently are often the ones who are the most disorganized and the most likely to surround themselves with distractions. In many instances, these students have a history of concentration problems that date back to elementary school.

Many students discover that by regulating distractions in the study environment, applying the commonsense "do's and don'ts" of effective studying, reducing disorganization, and developing practical attention-focusing procedures, they can significantly enhance their academic efficiency, productivity, and performance. When you conduct an objective experiment into whether a nondistracting study context improves your grades, you may find a clear and compelling argument for intentionally exerting control over your study environment.

SECTION TWO

Developing a School Success System

LEARNING HOW TO STUDY MORE PRODUCTIVELY

5

POWER READING

OBJECTIVES

- Learning how to speed-read
- Creating a mind-map
- Using critical and strategic intelligence when reading

A New Perspective

cience had never been one of Jeremy's favorite subjects. In fact, his biology course in high school had been a nightmare that had almost driven him over the edge. Despite hours and hours of studying, he had barely squeaked by with a C–.

Now as a second-year college student majoring in graphic arts, Jeremy was preoccupied with taking the required art classes for his degree. His dilemma was fulfilling the school's general education requirements. Needing one more science class to graduate, Jeremy had enrolled in a general science course, and it had been a downhill slide from the very first day.

After glancing at the assigned unit on nuclear energy, Jeremy began to panic. All of the negative feelings he had experienced in high school came flooding back. The material seemed so complicated and boring. Having absolutely no confidence in his ability to understand and recall scientific information, he felt overwhelmed and demoralized. Convinced that he was hopelessly "dumb," he slammed his textbook closed and decided to take his dog for a walk. He had to clear his head and figure out a way to pass the course.

When he returned to his apartment, Jeremy remembered that his cousin Jesse was a hospital lab tech who had a B.A. in chemistry and was now enrolled part-time in a master's degree program. His cousin had always been a great student, especially in science, and at the last family Thanksgiving get-together, Jesse had offered to help him if he had problems in school.

Fortunately, Jesse was home when Jeremy telephoned him.

Jeremy: Jesse, I'm in a real jam. I think I may flunk the general science course I need for my degree. I just don't understand science. It puts my toes to sleep.

Jesse: Well, you've somehow got to pass the course. Come on over now and bring your textbook. I have an idea that may help you.

Jeremy: What is it?

Jesse: The method is called mind-mapping. It helps you identify, understand, and remember information. I personally like this technique because it shows you how the information is tied together. It lets you see the links and it makes the facts and ideas easier to comprehend. I used mind-mapping throughout college, and if I hadn't, I would never have graduated with a 3.5 G.P.A. There's one other thing. The procedure can be very creative and artistic, so it's right up your alley.

Jeremy: I can't argue with that kind of success, Jesse, and I like the idea that the method is artistic. I'm for anything that can make a unit about nuclear energy interesting. I'll be there in 15 minutes.

As they sat at the kitchen table, Jesse began to explain the procedures. He then went to his room, returned with a binder, and showed Jeremy several mind-maps he had drawn for some of his college courses (see Figure 5.1 for an example).

The key to mind-mapping, Jeremy discovered, was to figure out what information was important and link this information so that it made sense and could be clearly understood and remembered. Jesse told Jeremy that the procedure of representing the data in an "information diagram" would improve his recall. Jeremy especially loved the idea of being able to use pictures, designs, and graphics to explain and represent the material he needed to learn.

Jesse told his cousin to use different colored pencils or pens when he recorded the data on a piece of unlined paper. He could link the information together with lines and arrows. If the method worked for him, the facts and the map would remain imprinted in his mind. These mental pictures would help him answer the questions on a test.

Jeremy learned that there were key preliminary steps that should be done before actually reading and mind-mapping the material in the textbook. **Step 1** was to read the title of the chapter and turn it into a question using three *main idea question words: how, why, or what.*

Turning the title of the science chapter—"Nuclear Energy: Harnessing the Atom"—into a question was a piece of cake. After reviewing the three *main idea questions,* Jeremy concluded that he could use either "how" or "why" to turn the title into a question. He selected the word "how." At the top of a separate piece of lined paper, he wrote: *"How was the atom harnessed to produce nuclear energy?"*

At Jesse's recommendation, Jeremy turned the paper so that it was horizontal and allowed more room for the mind-map. In the center of the page, he wrote in capital letters with a red felt pen *Nuclear Energy.* Then, using a green felt pen for contrast, he drew a circle around it. He copied his question at the top.

Jesse explained that **Step 2** was to *review mentally all that he already knew about nuclear energy.* Jeremy recalled newspaper articles and several movies and TV programs that dealt with nuclear reactors, meltdowns, bombs, waste, and accidents. He was surprised by how much he actually knew.

Step 3 had two parts. **Part 1** was to *speed-read the material very quickly while trying to note some of the key ideas and information.* **Part 2** was to *speed-read the material again.* Jesse explained that when you speed-read, you don't actually read *every* word; rather, you force your eyes to *skim* each line looking for "clumps" of information. He showed Jeremy how to use two fingers as a horizontal shutter to scan the lines quickly (see the illustration page 95). He told him to skim the material very rapidly and not to worry about pronouncing each word in his mind. He also told Jeremy not to be upset about what he didn't remember after the first skimming. The purpose of this initial scan was to get a basic overview of the material.

Jesse advised Jeremy to take a few minutes to examine the four illustrations in the unit before beginning to skim the material. The first illustration (entitled "Nuclear Fission") showed an atom splitting and releasing energy and other materials. The second (entitled "Nuclear Fusion") showed two nuclei fusing into one nucleus and releasing energy and other materials. The third (entitled "Chain Reaction") showed an atom splitting and triggering a chain reaction in which other atoms were split. Jeremy then examined the fourth illustration (entitled "Nuclear Reactor"), which showed how nuclear energy is produced in a nuclear reactor.

After briefly studying the illustrations, Jeremy began to speed-read the first several pages of the unit as Jesse had instructed. This required approximately three minutes. He then skimmed the material a second time. This also took three minutes.

The procedure was a little unsettling because Jeremy realized that he didn't remember very much. When he commented about this to Jesse, his cousin assured him that this was perfectly OK and reminded him that he was simply trying to get an overview of the material.

It was now time to do **Step 4.** This step involved reading the material slowly and carefully and actually mind-mapping the key information. In the middle of the blank paper where he had written the words *Nuclear Energy,* Jeremy began creating his mind-map. Realizing that there was a great deal of information in the unit and that he needed more room, Jeremy decided to discard his original piece of paper. Instead, he taped two pieces together, putting the tape on the reverse side of the pages. In the middle, he again wrote *Nuclear Energy* in big block letters with a red felt pen and drew a green circle around the words, and copied his question at the top.

Using different colored felt pens for each fact or chunk of information, Jeremy recorded everything he considered important. As he drew intricate and artistic circles, boxes, ovals, and squiggly chains around each information chunk; linked the facts together; and drew lines connecting the data to the green circle in the middle of the page, Jeremy was astonished by how much information he wanted to include in his map.

Jeremy completed the first part of the mind-map at Jesse's dining room table. From time to time, Jesse made suggestions about which facts should be included. Jeremy was delighted with the procedure and was amazed at how it helped him understand otherwise complex and intimidating scientific material. He couldn't wait to get home and complete his map.

zooming in on the issues

A Picture Can Be Worth a Thousand Words

Jeremy faced a major challenge: He needed one more science course to fulfill the general education requirements for his degree.

Go back to the story and underline the key decision Jeremy made about his cousin. Then, evaluate the decision.

1	2	3	4	5	6	7	8	9	10
not smart				fairly smart					very smart

Underline and number each of the mind-mapping procedures that Jesse described to Jeremy, and predict the effectiveness of the mind-mapping method in helping Jeremy handle the science unit.

1	2	3	4	5	6	7	8	9	10
ineffective				fairly effective					very effective

Why did you reach this conclusion?

_____

_____

_____

List any reservations you might have about the mind-mapping procedure:

1. _____

2. _____

3. _____

4. _____

Can you think of any other ideas that might have helped Jeremy deal with his problem?

1. _____

2. _____

3. _____

4. _____

How would you evaluate Jeremy's strategic thinking?

1	2	3	4	5	6	7	8	9	10
poor				fair					excellent

Why did you reach this conclusion? _____

_____

_____

Based on his behavior and attitude, predict the likelihood that Jeremy will fulfill the science requirement for his degree.

1	2	3	4	5	6	7	8	9	10
poor				fair					excellent

Why did you reach this conclusion? _____

_____

_____

Drawing a Conclusion from the Evidence

Having read about Jeremy's predicament, what specific conclusion can you draw from the information in the story? Using the *inductive method,* express in a well-crafted sentence what you have concluded. *Remember:* you are summarizing the **point** of the story.

The point of Jeremy's story: _____

_____

_____

_____

_____

Dealing with "Boring" Material

You're now going to read the same science unit that Jeremy was studying and practice the first three steps of the mind-mapping procedure. Before beginning, the issue of studying material that may appear boring or irrelevant must be addressed. Your first reaction to the prospect of reading a unit about nuclear energy may be quite negative. You may not be particularly interested in learning about the subject, especially if you don't like science or lack confidence in your ability to understand scientific material.

Throughout your education, you can expect to encounter material that seems uninteresting. Having to learn information that may not seem particularly relevant is a fact of life in school. To fulfill your degree requirements, you will have to take courses in science, social science, humanities, English, foreign language, and math. You may not like the content of a particular required course, but you must, nonetheless, do everything in your power to get a good grade. This is the essence of thinking strategically.

In school and in life, you have to get the job done even if a task or obligation is tedious, unpleasant, or boring (e.g., completing a financial aid application). Having the fortitude to complete the unpleasant jobs is a requisite to success in a highly competitive world that rewards those with grit; determination; and focused, goal-directed behavior and attitudes. There is, however, "a light at the end of the tunnel." The study method you are about to learn will make the challenge of studying content that you may consider boring, uninteresting, useless, or irrelevant less painful and difficult.

The following article about nuclear energy is *intentionally* included because it is difficult and contains complex technical information. Those who enjoy science are likely to find the material more appealing than those who prefer courses in art, foreign languages, or criminal justice. (Do not despair! Non-scientific subjects are used in subsequent chapters.) Students who are not scientifically oriented may have to work harder to understand and master the content, but the process of pushing yourself to the limit and knocking over, or detouring around, life's obstacles will challenge you to develop your ingenuity and your full range of abilities. Any serious athlete can confirm this. As you run a marathon, climb a mountain, or compete on a playing field, you could easily become exhausted and be sorely tempted to quit. Winners reach inside, remind themselves of their desire to prevail, and push on through the barrier. The real test of character is how you handle the tough situations—not how you handle the easy, comfortable ones.

Learning How to Create a Mind-Map

You are going to learn how to create a mind-map. If you already know the method, do the exercises anyway. You may learn something new, and it will be good practice. You will use the nuclear energy material in the next two chapters as you practice other study procedures, so the more you learn about the subject now, the better.

Practicing Mind-Mapping

NUCLEAR ENERGY: HARNESSING THE ATOM

Step 1. *Turn the title into a Main Idea Question using a question word: how, why, what.* (Use the *complete* title. You can add words so that the question makes sense.)

Main idea question: _____

_____

(*Hint:* One possibility is "How was the atom harnessed to produce nuclear energy?" You'll have many additional opportunities to practice turning titles into questions in subsequent chapters.)

Step 2. *Write down what you already know about the subject.* (You probably know something about nuclear energy from watching TV or reading the newspaper.) Record what you can recall *before* reading the material.

WHAT I ALREADY KNOW ABOUT NUCLEAR ENERGY

1. _____

2. _____

3. _____

4. _____

5. _____

6. _____

Step 3: *Speed-reading.* It's time to speed-read the nuclear energy unit, skimming for information. Look at the illustration below and notice how the fingers form a "shutter."

Using your fingers this way permits you to scan the words quickly and easily, *without reading or pronouncing each word in your mind.*

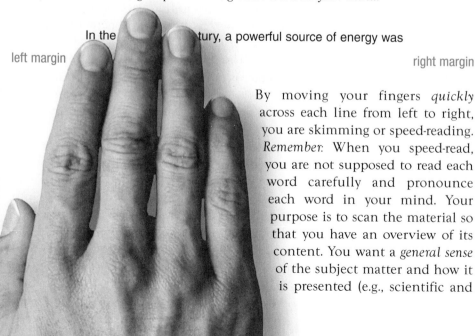

In the   tury, a powerful source of energy was

left margin   right margin

By moving your fingers *quickly* across each line from left to right, you are skimming or speed-reading. *Remember:* When you speed-read, you are not supposed to read each word carefully and pronounce each word in your mind. Your purpose is to scan the material so that you have an overview of its content. You want a *general sense* of the subject matter and how it is presented (e.g., scientific and technical, editorial or opinion, criticism). This skimming procedure may be challenging for you at first because you were taught to read every word carefully in elementary school. This early conditioning about the "proper way to read" can be an extremely difficult habit to break.

Speed-reading is a very different skill. It's a tool for becoming familiar with the subject matter when you *first* begin to read or study something new. When you actually study the material, you must, of course, read it slowly, carefully, and accurately. Your goal at this stage of the studying process is to digest, comprehend, recall, and apply the information you have to learn.

It's time to practice speed-reading—spend no more than *four minutes* scanning the material on the next four pages. *Remember:* You're not expected to remember a great deal of information from the first scanning. You simply want to get an idea about what you are being asked to read or study. Forcing yourself to scan the material quickly may be difficult at first because you are not used to the technique. With practice, the method will become easy, and your confidence in your ability to acquire a quick overview of the content of what you're reading will improve dramatically!

MIND-MAPPING: A PICTURE IS WORTH A THOUSAND WORDS

If you followed the instructions above, you've already completed **Step 1, Step 2,** and the first part of **Step 3** of the mind-mapping procedure. You've probably also learned some new information about nuclear energy from skimming the article.

It is now time to do the second part of **Step 3**—*speed-read the article again.* Skim quickly and spend no more than four minutes. After you've finished this skimming process, you'll probably discover that you've picked up more information about nuclear energy. **Don't worry if there are still many specific facts you can't remember.** You can't be expected to remember all of the facts after skimming the article only two times!

Now, you're ready to do **Step 4.**

Step 4: *Read the material carefully and mind-map.* You're going to become an artist! You'll need colored pencils or felt pens and a piece of unlined paper. Turn the paper horizontally and use one of your colored pens to write the question "How Can the Atom Be Harnessed to Produce Nuclear Energy?" at the top of the paper. Because you will be including a great deal of information, you might want to tape two pieces of paper together. Be as creative and artistic as you want when making designs around any of the information you write down. (If you don't want to be artistic, that's OK. You may prefer to make your diagram simple and straightforward.) Use colors you like. Write small so that you can fit the information on the paper. Include only the **key** ideas in your mind-map. Leave out unnecessary words. Plan ahead so you have enough room to draw the arrows, boxes, circles, and ovals. Draw connecting lines to show how the information is linked. If you have difficulty getting started, examine the partial model in Figure 5.1. Your mind-map may look quite different, but it should contain most of the facts in the model. Compare your completed mind-map to Figure 5.2. If your mind-map is missing information, consider why the missing facts are important and why your instructor might want you to understand and recall them.

NUCLEAR ENERGY: HARNESSING THE ATOM

In 1945, two atomic bombs were dropped over the cities of Nagasaki and Hiroshima. This devastating nuclear attack caused the Japanese forces to surrender. Although many people believe that the attack signaled the beginning of the nuclear age, atomic energy was actually discovered more than 50 years prior to the bombing.

Atoms are the smallest and most fundamental unit of matter, and everything in our world is comprised of this basic unit. This includes the clothes we wear, the air we breathe, the food we eat, the paper we write on, and the gasoline we put in our cars. Several important earlier discoveries led to the discovery of nuclear energy. In 1896, a French scientist named Antoine Henry Becquerel identified radioactivity. His scientific experiments revealed that certain elements released radioactive rays and that these elements possessed unique and fascinating properties.

In the late 1930s, scientists in Germany realized that by using a process called **nuclear fission,** it was possible to split the nucleus of an atom into two nuclei. To understand how fission works, it may help to imagine a chocolate chip being split in half by a cleaver. Now imagine that the energy holding the chocolate chip together is suddenly released by the splitting process, and this results in a massive explosion. (This image is intended only to help you understand the fission process. In the case of splitting a chocolate chip, *no* significant energy is actually released.) The discovery that energy is released when certain types of atomic material are split led to the first nuclear reactor being built in the early 1940s and, ultimately, to the first military use of nuclear fission. The two atomic bombs dropped over Japan to end World War II represent the only time in history that nuclear weapons have been used in war.

The development of the hydrogen bomb in the 1950s was an even more frightening use of atomic power. Hydrogen bombs release massive amounts of nuclear energy by combining (fusing) two hydrogen nuclei to form one nucleus. To understand the fusion process, imagine two chocolate chips sitting next to each other on a pan in an oven. As the oven gets hot, the two chips melt together (or fuse) to form one big chip, and in this combining process, a massive amount of energy is released. (Of course, two chocolate chips melting together do not actually produce a measurable release of energy!) Fusion occurs naturally in the sun where hydrogen nuclei are continually combining to produce enormous amounts of heat, light, and radiation (see the illustrations "Nuclear Fission" and "Nuclear Fusion").

Although nuclear technology has produced nuclear weapons that are capable of horrific destruction, this same technology

EXHIBIT 1 Nuclear fission

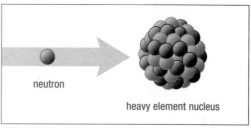

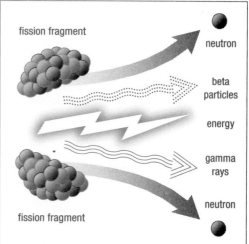

Neutron splits the nucleus of a heavy element such as uranium into two fission fragments, resulting in an energy release along with other materials.

EXHIBIT 2 Nuclear fusion

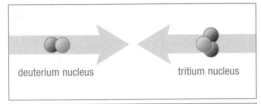

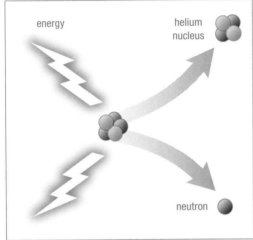

Two lighter nuclei unite to form a heavier nucleus which results in an energy release.

also has many peaceful applications. One of the most important involves the production of electricity. In 1956, the first nuclear power plant was built in England, and in 1957, the first U.S. plant was constructed. By the late 1980s, there were over 420 reactors operating throughout the world, and there were more than 110 nuclear reactors in production in the United States. Today, nuclear energy is second only to coal as the largest source of electricity—currently, more than 17 percent of our electricity is generated from nuclear energy.

Examining the Nuclear Atom

To understand nuclear power, we must examine the atom. At the center of every atom is a nucleus. This nucleus makes up most of the *mass* (weight) of the atom, but relatively little of its *volume* (size). Scientists discovered that in certain atoms a special energy binds the nucleus together. When the nucleus undergoes changes, the binding energy is released as *electromagnetic waves* (gamma radiation) and *energy particles* (e.g., neutron, protons). When an atomic nucleus begins to disintegrate spontaneously and gives off radiation, the process is called **nuclear decay.** Nuclear energy can also be released when an atomic nucleus is *intentionally* split or fused. This is precisely what happens when a nuclear weapon explodes (see Exhibits 1 and 2).

To understand how binding energy is released, consider what occurs when you burn a log in a fireplace. Before burning, the log may weigh eight pounds. After burning, the remaining ash and carbon weigh less than a pound. Weight (or mass) is lost because the fire has transformed the cellulose into smoke, heat (thermal energy), carbon, and ash. The released energy heats the room and escapes through the chimney. The ash is what remains from the original mass.

In an atomic nucleus (e.g., Uranium 235), the mass (weight) of the original nucleus (see Exhibits 1 and 2) is *greater* than the mass of the products that result when the binding energy breaks down. The lost mass is released as energy (e.g., radiation, neutrons, heat). After concluding that *matter is a type of energy*, Albert Einstein, the famous physicist who is considered by many to be the "father" of the nuclear age, explained the loss of mass with his famous equation $E=MC^2$ (energy = mass multiplied by the speed of light squared).

Nuclear energy is an awesome source of power. The energy released by a hydrogen bomb is thousands of times greater than the energy released by conventional bombs. The atomic energy contained in the core of a nuclear power plant is approximately one billion times greater than the energy produced by burning an equivalent amount (in terms of weight) of coal, oil, or gas.

Nuclear Weapons

In the 1930s, a frightening use for nuclear energy was recognized as scientists began to study and understand nuclear fission. When fission occurs, the nucleus of a heavy element such as enriched uranium splits in

EXHIBIT 3 Chain reaction   Continuing splitting of nuclei to produce a steady supply of energy.

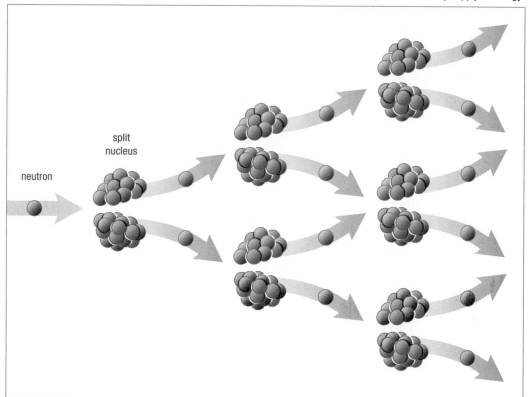

two. A chain reaction then occurs. As each nucleus splits, the released energy triggers another nucleus to split, and the chain reaction continues (see Exhibit 3). The released energy (*kinetic energy*) rapidly transforms into intense heat. This discovery led to the development of the atomic bomb.

An even more powerful way to release nuclear energy was discovered in the 1950s. Nuclear scientists and engineers realized they could use an atomic bomb to produce the necessary intense heat and energy to combine two light hydrogen nuclei into a larger nucleus. This process is called **nuclear fusion.** The released energy from a hydrogen fusion reaction (a hydrogen bomb) is many times more powerful than that released by nuclear fission (an atomic bomb).

Nuclear Reactors

Today, nuclear reactors are a major source of electrical energy in many countries throughout the world. In the core or center of a thermal nuclear reactor, fissionable fuel material (tiny pellets of nuclear fuel typically stacked end to end in 13-foot tubes) is combined with moderators (used to slow down the fission process), other materials, and safety systems to produce a continuing chain reaction. Coolants are also used to transfer heat and to start, maintain, and stop the chain reaction. Several different types of reactors are currently in production throughout the world. The energy from the nuclear chain reaction produces steam that runs the turbines and generators that produce electricity (see Exhibit 4).

The Pluses and Minuses of Nuclear Energy

Because of safety and environmental concerns, governments throughout the world are carefully weighing the advantages and disadvantages of nuclear energy. One major advantage is that nuclear power plants use much less fuel than plants that burn coal,

EXHIBIT 4   Fast breeder reactor

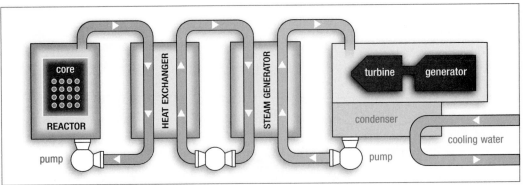

oil, or gas. The fission of one pound of uranium generates the equivalent energy of 1,140 *tons* of coal. Another advantage is that nuclear plants do not release the chemical and solid pollutants that many coal-burning electricity plants produce.

There are also important disadvantages to nuclear power. Nuclear plants cost far more to build than conventional plants, and the availability of atomic fuel is limited (usually Uranium 235). The risk of a serious accident, such as occurred in 1986 at Chernobyl in the former Soviet Union, has caused people throughout the world to have grave concerns about safety.

Accidents have also occurred in the United States. In 1978, there was a serious accident at the Three Mile Island Nuclear Power Plant. Because of human and mechanical error, the cooling system that regulated the heat in the core failed. Fortunately, scientists and technicians were able to prevent a total core meltdown (an uncontrolled nuclear reaction that produces intense heat and melts the nuclear containment vessels) and the massive release of radioactivity.

Other major concerns involve the safety risks related to the disposal of the spent fuel rods and other radioactive wastes. Radioactivity is extremely dangerous and can cause death. Even relatively limited exposure to radioactive material can cause cancer, genetic damage, and birth defects. Used uranium or plutonium from nuclear reactors and weapons plants can continue to produce radioactivity for centuries. Because of the fear that an accidental release of radioactivity will occur, many states do not want these wastes disposed of within their borders. Even the safe transportation of nuclear waste poses potential risks. If a train or truck was involved in an accident and overturned, dangerous radioactivity might be released, and its effects can linger for years.

Other Uses of Nuclear Energy

Nuclear energy has other applications besides the production of electrical energy and nuclear weapons. Atomic elements have become important tools in modern medicine. Radioactive Cobalt 60 is used to treat cancer. Radioactive tracers are used as diagnostic tools, and radioactive medicines are used to treat diseases. Radioactivity can also be used to kill bacteria, prevent plant diseases, preserve foods for long periods of time without refrigeration, and even provide a highly accurate way to keep track of time (the atomic clock).

Most scientists agree that many other medical and nonmedical uses of nuclear energy are yet to be discovered. Safety, of course, is still a very serious concern, but it's clear that a harnessed atom will play an increasingly important role in the lives of people throughout the world during the twenty-first century.

Sources: Material from *Encyclopedia Britannica (1998), World Book Encyclopedia (2001),* and *Encyclopedia Americana* (1998).

Partial model mind-map.   **FIGURE 5.1**

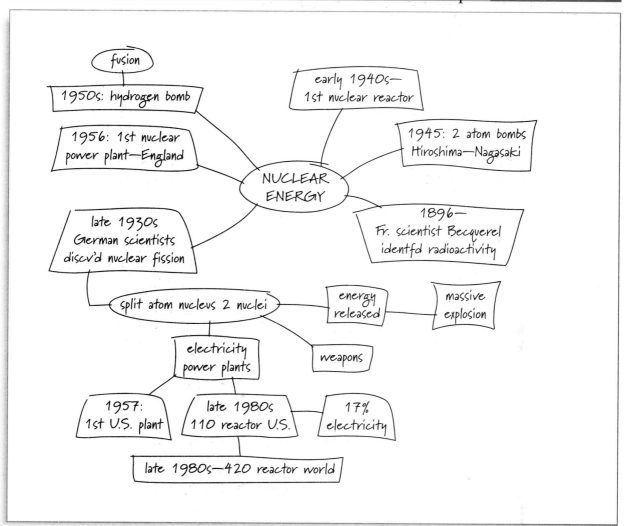

Step 5: *Answer the main idea question.* Writing a short essay to answer the main idea question you wrote at the top of your mind-map helps you tie together and remember the important information. Use your mind-map to help you write the essay. A sample topic sentence is provided to help you get started.

Recapping the Five Mind-Map Steps

Step 1: Turn the title into a main idea question.

Step 2: Write down everything you know about the subject before reading the material.

Step 3: Speed-read the material two times.

Step 4: Read the material carefully and mind-map.

Step 5: Answer the main idea question.

FIGURE 5.2   *Complete model mind-map.*

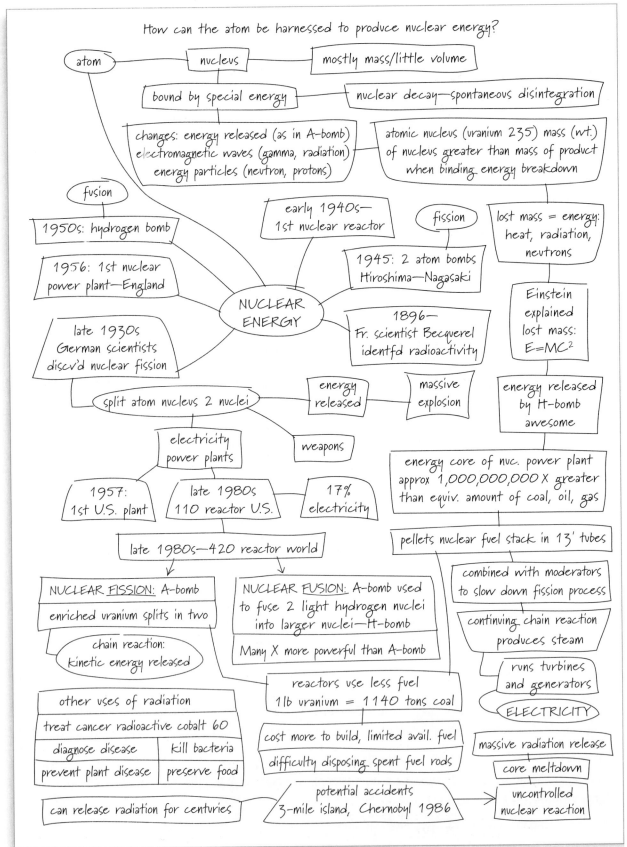

Answering the Main Idea Question

Use your mind-map to write a paragraph that answers the main idea question you posed before you began to read the article: "How was the atom harnassed to produce nuclear energy?" Begin with a powerful topic sentence and include in the paragraph the important facts recorded in your mind-map. You can use the following sample to begin your essay, or you can make up your own. Once you choose a topic sentence, incorporate the facts and data that explain how nuclear energy was discovered, how it works, and how it's used.

Sample topic sentence: *The discovery of radioactivity by a French scientist in 1896 led to a major scientific breakthrough—the harnessing of nuclear energy.*

HOW WAS THE ATOM HARNESSED TO PRODUCE NUCLEAR ENERGY?

_____

_____

_____

_____

_____

_____

_____

_____

_____

_____

_____

_____

_____

_____

Reviewing the Mind-Mapping Steps

Number the following mind-mapping steps in the proper order.

Step _____ : Answer the main idea question.

Step _____ : Speed-read the material two times.

Step _____ : Write down everything you know about the subject before reading the material.

Step _____ : Read the material carefully and mind-map.

Step _____ : Turn the title into a main idea question.

USING MIND-MAPPING TO PREPARE FOR A LECTURE

Let's assume that your assignment is to read certain pages in your psychology textbook. It's Thursday, and your instructor will give a lecture covering the assigned material on Monday (see Chapter 8 for suggestions on how to improve your lecture note-taking skills). You have several options:

- go to class without having read the material
- skim the material to get an overview
- read the material
- skim, read carefully, and mind-map the material

If you think strategically and want a good grade in the course, you should choose Option 4. Combining skimming, reading, and mind-mapping makes certain that you are prepared for class and allows you to derive maximum benefit from the lecture. The procedure also provides an overview and helps link the key information that the instructor will cover in class.

When preparing for a lecture, you can omit steps 1 and 5—asking and answering the title question. You can do this later when you're actually studying the material for a test. You should be able to complete the skimming, reading, and mind-mapping steps relatively quickly, and this preparation time will produce dividends down the road when you have to take a test that covers the assigned material.

Developing Your Critical Intelligence

Many students are willing to accept at face value whatever is written in a book. Recognizing that the author of a European history or psychology textbook obviously knows more about the subject than they do, they are reluctant to question or challenge the author's statements, interpretations, and conclusions. Because authors have advanced degrees and have done research in their area of specialization, some students regard them as experts who cannot be challenged. They are also aware that their instructor would not have selected a particular textbook if he or she was not convinced of the book's merit and validity.

That textbook authors are authorities in their field is generally beyond dispute. At issue is whether these experts are always objective and whether their contentions are balanced and fair. Some authors—even historians—may have subtle or not-so-subtle biases and may perceive events and data from their own personal perspective. For example, a scholar who grew up in a ghetto and then attended a prestigious university to earn a Ph.D. might interpret certain aspects of the Civil War quite differently than a middle-class scholar who went to an elite private school and earned a Ph.D. from the same university. Despite the assumption of objectivity, an author's life experiences, training, and values can influence how facts are interpreted and information is distilled.

Once you establish the habit of critically analyzing and questioning what you are reading in books and hearing in class, you will become more cautious about accepting information or statements simply because the assertions are made by an expert. This "delving beneath the surface" process enhances your active involvement in what you are studying, and it plays an instrumental role in improving your comprehension and ability to assimilate information. Examples of probing questions that demonstrate active critical thinking include:

- What is the significance of this material?
- Do I agree with the author's or instructor's interpretation of the facts?
- Do I perceive personal biases in what is written or expressed verbally?
- Do I believe the author or instructor has chosen to disregard certain facts and weigh information subjectively and, perhaps, inaccurately?
- What issues have been addressed and what questions are still unanswered?
- Is there more than one legitimate way to evaluate these facts and data?
- After carefully analyzing this information, are my conclusions and interpretations different from those of the expert?
- Can I defend my position logically?
- Can I express my conclusions persuasively and without triggering resentment?

When you establish the habit of asking incisive questions and when you read and think critically, you are using your mind as an analytical tool. By weighing the pluses and minuses of a position, you are thinking independently. This analytical procedure indicates your unwillingness to accept at face value everything that you read or hear. Because you think critically, no one can sell you the Brooklyn Bridge! No one can incite you to participate in a riot! No one can persuade you to commit a crime. No one can induce you to experiment with drugs. You are too smart to react mindlessly to flawed logic, irrational arguments, and skewed information that lacks legitimate substance, no matter how convincing the "pitch man" is.

Once you have trained yourself to think critically, you'll discover that you automatically question premises, suppositions, and contentions. If the data do not compute, you'll challenge the statements and conclusions, even if they are written in a textbook or periodical or expressed by an expert.

At the same time, it is important to realize the value of diplomacy when challenging another person's statements, conclusions, or positions in public, especially if the disputed statements are made by an instructor. You may decide to speak out and express your reservations, or you may decide to reject a statement or conclusion without actually challenging your instructor in class. If you feel that you must express your position, you may decide that it is more strategic to speak with your instructor after class or during office hours. You must gauge the situation, and you must gauge your instructor. You must also think about how you can most effectively present your conclusions without coming across as hostile, confrontational, or arrogant and without pressing "hot buttons." Whether or not you choose to challenge an "authority" openly, you will have, at least, questioned in your own mind the plausibility of the statements, applied your critical intelligence, and formed your own opinions and conclusions.

By delving beneath the surface, examining and analyzing the subject matter carefully, asking penetrating questions, and arriving at your own conclusions, you are learning and studying actively, thinking critically, and

Critical intelligence: The ability to look beneath surface appearances to identify the underlying issues and evaluate the logic used to support a particular position, interpretation, or argument.

How Critical Intelligence Functions

- **probing** beneath surface appearances
- **asking** penetrating questions
- **searching** for underlying issues
- **applying** reason and logic
- **recognizing** and **understanding** key points and ideas
- **analyzing** information and available data
- **questioning** the validity of data, assumptions, and statements
- **identifying** contradictions, inconsistencies, and deceptions
- **viewing** issues from different perspectives
- **perceiving** flaws in arguments, conclusions, and advice
- **assessing** issues objectively and logically
- **considering** the pluses and minuses of events and decisions
- **weighing** options
- **predicting** potential consequences
- **responding** skeptically to simplistic statements
- **relating** new information to previously assimilated information

functioning *at cause* (i.e., with active mental involvement) and not *at effect* (i.e., with passive mental involvement). This active participatory learning makes the content of what you are studying more relevant and meaningful and significantly improves the likelihood that you will comprehend, recall, and utilize the information. Your mind becomes a powerful tool that you can activate on command and use productively—not only in school, but in all aspects of your life.

A *note of caution:* Guard against becoming too smug about your critical intelligence. You may examine the facts, interpret the evidence, add up the pros and cons, and arrive at a conclusion. It is possible, however, that your conclusion is incorrect. Keep an open mind and be willing to admit when your position is wrong if the evidence so indicates or if another person's arguments are more compelling. This is the essence of *intellectual honesty.*

POWERHOUSE THINKING

Basic Tenets of Applied Critical Intelligence

- Analyze objectively.
- Question premises, opinions, conclusions, and statements.
- Reject defective logic, fallacies, and inconsistencies.
- Think for yourself!

PRACTICE APPLYING CRITICAL THINKING

Examine the following description of an historical event and apply critical intelligence when analyzing and evaluating the content.

> The Cherokee, Apache, and Shawnee tribes hated the settlers who crossed their territory, appropriated their land, and carved out homesteads for themselves. Ferocious attacks on wagon trains were common, and many settlers were killed. Farms and ranches were burned to the ground by marauding war parties. In retaliation, federal troops frequently attacked and burned Indian villages. To resolve this difficult problem, the United States government set aside reservations for the Indians, signed treaties that promised the Indians land and food, and then resettled entire tribes in these designated areas.

As you read this passage you may have become disturbed or even angry. Ideally, you should ask questions about the content and the author's statements, including:

1. Why *shouldn't* the Indians resist the settlers who were crossing and taking *their* land?
2. Why were the Indian villages destroyed and why were innocent women and children killed?
3. What about the trappers who cheated the Indians, and the hunters who killed millions of buffalo that were the primary source for food and clothing for the Plains Indians?
4. What right did the United States government have to force entire tribes of Indians from their land and what right did they have to "resettle" them on reservations?
5. What about all of the treaties that the U.S. government broke?
6. How many settlers were killed in comparison to the number of Native Americans who were killed?

If these questions occurred to you as you read the passage, you are thinking critically. This intellectual process is a requisite to comprehending the underlying issues and acquiring insight. Your active involvement and penetrating questions will produce more meaningful long-term learning than will the temporary and fragmentary short-term assimilation of data.

Mastery: Additional Practice
Applying Critical-Thinking Skills

Read the following article. As you read, examine the information critically and look for any biases (personal positions) that the author may have. Does he slant the facts? Has he failed to address important issues to your satisfaction? When you finish reading, you will be asked to pose some probing questions about the content of the passage and the underlying issues. The objective of this exercise is to underscore the importance of *thinking actively and critically* when you read. If this article was assigned in a criminal justice or psychology course, your questions and comments, and those of your classmates, about the key legal, moral, and ethical issues would undoubtedly trigger a lively class discussion!

INNOCENT BY REASON OF INSANITY

On November 6, 2002, in a response to an eleventh-hour appeal, the Supreme Court granted a stay of execution to a convicted killer named James Colburn. The appeal was received by Justice Scalia minutes before Colburn was to be led to the Texas execution chamber and strapped to a gurney.

Colburn had been sentenced to death for fatally stabbing a hitchhiker in 1994 during an attempt to rape her. Diagnosed as a paranoid schizophrenic, Colburn was reported to have been so heavily sedated during his trial that he slept through much of it. Colburn claimed that he was hearing voices at the time of the murder and that when he realized what he had done, he surrendered to the police.

Colburn had been institutionalized several times after first being diagnosed as schizophrenic at the age of 14. Despite this documented history of severe mental illness, two psychologists concluded that he was competent to stand trial. When he was tried in 1995, it took the jury only 20 minutes to convict him of capital murder, and during the penalty phase, just two hours to sentence him to death.

In a previous appeal to the Supreme Court, Colburn's attorneys had argued that their client was too mentally ill to assist in his defense at his murder trial. The justices rejected this appeal in a seven to two ruling. Despite having recently banned the execution of the mentally retarded as unconstitutionally cruel, the Court refused to grant blanket protection from the death penalty to the mentally ill.

The argument offered in Colburn's last-minute appeal took a different tack. His attorneys argued that the execution of the mentally ill defendant would constitute cruel and unusual punishment and, as such, would violate the Eighth amendment and be unconstitutional.

Colburn's appeals raise two critically important legal issues: namely, how does the Court define insanity and how should the state punish the mentally ill who commit crimes? The American judicial system has been wrestling with this conundrum for decades, and many legal scholars believe that it has made little progress in defining a nationally acceptable standard for determining mental competence.

At the heart of the mental health assessment that is required in most states when a defendant's sanity is at issue is a core point of law: *Did the accused know the difference between right and wrong?* The challenge in making this determination is compounded by the fact that psychiatrists and psychol- ogists representing the prosecution and the defense often come to diametrically opposed conclusions.

The debate about insanity has its origins in English law. During the Middle Ages, an accused was considered mad if he didn't know what he was doing and lacked the ability to reason. In the sixteenth century, the criteria focused on behaviors that would today be considered indications of mental retardation. If the defendant couldn't perform basic functions such as counting or couldn't recognize his immediate family, he was considered mad.

Another shift occurred more than 300 years later. In 1843, Daniel M'Naghten murdered Edward Drummond, the secretary to the English prime minister. During his trial, M'Naghten pleaded that he was insane. Medical testimony indicated that the defendant was delusional (unable to distinguish reality from fantasy), driven to murder, and incapable of understanding the difference between right and wrong. Found not guilty by reason of insanity, the verdict led to what is now referred to as the "M'Naghten Rule."

Because the M'Naghten rule excludes the actions of severely disturbed defendants who may realize that what they are doing is wrong but cannot control themselves, some states have developed broader criteria. These incorporate a volitional standard (i.e., a compulsion to act because of mental disorder) and a cognitive standard (i.e., knowing right from wrong).

That tens of thousands of prisoners in the United States are suffering from severe mental disorders and require treatment is indisputable. Included are a large number of schizophrenics, such as James Colburn, who, unless medicated, are out of touch with reality. At issue is whether convicted felons with severe mental disorders are being sent to prison because we lack the psychiatric facilities and/or desire to treat them, or because we feel compelled to punish felons for their crimes irrespective of their mental illness.

During Colburn's trial in Montgomery County, Texas, Assistant District Attorney Jay Hileman told the jury that Colburn should be held accountable for his crime. "Attributing this violence, this horrible cruelty . . . to paranoid schizophrenia is naïve and simplistic. . . . He did it because he is mean."

Philip H. Hilder, one of Colburn's appellate lawyers, summarized the legal issue very differently. "In blunt terms, he is out of his mind from a condition not of his doing. We're not asking that he be excused for a murder. We're asking that he be treated."

The current stay of execution allows Colburn's attorneys 90 days to file a brief that details why the Supreme Court should grant a full hearing on the competency issue.

Update: James Colburn was executed by the State of Texas on March 26, 2003.

The preceding article does not take an obvious position on the validity of the death penalty, nor does it take an obvious position on the appropriateness of executing or imprisoning mentally ill felons. You may, however, have discerned a bias or slant regarding the current judicial standards that are commonly used to determine insanity.

After reading the material, did you conclude that the author is opposed to executing the mentally ill despite the fact that a convicted person may not meet the legal criteria of insanity?

   ◯ yes   ◯ no   ◯ not sure

If you answered "yes," what led you to this conclusion?

1. _____

2. _____

3. _____

4. _____

After critically evaluating the information in the article, did any questions about the underlying issues occur to you? For example, you might have wondered:

- Why is the judicial system in the United States having so much difficulty arriving at a nationally acceptable standard for defining insanity?

- Is it morally correct to execute a mentally ill person who must be medicated in order to comprehend that he or she is condemned to death?

Pose five additional questions that raise or probe important topics relevant to an objective evaluation of the insanity defense.

1. _____

2. _____

3. _____

4. _____

5. _____

You may be able to answer the questions you posed by referring to information in the article and by applying your analytical and critical-thinking skills. Other questions may require clarification by someone who is more knowledgeable about the legal and psychological issues.

Most instructors are committed not only to providing you with important information, but also to training your mind and teaching you how to think. Wise instructors realize that critical thinking and proactive involvement in assimilating the course content invariably enhance their students' comprehension, retention, and mastery.

Using DIBS

A conscientious student receives several marginal grades on essays in an upper-level political science course. Distressed, he makes an appointment to discuss the matter with his instructor. The instructor tells him that his papers are basically well-written and contain adequate facts but that he is not demonstrating that he can critically evaluate the key topics. The instructor reminds the student that she announced at the beginning of the semester that the ability to think critically would be a primary criterion for assessing performance in the course.

Pretend you are the student, and use DIBS to handle the problem. Remember to use "I" messages.

Define: _____

Investigate: _____

_____

_____

Brainstorm: _____

_____

_____

Select: _____

Assess the likelihood that the selected solution will resolve the dilemma.

1	2	3	4	5	6	7	8	9	10
unlikely				fairly likely					very likely

For Your Information

When you first learned to read, most of your effort was directed toward figuring out how to decipher letters and words accurately. Most students progress from the basic decoding of symbols and phonemes to more advanced reading comprehension with relatively little difficulty. (*Please note:* Students with learning problems such as dyslexia may continue to have significant difficulty decoding words accurately. If they are emotionally and physically depleted by the battle to read, they may have little energy left to devote to understanding and remembering what the words actually mean. The consequences are predictable: poor comprehension, frustration, demoralization, and negative associations with reading. If you identify with this condition, discuss the matter with your academic advisor and request information about being diagnostically evaluated.)

There are three major levels of reading comprehension.

MOST BASIC LEVEL: LITERAL COMPREHENSION

On this level you must be able to remember information.

Example: The scientist carried the chemicals to the scale, weighed them carefully, placed the measured materials in the flask, ignited the Bunsen burner, and set the flask on the tripod above the burner.

Literal question: What were the steps in the scientist's procedure?

SECOND LEVEL: INFERENTIAL COMPREHENSION

On this level, you must be able to understand information that is implied, but not directly stated.

Example: The scientist carried the chemicals to the scale, weighed them carefully, placed the measured materials in the flask, ignited the Bunsen burner, and set the flask on the tripod above the burner.

Inferential question: What was the scientist doing?

THIRD LEVEL: APPLICATIVE COMPREHENSION

On this level, you must be able to utilize information.

Example: The scientist carried the chemicals to the scale, weighed them carefully, placed the measured materials in the flask, ignited the Bunsen burner, and set the flask on the tripod above the burner.

Applicative   If you were doing the same experiment, what procedures
question: would you follow?

College instructors expect students to understand the content in their textbooks and answer test questions that require all three levels of comprehension. Simply being able to memorize facts, rules, and formulas (the literal level) may be an asset in courses that emphasize the retention of data, but the *capacity to memorize does not guarantee success in all courses.* Most instructors want their students to demonstrate insight and document their ability to *apply* what they are learning. They also want their students to prove that they can think analytically and critically and can identify, understand, and assimilate the important underlying issues and concepts.

To acquire the advanced reading comprehension and analytical-thinking skills necessary for success in college, you must be able to:

- identify important information
- distinguish main ideas from details
- understand essential issues and concepts
- evaluate and make critical judgments
- recall facts
- organize and classify information
- perceive the connections between what you are currently learning and what you have already learned
- apply what you've learned

Students who possess a full range of reading comprehension skills are likely to perform better in college. Being able to comprehend and retain the content of textbooks and course material significantly improves the probability of academic success and puts students on a track leading to superior grades and expanded educational and vocational opportunities.

Mind-mapping (also referred to as "chunking") is a practical tool for representing, organizing, understanding, and recalling the information you are studying. The method is intended to help you recognize how ideas and data are linked. Ideally, you will find mind-mapping enjoyable, and this will encourage you to become more actively involved in reading and studying. *Active learning*—as opposed to *passive learning*—stimulates interest, motivation, and effort and improves mastery and assimilation of the course content.

Effective mind-mapping requires practice, but you should be able to master the procedure quickly and with relative ease. The challenge is to decide what information is important and to figure out how to represent and link this key information.

Once you've mastered the mind-mapping method, you should adjust the procedure so that it works with your personal learning style and helps you meet the specific requirements of each of your courses. You may ultimately decide that you prefer a more traditional note-taking system. (Traditional note-taking methods are described in Chapter 7.) For now, experiment with mind-mapping. Use the method during the next several weeks. You may be quite pleasantly surprised to discover that your grades and comprehension have significantly improved.

Critical thinking is another requisite to acquiring first-rate reading comprehension skills. By questioning and probing the content of what you are studying, you are proactively involving yourself in the learning process, and this cannot help but enhance your insight, understanding, and recall. Your mind will operate on all eight cylinders and generate maximum intellectual RPM. This cerebral efficiency will provide you with a distinct competitive edge over students who are in the habit of thinking and learning passively.

TURBOCHARGING YOUR READING COMPREHENSION

OBJECTIVES

- Responding strategically to setbacks
- Mastering another system for understanding and recalling information in your textbooks
- Writing effective essays that document your comprehension

A Plan That Didn't Work

Ashley desperately wanted at least a B+ on her American history final. She spent more than nine hours studying for the exam, and she believed that she could answer any question her instructor might ask. While waiting for the test to be handed out, she imagined getting her test back the following week with a B+, or perhaps even an A–, written at the top in red ink. According to her calculations, the B+ on the final guaranteed a B in the course. A straight A on the final guaranteed an A– in the course. Getting an A– would be fantastic, Ashley thought, but she would be content with a B.

When the instructor finally handed her the exam, Ashley felt a sense of relief. "Let's get this over with," she thought. After scanning the questions, her initial sense of relief and confidence quickly turned to panic. Fear surged through her body. It was as if she were looking at a test covering material she had never seen before! As she tried to answer the questions, her panic grew. She thought that she could only answer 60 percent of the questions! The more upset she became, the more she forgot.

When Ashley handed in the exam, she felt she'd be lucky to get a C–. Badly shaken, she quickly left the room. Her fantasy of a B in the course was shattered.

zooming in on the issues

Dealing with a Setback

Having misjudged how she would do on the test, Ashley found herself at a critical crossroads. Certain she would get a poor grade on the exam, she had to decide how she was going to respond to the setback. She had several options:

Option 1: She could give up, conclude that she was incompetent, and resign herself to getting bad grades on future tests.

Option 2: She could continue to use the same study strategy and hope to do better next time.

Option 3: She could examine her miscalculation analytically (perhaps with help from her instructor), identify the probable reasons for doing poorly, and make tactical adjustments in her study strategy.

Evaluate Option 1.

1	2	3	4	5	6	7	8	9	10
not smart				fairly smart					very smart

Why did you make this evaluation? _____

_____

_____

Predict the probable consequence of choosing this option: _____

_____

Evaluate Option 2.

1	2	3	4	5	6	7	8	9	10

not smart   fairly smart   very smart

Why did you make this evaluation? _____

_____

_____

Predict the probable consequence of choosing this option: _____

_____

Evaluate Option 3.

1	2	3	4	5	6	7	8	9	10

not smart   fairly smart   very smart

Why did you make this evaluation? _____

_____

_____

Predict the probable consequence of choosing this option: _____

_____

Based on the description of Ashley's behavior and attitude, do you think she will bounce back from the setback and make strategic adjustments in her study methods?

  ○ yes   ○ no   ○ not sure

Why did you reach this conclusion? _____

_____

_____

Drawing a Conclusion from the Evidence

Having read about Ashley's setback, what specific conclusion can you draw from the information in the story? Using the *inductive method*, express in a well-crafted sentence what you have concluded. *Remember:* you are summarizing the **point** of the story.

The point of Ashley's story: _____

_____

_____

_____

_____

Learning from Mistakes

No one can accuse Ashley of not being responsible. She established her goal for the exam, and she studied conscientiously. After spending hours preparing, she felt justifiably confident. Then, the unexpected happened: Ashley discovered she wasn't as prepared as she thought. There are four possible explanations for the setback:

1. She hadn't learned the information as well as she believed.
2. She hadn't identified the information her teacher considered important.
3. She didn't fully understand the material.
4. She "clutched" during the test and couldn't recall what she had studied.

You may have experienced a similar test-taking nightmare. You studied diligently for an exam and expected to do well, but you ended up doing poorly.

Setbacks and disappointments are part of life. Everyone occasionally miscalculates, and everyone occasionally experiences disappointments. How you respond to these reversals plays a pivotal role in what happens to you in life. When confronted with a setback, you can choose to respond *passively* and allow yourself to feel defeated and demoralized, or you can choose to respond *actively* and create a methodical plan for getting back on your feet and moving forward again.

Students who are not in the habit of thinking strategically are often overwhelmed by setbacks. They may complain that life is unfair or blame others for their missteps. They may begin to doubt themselves and their capabilities. Rather than developing a logical plan to handle predicaments and avoid similar miscues, they accept marginal performance as their fate in life and lower their expectations and aspirations accordingly. Defeatist attitudes and catastrophic expectations drive their counterproductive attitudes and behaviors and fuel their negative mind-set. If they receive a poor grade, these non-strategically minded students are likely to conclude, *"I flunked the last test, and I know I'm going to flunk the course. What's the sense of studying? It doesn't make any difference."*

Students who think strategically respond very differently. They learn from their mistakes, setbacks, and failures. Rather than wallow in self-pity or become depressed, they confront the problem head-on, assess the damage, identify what went wrong, examine their miscalculations, figure out how to overcome or bypass the obstacle, and do everything they can to avoid repeating the same errors. This is the essence of *thinking smart and strategically* (refer to Chapter 2 to review additional information about strategic thinking).

A strategic student who receives a poor grade because she studied the wrong material or didn't include important information in an essay might feel upset, as anyone would under the circumstances, but she wouldn't allow her upset to control her. She would make the appropriate adjustments in her study procedures and do everything in her power to make things turn out better the next time. Rather than give up, conclude she's "dumb," and feel sorry for herself, she develops a plan for improving her grade on the next exam or essay.

Students who overcome challenges and surmount barriers invariably share five distinct traits that significantly enhance the likelihood that they will ultimately attain their objectives. These students are:

1. motivated to succeed
2. capable of thinking and acting analytically and strategically
3. willing to learn from failures, defeats, and mistakes
4. able to capitalize on their strengths and neutralize the weaknesses
5. intent on persevering

This "let's get the problem fixed" mind-set directly reflects *grit and character.*

Grit and character:
Unfailing determination, dogged persistence, and an intense desire to prevail.

Using DIBS

Pretend you are Ashley. You have gotten a poor grade on an exam and feel demoralized. Use DIBS to develop a strategy for improving your performance on future tests. Remember to use "I" messages.

Define:

_____

_____

Investigate:

_____

_____

_____

_____

Brainstorm:

_____

_____

_____

_____

Select:

_____

_____

Let's assume you defined the problem as "Ashley got a poor grade on her history final." Let's also assume that you listed "study harder" as a possible solution. Although this is a reasonable recommendation, the solution is *too general to be of significant value.* For Ashley to avoid getting low test grades in the future, she has to develop a more specific study plan. Then she has to try it out and evaluate its effectiveness. If the plan doesn't work, she should continue experimenting with other plans from her brainstormed list until she finds one that improves her grade.

The key to successful problem solving is precision. The more precisely you define Ashley's problem and the more precise the proposed solutions, the more likely you can develop an effective study strategy to improve her test performance.

The priority for any student who consistently does poorly on tests is to develop more productive methods for identifying, understanding, and remembering important information. You are about to learn methods that are specifically designed to improve your reading comprehension and your retention of key information in your textbooks. These capabilities are requisites to doing well on exams.

POWERHOUSE THINKING

Basic Tenets for Handling Setbacks

- Objectively analyze what went wrong.
- Develop a new strategy that addresses specific deficiencies and improves the likelihood of success next time.
- Apply determination, grit, and character and persevere despite frustration and discouragement.

Reading: More Than Just Deciphering Words

As you scanned, read, and mind-mapped the material about nuclear energy in Chapter 5, your brain absorbed the visually encoded information (i.e., letters, words, and sentences) that was perceived by your eyes. In a sense, your eyes function like a camera transmitting "pictures" (i.e., the words on the page) to your brain, which in turn functions like a high-speed computer. The neurological circuitry in your brain instantaneously receives the words on the page, runs the data through stored memory, and links the transmitted words (or symbols) with their meaning. For example, when you read the word "scientist," your mind made an immediate association with the word because you're familiar with scientists. Without realizing it, you may have even formed a mental picture of a scientist in a white lab coat working in a laboratory.

In the passage, you also read the word "fission." If you had never seen this word before, you would not have immediately linked the word and its meaning. Although *fission* is defined in the passage, you might have to think more carefully about it than the word *scientist*. If you are an auditory learner, you might remember the definition of fission by saying the word several times while deliberately repeating the verb "to split." If you are a visual learner, you might also remember the definition by visualizing a nucleus being split into two parts. You might enhance your mental picture by visualizing someone with a hammer and chisel about to break a slab of marble in half, or you might mentally imprint the metaphor used in the passage of a chocolate chip being split in half. You might also see in your mind a graphic representation of an atom being split by a bolt of energy. (Methods that incorporate visual association to recall information are discussed in Chapter 9.)

You may not be consciously aware that your brain is continually receiving signals from two of your primary sensory receptors: your eyes and ears. (Your brain also receives signals from your other primary senses—touch, taste, and smell.) Your mind absorbs the sensory data, deciphers it, and then tells you what to do with the information. Under most circumstances, the brain processes sensory stimuli with astonishing quickness and effectiveness and can usually respond within a millisecond to the stimuli. For example, if someone asks you, "Who was the first President of the United States?" or "How much is 9 times 9?" you would immediately reply George Washington and 81. However, if you are sleepy and your brain is not working at peak efficiency, you might not recall the information as quickly. When your brain's operating system is not functioning optimally, you may have to struggle to *decode* (i.e., process, assimilate, comprehend, and link) new data and *encode* (express verbally or in writing) your knowledge, understanding, and thoughts. Under such less-than-perfect circumstances, you may say, "I'm too sleepy to answer right now. Ask me in the morning!"

When you study, you want your brain to operate at maximum efficiency, and you want to generate maximum mental power. This mental stamina and efficiency must be developed through training, practice, and conditioning. At the same time, other key ingredients must be added to the equation. To study productively, you must also possess a range of highly effective learning tools and the ability to select and use the best resource for each learning situation.

Acquiring a New Study Resource

You've already mastered a powerful study tool—mind-mapping—that is designed to help you understand and recall important information. It's time to learn another method for "powering up" your brain's computer. It's called the **"chewing-up information" method.**

You may be wondering "Why learn another method?" The answer is simple. If you practice and master several different techniques for reading and studying effectively, you can choose the system that works best for you. You can also combine parts of different methods and create your own personalized study system.

To practice the chewing-up information method, you will use the nuclear energy article presented in Chapter 5—the material is reprinted so that you do not have to flip back and forth. The reason for revisiting this material is to demonstrate how you can comprehend and recall dense, complex information if you take the time to examine and *digest* the content systematically. The mastery of any challenging pursuit or subject matter requires motivation, effort, technique, and practice. Once your ability to assimilate the academic content of your courses improves, you can learn virtually anything. The mastery process is sequential. You must first become competent. With sufficient practice and consistent application of the relevant skills, you will discover that you are increasingly proficient.

For now, do not reread the nuclear energy material reprinted next. Skip ahead to the chewing-up information method explanation on page 124.

NUCLEAR ENERGY: HARNESSING THE ATOM

In 1945, two atomic bombs were dropped over the cities of Nagasaki and Hiroshima. This devastating nuclear attack caused the Japanese forces to surrender. Although many people believe that the attack signaled the beginning of the nuclear age, atomic energy was actually discovered more than 50 years prior to the bombing.

Atoms are the smallest and most fundamental unit of matter, and everything in our world is comprised of this basic unit. This includes the clothes we wear, the air we breathe, the food we eat, the paper we write on, and the gasoline we put in our cars. Several important earlier discoveries led to the discovery of nuclear energy. In 1896, a French scientist named Antoine Henry Becquerel identified radioactivity. His scientific experiments revealed that certain elements released radioactive rays and that these elements possessed unique and fascinating properties.

In the late 1930s, scientists in Germany realized that by using a process called **nuclear fission,** it was possible to split the nucleus of an atom into two nuclei. To understand how fission works, it may help to imagine a chocolate chip being split in half by a cleaver. Now imagine that the energy holding the chocolate chip together is suddenly released by the splitting process, and this results in a massive explosion. (This image is intended only to help you understand the fission process. In the case of splitting a chocolate chip, *no* significant energy is actually released.) The discovery that energy is released when certain types of atomic material are split led to the first nuclear reactor being built in the early 1940s and, ultimately, to the first military use of nuclear fission. The two atomic bombs dropped over Japan to end World War II represent the only time in history that nuclear weapons have been used in war.

The development of the hydrogen bomb in the 1950s was an even more frightening use of atomic power. Hydrogen bombs release massive amounts of nuclear energy by combining (fusing) two hydrogen nuclei to form one nucleus. To understand the fusion process, imagine two chocolate chips sitting next to each other on a pan in an oven. As the oven gets hot, the two chips melt together (or fuse) to form one big chip, and in this combining process, a massive amount of energy is released. (Of course, two chocolate chips melting together do not actually produce a measurable release of energy!) Fusion occurs naturally in the sun where hydrogen nuclei are continually combining to produce enormous amounts of heat, light, and radiation (see the illustrations "Nuclear Fission" and "Nuclear Fusion").

Although nuclear technology has produced nuclear weapons that are capable of horrific destruction, this same technology

EXHIBIT 1   Nuclear fission

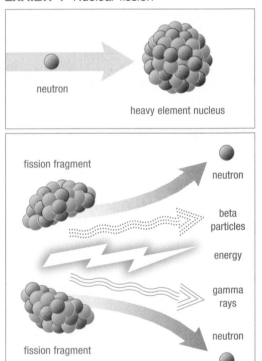

Neutron splits the nucleus of a heavy element such as uranium into two fission fragments, resulting in an energy release along with other materials.

EXHIBIT 2 Nuclear fusion

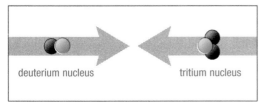

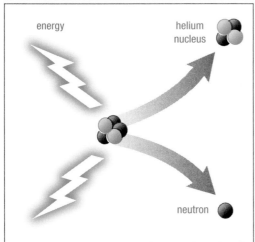

Two lighter nuclei unite to form a heavier nucleus which results in an energy release.

also has many peaceful applications. One of the most important involves the production of electricity. In 1956, the first nuclear power plant was built in England, and in 1957, the first U.S. plant was constructed. By the late 1980s, there were over 420 reactors operating throughout the world, and there were more than 110 nuclear reactors in production in the United States. Today, nuclear energy is second only to coal as the largest source of electricity—currently, more than 17 percent of our electricity is generated from nuclear energy.

Examining the Nuclear Atom

To understand nuclear power, we must examine the atom. At the center of every atom is a nucleus. This nucleus makes up most of the *mass* (weight) of the atom, but relatively little of its *volume* (size). Scientists discovered that in certain atoms a special energy binds the nucleus together. When the nucleus undergoes changes, the binding energy is released

as *electromagnetic waves* (gamma radiation) and *energy particles* (e.g., neutron, protons). When an atomic nucleus begins to disintegrate spontaneously and gives off radiation, the process is called **nuclear decay.** Nuclear energy can also be released when an atomic nucleus is *intentionally* split or fused. This is precisely what happens when a nuclear weapon explodes (see Exhibits 1 and 2).

To understand how binding energy is released, consider what occurs when you burn a log in a fireplace. Before burning, the log may weigh eight pounds. After burning, the remaining ash and carbon weigh less than a pound. Weight (or mass) is lost because the fire has transformed the cellulose into smoke, heat (thermal energy), carbon, and ash. The released energy heats the room and escapes through the chimney. The ash is what remains from the original mass.

In an atomic nucleus (e.g., Uranium 235), the mass (weight) of the original nucleus (see Exhibits 1 and 2) is *greater* than the mass of the products that result when the binding energy breaks down. The lost mass is released as energy (e.g., radiation, neutrons, heat). After concluding that *matter is a type of energy,* Albert Einstein, the famous physicist who is considered by many to be the "father" of the nuclear age, explained the loss of mass with his famous equation $E=MC^2$ (energy = mass multiplied by the speed of light squared).

Nuclear energy is an awesome source of power. The energy released by a hydrogen bomb is thousands of times greater than the energy released by conventional bombs. The atomic energy contained in the core of a nuclear power plant is approximately one billion times greater than the energy produced by burning an equivalent amount (in terms of weight) of coal, oil, or gas.

Nuclear Weapons

In the 1930s, a frightening use for nuclear energy was recognized as scientists began to study and understand nuclear fission. When fission occurs, the nucleus of a heavy element such as enriched uranium splits in

EXHIBIT 3 Chain reaction   Continuing splitting of nuclei to produce a steady supply of energy.

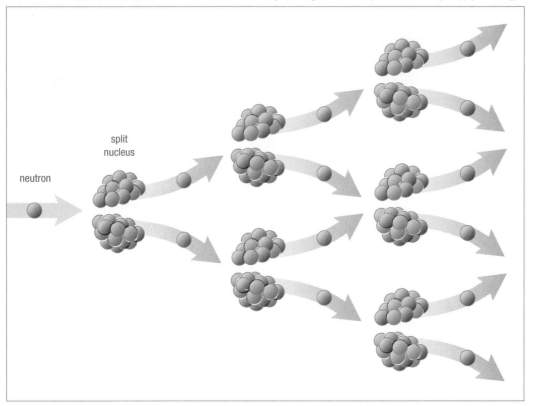

two. A chain reaction then occurs. As each nucleus splits, the released energy triggers another nucleus to split, and the chain reaction continues (see Exhibit 3). The released energy (*kinetic energy*) rapidly transforms into intense heat. This discovery led to the development of the atomic bomb.

An even more powerful way to release nuclear energy was discovered in the 1950s. Nuclear scientists and engineers realized they could use an atomic bomb to produce the necessary intense heat and energy to combine two light hydrogen nuclei into a larger nucleus. This process is called **nuclear fusion.** The released energy from a hydrogen fusion reaction (a hydrogen bomb) is many times more powerful than that released by nuclear fission (an atomic bomb).

Nuclear Reactors

Today, nuclear reactors are a major source of electrical energy in many countries throughout the world. In the core or center of a thermal nuclear reactor, fissionable fuel material (tiny pellets of nuclear fuel typically stacked end to end in 13-foot tubes) is combined with moderators (used to slow down the fission process), other materials, and safety systems to produce a continuing chain reaction. Coolants are also used to transfer heat and to start, maintain, and stop the chain reaction. Several different types of reactors are currently in production throughout the world. The energy from the nuclear chain reaction produces steam that runs the turbines and generators that produce electricity (see Exhibit 4).

The Pluses and Minuses of Nuclear Energy

Because of safety and environmental concerns, governments throughout the world are carefully weighing the advantages and disadvantages of nuclear energy. One major advantage is that nuclear power plants use much less fuel than plants that burn coal,

EXHIBIT 4 Fast breeder reactor

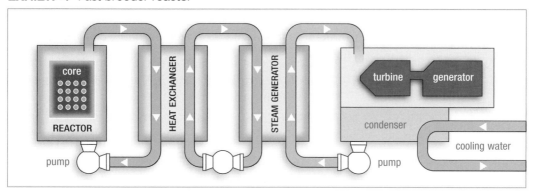

oil, or gas. The fission of one pound of uranium generates the equivalent energy of 1,140 *tons* of coal. Another advantage is that nuclear plants do not release the chemical and solid pollutants that many coal-burning electricity plants produce.

There are also important disadvantages to nuclear power. Nuclear plants cost far more to build than conventional plants, and the availability of atomic fuel is limited (usually Uranium 235). The risk of a serious accident, such as occurred in 1986 at Chernobyl in the former Soviet Union, has caused people throughout the world to have grave concerns about safety.

Accidents have also occurred in the United States. In 1978, there was a serious accident at the Three Mile Island Nuclear Power Plant. Because of human and mechanical error, the cooling system that regulated the heat in the core failed. Fortunately, scientists and technicians were able to prevent a total core meltdown (an uncontrolled nuclear reaction that produces intense heat and melts the nuclear containment vessels) and the massive release of radioactivity.

Other major concerns involve the safety risks related to the disposal of the spent fuel rods and other radioactive wastes. Radioactivity is extremely dangerous and can cause death. Even relatively limited exposure to radioactive material can cause cancer, genetic damage, and birth defects. Used uranium or plutonium from nuclear reactors and weapons plants can continue to produce radioactivity for centuries. Because of the fear that an accidental release of radioactivity will occur, many states do not want these wastes disposed of within their borders. Even the safe transportation of nuclear waste poses potential risks. If a train or truck was involved in an accident and overturned, dangerous radioactivity might be released, and its effects can linger for years.

Other Uses of Nuclear Energy

Nuclear energy has other applications besides the production of electrical energy and nuclear weapons. Atomic elements have become important tools in modern medicine. Radioactive Cobalt 60 is used to treat cancer. Radioactive tracers are used as diagnostic tools, and radioactive medicines are used to treat diseases. Radioactivity can also be used to kill bacteria, prevent plant diseases, preserve foods for long periods of time without refrigeration, and even provide a highly accurate way to keep track of time (the atomic clock).

Most scientists agree that many other medical and nonmedical uses of nuclear energy are yet to be discovered. Safety, of course, is still a very serious concern, but it's clear that a harnessed atom will play an increasingly important role in the lives of people throughout the world during the twenty-first century.

Sources: Material from *Encyclopedia Britannica (1998), World Book Encyclopedia (2001),* and *Encyclopedia Americana* (1998).

The "Chewing-Up Information" Method

Like the mind-mapping method, the chewing-up information method consists of five steps.

Step 1: *Turn the title into a question before scanning and reading the material.*

Reason:	Asking a question about what you are about to read before actually beginning to read helps you *think about* and *understand* the information.
TITLE:	"Nuclear Energy: Harnessing the Atom"
Question:	How was the atom harnessed to produce nuclear energy?
Answer:	Because you're asking this question before reading the material, you don't have enough information to answer the question. *Don't try to answer it yet. Simply let your mind think about it while you are scanning.* This will help you focus your thinking while reading the material.

Some questions deal with **main ideas** and may require many sentences or paragraphs to answer; for example, **"Why** did scientists want to harness nuclear energy?" Other questions focus on **details** and can often be answered with a word or two; for example, **"When** was radioactivity discovered?"

Question words: how, when, where, why, what, which, who

Main idea question words: how, why, what

> Examples: *Why* did the United States go to war with Japan in 1941?
>
> *What* are the major risks associated with nuclear energy?

Detail question words: when, where, which, who, what

> Examples: *Who* discovered radioactivity?
>
> *What* was Einstein's formula for relativity?

Now it's time to practice Step 1. Use one of the *main idea question words* to change the following titles into questions.

TITLE:	"A New Method of Irrigation"
Question:	*What was the new irrigation method?*

TITLE:	"Techniques for Reducing Pollution"
Question:	_____ ?

TITLE:	"Salk Discovers a Vaccine That Fights Polio"
Question:	_____ ?

TITLE:	"The AIDS Epidemic"
Question:	_____ ?

TITLE:	"The Dangers of Drug Addiction"
Question:	_____ ?

TITLE:	"Three Different Methods of Taxation"
Question:	_____ ?

TITLE: "Methods for Providing Protection Against Urban Terrorism"

Question: _____ ?

Now, figure out the title from the question.

Question: What were the causes of the Civil War?

TITLE: *"The Causes of the Civil War"* _____

Question: Why did the American colonies rebel against England?

TITLE: _____

Question: What are the two houses of Congress?

TITLE: _____

Question: How does the American court system work?

TITLE: _____

Question: Why do cars pollute the environment?

TITLE: _____

Question: What did Einstein discover?

TITLE: _____

You completed Step 1 of the chewing-up information method in Chapter 5 when you converted the title of the nuclear energy article into a main idea question: *"How was the atom harnessed to produce nuclear energy?"* You're now going to learn the remaining steps.

Step 2: *Turn each subtitle into a question before reading the section.*

Reason: This helps you think about the content of the material
                you're about to read *before* you actually scan and read it.
                The process of raising questions before you read helps you
                focus on the content and improves comprehension.

SUBTITLE 1:   Examining the Atom's Nucleus

Question: What is the atom's nucleus?

Don't attempt to answer this question yet. Let your mind think about it as you scan. Before speed-reading, go through the entire unit and turn each subtitle into a main idea question.

SUBTITLE 2:   Nuclear Weapons

Question: What are nuclear weapons?

SUBTITLE 3: _____

Question: _____

SUBTITLE 4: _____

Question: _____

SUBTITLE 5: _____

Question: _____

Even though you've already done the next step, it's important to redo it because it has been a while since you first read the passage.

Step 3: *Speed-read the material one time (see page 90 to review the method).*

Step 4: *Reread the material carefully using a highlighter or pencil to underline key ideas and important facts in each paragraph.*

Let's see how the first seven paragraphs might look after you underline or highlight the key ideas (Step 4).

NUCLEAR ENERGY: HARNESSING THE ATOM

In 1945, two atomic bombs were dropped over the cities of Nagasaki and Hiroshima. This devastating nuclear attack caused the Japanese forces to surrender. Although many people believe that the attack signaled the beginning of the nuclear age, atomic energy was actually discovered more than 50 years prior to the bombing.

Atoms are the smallest and most fundamental unit of matter, and everything in our world is comprised of this basic unit. This includes the clothes we wear, the air we breathe, the food we eat, the paper we write on, and the gasoline we put in our cars. Several important earlier discoveries led to the discovery of nuclear energy. In 1896, a French scientist named Antoine Henry Becquerel identified radioactivity. His scientific experiments revealed that certain elements released radioactive rays and that these elements possessed unique and fascinating properties.

In the late 1930s, scientists in Germany realized that by using a process called **nuclear fission,** it was possible to split the nucleus of an atom into two nuclei. To understand how fission works, it may help to imagine a chocolate chip being split in half by a cleaver. Now imagine that the energy holding the chocolate chip together is suddenly released by the splitting process, and this results in a massive explosion. (This image is intended only to help you understand the fission process. In the case of splitting a chocolate chip, *no* significant energy is actually released.) The discovery that energy is released when certain types of atomic material are split led to the first nuclear reactor being built in the early 1940s and, ultimately, to the first military use of nuclear fission. The two atomic bombs dropped over Japan to end World War II represent the only time in history that nuclear weapons have been used in war.

The development of the hydrogen bomb in the 1950s was an even more frightening use of atomic power. Hydrogen bombs release massive amounts of nuclear energy by combining (fusing) two hydrogen nuclei to form one nucleus. To understand the fusion process, imagine two chocolate chips sitting next to each other on a pan in an oven. As the oven gets hot, the two chips melt together (or fuse) to form one big chip, and in this combining process, a massive amount of energy is released. (Of course, two chocolate chips melting together do not actually produce a measurable release of energy!) Fusion occurs naturally on the sun where hydrogen nuclei are continually combining to produce enormous amounts of heat, light, and radiation.

Although nuclear technology has produced nuclear weapons that are capable of horrific destruction, this same technology also has many peaceful applications. One of the most important involves the production of electricity. In 1956, the first nuclear power plant was built in England, and in 1957, the first U.S. plant was constructed. By the late 1980s, there were over 420 reactors operating throughout the world, and there were more than 110 nuclear reactors in production in the United States. Today, nuclear energy is second only to coal as the largest source of electricity—currently, more than 17 percent of our electricity is generated from nuclear energy.

UNDERLINING OR HIGHLIGHTING ON YOUR OWN

Using the preceding model as a guide, underline or highlight *only* the **key information** in the first seven paragraphs of the nuclear energy article. Do it on your own without looking at the sample. Refer to the model after you finish to verify that you included the important facts. **Then, continue underlining or highlighting the key information in the entire unit.** Remember to leave out words such as "a," "the," "their," and "of." Highlight *only* the most important words.

ANSWERING THE SUBTITLE AND TITLE QUESTIONS

Once you have finished highlighting or underlining, it's time to answer the subtitle and title questions you posed in **Step 2** of the "Chewing-Up Information" method. The first two questions are answered for you below. Answer the remaining questions on your own. You can refer back to the article and the information you highlighted to help you answer the questions.

Step 5: *Answer subtitle questions and title question.*

Subtitle question 1: *What is the nuclear atom?*

Sample answer: There's a nucleus at the center of every atom. This nucleus makes up most of the mass or weight, but relatively little of the volume or size of the atom. A special energy binds certain nuclear atoms. If the nucleus changes its structure, the binding energy is released as radiation, heat, and particles of energy. When this happens naturally, it is called nuclear decay. When it happens artificially in the case of an atomic weapon, the nucleus is bombarded from the outside and the binding energy is released as a powerful explosion.

Subtitle question 2: *What are nuclear weapons?*

Sample answer: There are two types of nuclear weapons: fission bombs (the atomic bomb) and fusion bombs (the hydrogen bomb). In a fission bomb, the nucleus is split in two. This starts a chain reaction. The lost mass and binding energy are released as radiation, energy particles, and intense heat. In a fusion bomb, an atomic bomb is exploded to fuse (cause to melt together) two light hydrogen nuclei into a larger nucleus. The energy released by this fusion is many times more powerful than the energy from a fission bomb.

Subtitle question 3: _____ ?

Your answer:

_____

_____

_____

_____

_____

_____

Subtitle question 4: _____ ?

Your answer:

_____

_____

_____

_____

_____

_____

_____

Subtitle question 5: _____ ?

Your answer:

_____

_____

_____

_____

_____

_____

_____

Title question: _How was the atom harnessed to produce nuclear energy?_

You already answered this question in Chapter 5, so you don't have to answer it again. You should now be able to write a first-rate and organized essay to answer this question if you were asked to do so.

You've now learned the mind-mapping method and chewing-up information method, and you undoubtedly now know a great deal about nuclear energy. You've done your studying, and you've done a thorough and comprehensive job. _It's time to take a practice quiz to see how much you have learned._ Put away your books and your mind-map. _Please note:_ Some of the questions are tricky, so think carefully about your answers and be on the lookout for "zingers."

QUIZ ON THE NUCLEAR ENERGY ARTICLE

1. The science of nuclear energy:
   A. started with the dropping of an atomic bomb in World War II.
   B. exclusively concerns the production of energy in nuclear reactors.
   C. began with the discovery of radiation.
   D. deals exclusively with how to split an atomic nucleus.
   E. all of the above.

2. When an atomic weapon explodes, the mass is reduced because of the loss of binding energy. ○ True ○ False

3. In a fission chain reaction, many nuclei fuse to form one nuclei.

4. Nuclear energy is the largest source of electricity in the United States.
   ○ True   ○ False

5. Released binding energy assumes the form of:
   A. gamma radiation.
   B. energy particles.
   C. intense heat.
   D. all of the above.

6. The nucleus makes up most of the volume of an atom.
   ○ True   ○ False

7. The mass (weight) of the end products of a nuclear explosion weighs more than the mass of the original nucleus.   ○ True   ○ False

8. Einstein's famous formula about the relationship between mass and energy is: _____

9. Nuclear reactors were first built in the 1930s.   ○ True   ○ False

10. When fusion occurs:
    A. two heavy hydrogen nuclei combine in a chain reaction.
    B. one heavy hydrogen nucleus splits into two light nuclei.
    C. two light hydrogen nuclei combine in a chain reaction.
    D. none of the above.

11. Fission is used to produce fusion.   ○ True   ○ False

12. Fuel rods in the core of a nuclear reactor produce a nuclear chain reaction that generates heat and steam.   ○ True   ○ False

13. Electricity is produced when steam in a nuclear reactor powers a generator, which, in turn, powers a turbine.   ○ True   ○ False

14. Two dangers posed by nuclear energy are:

    _____

    _____

15. List two medical uses of nuclear energy:

    _____

    _____

16. List four other uses of nuclear energy:

    _____

    _____

    _____

    _____

EXAMINING YOUR PERFORMANCE ON THE QUIZ

The answers to the test questions are located on page 131. Check your answers to determine how you did.

> Possibility #1: You did very well on the test (no more than 1 incorrect answer).
>
> Possibility #2: You did relatively well on the test (no more than 3 incorrect answers).
>
> Possibility #3: You had difficulty with the test (4 or more incorrect answers).

If you had several incorrect answers on the test, you should do some analytical and strategic thinking. First, review the information you highlighted. Did you highlight the information that was covered in the quiz? Did you have difficulty remembering important facts or understanding concepts? Are there are any changes that you can make in your study process to improve your understanding and recall? A setback on one quiz is not a disaster. You should learn from the experience and do everything in your power to prevent the situation from recurring. This is the essence of thinking and acting smart.

Mastery: Using DIBS to Handle a Disappointment

If you didn't do as well as you wanted on the test, use DIBS to help you analyze and solve the problem. Your DIBS analysis might look something like this:

Define: I didn't do as well on the test as I wanted.

Investigate: I didn't remember the information.

I panicked when I took the test and forgot what I studied.

The test was too hard.

Brainstorm: I could look more carefully for key information when I study.

I could learn some new methods for remembering information.

I could learn relaxation techniques so I don't panic and forget what I've learned.

Select: I'll identify important information more carefully when studying and experiment with new techniques for recalling this information.

If you had difficulty on the test, don't worry. Chapter 9 presents many more test preparation methods. But, before you learn those techniques, you must learn how to take good notes from your textbooks.

In the next chapter, you'll practice taking "standard notes." You'll also practice answering title and subtitle questions. Because you've already highlighted or underlined the nuclear energy material, *you have actually done most of the work involved in taking notes.* You'll discover that note taking is easy! All you have to do is transfer the information to your binder.

Reviewing the Chewing-Up Information Method

Number in proper order the five steps you learned in the chewing-up information method.

Step ___ : Turn each subtitle into a question.

Step ___ : Reread the material carefully and highlight or underline key information.

Step ___ : Turn the title into a question using a main idea question word.

Step ___ : Speed-read the material.

Step ___ : Answer the subtitle and title questions.

The main idea question words are: _____

The detail question words are: _____

For Your Information

Many students who are having difficulty working up to their full potential in school are actually very conscientious and spend long hours studying. Unfortunately, these students often do little more than "go through the motions" of studying. Because they don't participate actively in the learning process, they understand and recall very little of what they are studying. The consequences are predictable: poor reading comprehension, marginal academic performance, and low grades.

It's easy to fall into the habit of thinking, studying, and learning passively and allowing your brain to go to sleep when you study. You may be spending adequate time doing your homework and preparing for tests, but you may derive little benefit from studying because your mind is not operating optimally.

There is a powerful antidote for passive learning, poor comprehension, and difficulty with recall. This antidote requires that you intentionally transform yourself into an active learner and deliberately engage your mind when you study.

To learn actively, you must:

- ask penetrating questions about the content as you read and study
- identify important information, especially information your instructor is likely to include on a test
- use the key information you've identified to answer the questions you pose about the content of the material you're studying

Good reading comprehension is a skill that can be systematically developed. As is the case with acquiring any new capability, your proficiency will improve with focused effort, motivation, practice, and good coaching.

ANSWERS TO QUIZ:

1. C; 2. T; 3. F; 4. F; 5. D; 6. F; 7. F; 8. E=MC^2; 9. F; 10. C; 11. T; 12. T; 13. T; 14. nuclear accidents, risks in disposing of wastes; 15. treat cancer, diagnose disease; 16. kill bacteria, prevent plant disease, preserve food, keep track of time

TAKING NOTES FROM TEXTBOOKS

OBJECTIVES

- Taking standard notes
- Speed-writing that incorporates abbreviations
- Writing effective essays
- Distinguishing main ideas and details

Getting What's Important
Down on Paper

For as long as he could remember, Darnel wanted to be a lawyer. As his parents and friends made a point of repeatedly pointing out, he *loved* to argue, and everyone was convinced that he would make a great attorney. Darnel especially enjoyed movies and TV shows that depicted courtroom scenes. The idea of defending someone seemed unbelievably exciting. It was like being an actor on stage. Of course, he understood that in the real world, it wasn't pretending. As a criminal attorney, his client's fate lay in his hands, and his skills could determine whether the person was acquitted or ended up in prison.

Realizing he would have to go to college and law school, Darnel was intent on getting good grades. His desire to excel academically was also driven by a key economic reality: His family was poor, and he would need a scholarship when he transferred to a four-year college. Darnel realized that he would never be admitted to a good university and earn a scholarship unless he had an excellent G.P.A. and top-notch letters of recommendation from his instructors.

Darnel's immediate goal was to get an A on the next U. S. government test. He had seven days to prepare. After his last class, Darnel drove home, went to his room, and wrote down his study plan:

MONDAY:

- speed-read assigned chapter twice
- make up main idea and detail questions from title and subtitles
- mind-map each unit in chapter

TUESDAY:

- reread chapter carefully
- expand mind-map to improve comprehension

WEDNESDAY:

- take notes in "standard form"
- answer questions from title and subtitles
- review class notes
- put key facts on index cards for easy access and review
- memorize important information

THURSDAY:

- make up practice test questions from notes based on the types of questions asked on previous history chapter tests

WEEKEND:

- review class notes, textbook notes

- mind-map the chapter as a review
- review and memorize key facts on index cards

Darnel estimated that, to make his plan work, he would need to allocate approximately six hours of study time. If he spent 45 minutes studying every evening and spent an additional three hours studying over the weekend, he felt confident that he would be prepared. A six-hour time investment didn't seem like too high a price for getting a good grade on an important test, especially when his grade could determine whether he would get an A or a B in the course.

Targeting What You Want

How significant a role did Darnel's goals play in his effort and academic performance?

1	2	3	4	5	6	7	8	9	10
insignificant				fairly significant					very significant

Why did you make this evaluation? _____

_____

_____

Do you believe he would have been as conscientious if he didn't have clearly defined career goals?

○ yes   ○ no   ○ perhaps

Evaluate the effectiveness of Darnel's study strategy.

1	2	3	4	5	6	7	8	9	10
ineffective				effective					very effective

Why did you make this evaluation? _____

_____

_____

Predict the likelihood that Darnel will attain his career objectives.

1	2	3	4	5	6	7	8	9	10
unlikely				fairly likely					very likely

Why did you make this evaluation? _____

_____

_____

Drawing a Conclusion from the Evidence

Having read about Darnel's strategy, what specific conclusion can you draw from the information in the story? Using the *inductive method*, express in a well-crafted sentence what you have concluded. *Remember:* You are summarizing the **point** of the story.

The point of Darnel's story:

_____

_____

_____

_____

Using DIBS

In addition to his other homework, Darnel had allocated three additional hours during the weekend to study for the history exam. Let's say Darnel tells his girlfriend that he is planning on studying the entire weekend. Upon hearing this, she becomes very upset. She reminds him that she's having a big party Saturday night and that he has agreed to help her prepare for it. He had promised to be at her apartment at 11:00 A.M. Saturday morning. Darnel clearly is in a bind. He has to study, but he certainly doesn't want his girlfriend to be angry at him.

Pretend that you are Darnel and use DIBS to resolve the problem. Remember to use "I" messages.

Define: _____

_____

Investigate: _____

_____

_____

_____

Brainstorm: _____

_____

_____

_____

Select: _____

_____

Assess the likelihood that the selected solution will resolve Darnel's dilemma.

1	2	3	4	5	6	7	8	9	10
unlikely				fairly likely					very likely

zooming out *on the issues*

Taking Effective Notes from Textbooks

You've already learned many powerful study techniques, including:

- scheduling time
- asking questions about the content
- mind-mapping
- using the chewing-up information method

You also know how to **identify important information** and how to **organize** this information into a mind-map so you can understand, connect, and remember it. In Chapter 6, you practiced the chewing-up information method. In Step 4, you learned to highlight or underline important information.

You're now going to learn another effective method for organizing and recording key information from your textbooks. The rationale for learning alternative methods is that once you've been exposed to several techniques, you can select the one that works best for you. You can also combine components of different methods and create a personalized study strategy that capitalizes on your particular learning strengths. (Refer to Chapter 1 to review how to identify your preferred and most effective learning modality.)

STANDARD NOTE TAKING

The new method you are going to practice is called *standard note taking*. You've probably already used some type of standard note taking in high school, although you probably didn't use this name to describe it. Even though you did use standard note taking in one form or another, you may not have used it effectively.

The first three steps in standard note taking are exactly the same as those in the chewing-up information method. In Step 4, you transfer the important information you highlighted or underlined into traditional notes.

Let's review the chewing-up information steps:

Step 1: *Turn the title into a question before reading the material.* (Main Idea Question Words: *How, Why, What.*) Write the question on the top line of your notebook paper and begin writing at the left red-lined margin.

Step 2: *Turn each subtitle into a question before reading the material.* Indent below the title question and leave plenty of space to put your notes under each question. When taking notes under each subtitle question, *do not try to answer the question in your notes.* Write down only the key information that deals with the subject. *When you finish taking notes, you'll use your notes to answer each subtitle question.* It is advisable to use a pencil or erasable ink in case you want to make changes.

Step 3: *Speed-read the material.* In Step 4, you can still highlight the important information if you wish. You may also choose to skip highlighting and proceed directly to taking notes.

Step 4: *Read the material carefully. Write down key information in note form as you read.* (A sample of standard note taking can be found on page 141).

POWERHOUSE THINKING

Basic Procedures for Taking Notes from Textbooks

- Write down only the key information.
- Leave out unnecessary words.
- Abbreviate whenever possible.
- Write neatly and legibly.
- Indent your notes under each subtitle question.

USING ABBREVIATIONS

You can save a great deal of time by using abbreviations, but it's essential that you understand what you've written. Below are some common abbreviations you may want to use. You may know others that are not on this list—add them to the bottom. Also, feel free to make up your own. (*Please note:* Another list of abbreviations for words relating to recording assignments is found on page 41. Although some abbreviations appear on both lists, the following are relevant to taking notes.)

SPEED-WRITING

Most words can be intelligibly abbreviated in your notes and easily understood if you leave out the vowels (e.g., vrtlly, rcgnzd, vwls). If the word begins (bgns) with a vowel, you should include it (e.g., abbrvtd). Include a middle vowel if this makes it easier to decipher a particular word (e.g., decphr). For new words or concepts (e.g., fission), you should *not* speed-write these words the *first* time you put them in your notes. Once you know you're dealing with fission, you could then write "fissn" or "fis." and feel confident you could recognize it when reviewing your notes. Your ability to *speed-write* and decipher what you've written will improve with practice.

Practicing Note Taking

Look at the information you highlighted or underlined in the first seven paragraphs of the nuclear energy article. This unit is being *intentionally* used again to demonstrate how complex information can be understood, assimilated, and recalled when you can access a range of effective study techniques.

After practicing the different methods, you may choose to use one technique exclusively, or you may decide to combine different methods and create your *own personalized system*. As you well know, studying for a math or physics test requires a different studying method than the one used to study for a general science or history test. On a math or physics test, you are asked to solve problems. On a general science or history test, you'll have to answer multiple-choice, short-answer, true–false, and/or essay questions.

Abbreviations

th	=	the	exp	=	explain	w/o	=	without	t/o	= throughout
p	=	page	v	=	very	thru	=	through	info	= information
"	=	inch	'	=	foot	gd	=	good	comp	= complete
w	=	with	<	=	less than	>	=	more than	2 gthr	= together
ht	=	height	blw	=	below	abv	=	above	exer	= exercise
u	=	you	2	=	to	wdth	=	width	mny	= many
tm	=	time	hr	=	hour	cen	=	century	dur	= during
wh	=	what	wn	=	when	gd	=	good	sect	= section
nt	=	not	un	=	unit	min	=	minute	n/t	= next to
ex	=	example	cmpr	=	compare	imp	=	important	ques	= question
mo	=	month	yr	=	year	sm	=	small	diff	= difficult
y	=	why	whr	=	where	bg	=	big	⟶	= leading to
fr	=	for	wh	=	who	nxt	=	next	sec	= second
wch	=	which	thru	=	through	bot	=	bottom	mid	= middle
frm	=	from	ch	=	chapter	dy	=	day	per	= person
fn	=	finish	his	=	history	Sp	=	Spanish	chem	= chemistry
Fr	=	French	Eng	=	English	Amer	=	American	bio	= biology

Personalized abbreviations:

___ = _____   ___ = _____   ___ = _____   ___ = _____

___ = _____   ___ = _____   ___ = _____   ___ = _____

___ = _____   ___ = _____   ___ = _____   ___ = _____

___ = _____   ___ = _____   ___ = _____   ___ = _____

Having access to a range of effective study techniques and "tricks" allows you to tailor your test preparation to the course content and the instructor's teaching and testing style.

You've undoubtedly taken notes in high school, and you may be quite satisfied with your current note-taking system. If you're convinced that this system works, you are under no obligation to change. You might discover, however, that the procedure used in this book is more effective. Be open-minded. You may ultimately decide use to your own method, or you may decide to incorporate all, or selected parts, of the methodology presented here. You can then objectively assess the results and decide what changes, if any, you want to make.

It's now time to transfer the information you highlighted in the nuclear energy article into *standard notes*. The first seven paragraphs of the unit, complete with important highlighted (actually, underlined) information, is reproduced below. Sample notes for these seven paragraphs follow. Once you "get the hang" of standard note taking, continue transferring the highlighted or underlined information into the note-taking format.

NUCLEAR ENERGY: HARNESSING THE ATOM

In 1945, two atomic bombs were dropped over the cities of Nagasaki and Hiroshima. This devastating nuclear attack caused the Japanese forces to surrender. Although many people believe that the attack signaled the beginning of the nuclear age, atomic energy was actually discovered more than 50 years prior to the bombing.

Atoms are the smallest and most fundamental unit of matter, and everything in our world is comprised of this basic unit. This includes the clothes we wear, the air we breathe, the food we eat, the paper we write on, and the gasoline we put in our cars. Several important earlier discoveries led to the discovery of nuclear energy. In 1896, a French scientist named Antoine Henry Becquerel identified radioactivity. His scientific experiments revealed that certain elements released radioactive rays and that these elements possessed unique and fascinating properties.

In the late 1930s, scientists in Germany realized that by using a process called **nuclear fission,** it was possible to split the nucleus of an atom into two nuclei. To understand how fission works, it may help to imagine a chocolate chip being split in half by a cleaver. Now imagine that the energy holding the chocolate chip together is suddenly released by the splitting process, and this results in a massive explosion. (This image is intended only to help you understand the fission process. In the case of splitting a chocolate chip, *no* significant energy is actually released.) The discovery that energy is released when certain types of atomic material are split led to the first nuclear reactor being built in the early 1940s and, ultimately, to the first military use of nuclear fission. The two atomic bombs dropped over Japan to end World War II represent the only time in history that nuclear weapons have been used in war.

The development of the hydrogen bomb in the 1950s was an even more frightening use of atomic power. Hydrogen bombs release massive amounts of nuclear energy by combining (fusing) two hydrogen nuclei to form one nucleus. To understand the fusion process, imagine two chocolate chips sitting next to each other on a pan in an oven. As the oven gets hot, the two chips melt together (or fuse) to form one big chip, and in this combining process, a massive amount of energy is released. (Of course, two chocolate chips melting together do not actually produce a measurable release of energy!) Fusion occurs naturally on the sun where hydrogen nuclei are continually combining to produce enormous amounts of heat, light, and radiation.

Although nuclear technology has produced nuclear weapons that are capable of horrific destruction, this same technology also has many peaceful applications. One of the most important involves the production of electricity. In 1956, the first nuclear power plant was built in England, and in 1957, the first U.S. plant was constructed. By the late 1980s, there were over 420 reactors operating throughout the world, and there were more than 110 nuclear reactors in production in the United States. Today, nuclear energy is second only to coal as the largest source of electricity—currently, more than 17 percent of our electricity is generated from nuclear energy.

SAMPLE NOTES

1. How was the atom harnessed to produce nuclear energy? (This is the main idea question derived from the title.)

   - 1945: 2 atomic bmbs drppd Nagasaki & Hiroshima ⟶ forced Japan surrndr
   - Atmic enrgy discvrd 50 yrs prior
   - Atoms smallest most basic unit matter
   - Evrythng cmprsed thse units: clothes, air, food, gas
   - 20th cen. ⟶ nuc. enrgy mst powrfl source enrgy discov
   - pwer frm atom
   - earlier discov. led devlpmnt nuc. enrgy
   - 1896: Becquerel idntfd radioactivty
   - crtn elmnts possess unique prprties
   - late 1930s nuc. fssion discov. Ger. (split nuc. atom)
   - early 1940s 1st nclr reactr
   - ⟶ 2 atm bmbs drppd on Japan ⟶ only tme war use
   - 1950: fusion hydrogen bomb ⟶ combine 2 hydro. nuclei ⟶ 1 nucleus ⟶ release mssive nclr enrgy
   - fusion natrlly frm sun ⟶ heat, lght, radiation
   - peacefl applic: electrcty
   - 1956: 1st nuc. plant England
   - 1957: 1st U.S. plnt
   - By late 80s 420 reactors world ⟶ 110 in U.S.
   - Nuc. enrgy ⟶ 2nd only to coal ⟶ 17% U.S. elctrcty

2. What is the nuclear atom? (subtitle question)
   (continue taking notes)

Copy the notes modeled above onto binder paper and finish taking notes on the entire article. *Remember:* Turn each subtitle into a question, indent, and put down only the important information. You want to write down key details and facts. As you take notes, *think about what the information means.* If you understand the content of what you're studying, you're far more likely to remember it, and you're far more likely to do well on an exam. (Methods for identifying and memorizing key facts and information are presented in Chapter 9.)

Mastery: More Practice Taking Notes

Use the chewing-up information method to study the history passage that follows. The system may seem very time consuming, but the only way for you to master note taking is to practice. As you become increasingly proficient at taking notes, your speed will increase.

Remember: **Do not highlight or underline this time. After completing Steps 1–3, start taking notes without highlighting.** Later, if you find highlighting a helpful preliminary step, you can certainly do so *before* you begin to take notes. You may conclude that a preliminary highlighting step helps you identify key information, and the actual note taking helps you better understand, organize, and remember the information. Spending the extra time to highlight before taking notes might be well worth the effort.

Complete Steps 1–3, copy the sample notes from p. 145 onto binder paper, and continue taking notes on the entire passage. Write neatly and use abbreviations you can understand.

THE FRENCH REVOLUTION: A TIME BOMB WAITING TO EXPLODE

The French Revolution lasted from 1789 until 1799. It was one of the most important events in European history. What began as a government financial crisis produced lasting radical changes in French society and government. As a result of the revolution, the rule of French kings ended, and the rights of the middle class (e.g., merchants, lawyers, and government officials) were strengthened. The social conditions of the peasants (small farm owners and farm workers) improved, and democratic ideals were incorporated into a constitution.

Factors Leading to the Overthrow of the Monarchy

There are many theories about what caused the French people to overthrow the monarchy, but it is clear that political conflicts and economic problems were major sources for the discontent that led to the revolution. France was bankrupt in 1789, and the different French classes were entangled in a struggle for power.

Louis XVI was king during this period. Like all French kings, he was an absolute monarch. This meant his authority was unlimited and that his subjects considered his right to rule to be a "divine right" derived directly from God.

Seven years of almost continual warfare produced France's economic crisis. Paying for these wars and providing financial support for the American Revolution (1775–83) created severe economic pressures that exploded in unrest and riots. Because discipline in the army had broken down, efforts by the King to restore order were unsuccessful. The army's weakness encouraged the revolutionary leaders.

Prior to the revolution, the French social classes had been separated for hundreds of years. There were three classes or *estates*: the clergy (the first estate), the nobles (the second estate), and the common people (the third estate). The third estate consisted of the majority of the French population: peasants, workers, and the middle class.

There is no doubt that the system for collecting taxes to support the government was biased and unfair. Whereas the clergy and nobles contributed little, the common people provided the bulk of the taxes. Because the middle class was considered part of the third estate, which was not respected, their considerable fiscal contributions in the form of taxes were never fully appreciated by the government.

Although the French aristocracy was very powerful, they believed that the King would not accept their influence. At the same time, the third estate wanted to limit the aristocracy's power and end a system that awarded power on the basis of inherited birth rights and social status. The common people desired a democratic system that would respond to the will of the people. Clearly, the conditions that existed were a powder keg requiring only a spark to explode.

The Will of the People: Representative Government

Because of the nation's enormous debts, the King had to raise money. The Parliament of Paris, however, refused to allow him to borrow money or raise taxes without calling a meeting of the Estates General. This body was comprised of representatives of all three estates and had not met for more than 170 years. Reluctantly, King Louis XVI agreed to the meeting.

The third estate wanted equal representation in which each delegate had one vote. They also wanted a national assembly and a constitution. Because they feared losing their power and influence, the King, clergy, and aristocracy refused this demand. In 1779, the third estate declared themselves a National Assembly. They informed the King that they wouldn't disband until a formal constitution was written.

Clearly, the American Revolution in 1775 and the American Constitution and Bill of Rights had a powerful effect on the French people. The writings by philosophers about freedom, democracy, and human rights heightened the people's awareness of the injustice in French society and fanned the discontent. Rousseau, a famous French philosopher, challenged the idea that a king's rights are divine. He argued that the right to govern comes from the people and is not given by God to a king.

In response to the social and political pressure, the King allowed the three estates to band together and form a National Assembly. Although he permitted this to happen, he was, at the same time, massing troops to break up the Assembly.

The third estate learned of the King's plot, and on July 14, 1789, they stormed and captured the Bastille, a military fortress in Paris. At the same time, there was a massive uprising of peasants. The rebellious citizens of Paris formed a revolutionary city government. Many of the nobles became fearful for their safety and began to flee the country. The popular uprising succeeded and saved the National Assembly from being disbanded by the King.

Profound Changes in French Society

In August 1789, the National Assembly produced a Declaration of the Rights of Man and of the Citizen. It stated that the French people had the right of liberty, property, security, resistance to oppression, and a representative government. The clergy and nobility were now required to pay taxes. Some of the feudal dues the peasants had to pay were eliminated.

A constitution was drafted that placed limits on the monarchy. Eighty-three regions were created. These *departments* were the equivalent of the separate states in America. Elected local councils were responsible for running each local government.

Despite the many changes, the right to vote and hold public office was limited to citizens who paid taxes. To pay France's enormous debts, lands belonging to the Catholic Church were seized and sold to the peasants and middle class. For the first time, it was decreed that priests and bishops were to be elected. Convents and monasteries were closed and religious tolerance was guaranteed to Protestants and Jews. It was also decreed that judges were to be elected. A Legislative Assembly replaced the National Assembly. This new governing body was comprised mainly of the middle class.

Louis XVI remained opposed to the revolution and plotted against it. Public opinion was divided. Some citizens were opposed to the measures taken against the Catholic Church. Others wanted even harsher measures taken against those who opposed the revolution.

During this period, there were also foreign threats to France's sovereignty. The French army had suffered defeats, and foreign forces invaded France. The King actually wanted the invaders to be victorious. This infuriated the revolutionaries, and they demanded that the King be dethroned. In 1792, three years after the storming of the Bastille, Louis XVI and his family were imprisoned.

On September 21, 1792, the National Convention declared France a republic. Its slogan was "Liberty, Equality, Fraternity." For the first time in French history, peasants, shopkeepers, and workers began to shape the political system. Public assistance for the poor was provided, as well as free elementary education, for both sexes, price controls to protect people from rapid inflation (money losing its value and buying power), tax reform, and the abolition of slavery in the colonies. A new citizen's army was created to control rebellions and repel foreign enemies.

The Reign of Terror

Louis XVI was condemned to death because of his attempts to help France's enemies. The revolution grew more radical and violent. More than 18,000 supporters of the King and the real and imagined enemies of the republic were executed by guillotine. Even Robespierre, an important leader of the revolution, was executed in 1794.

A new democratic constitution was written in 1795, but there were still turmoil and discontent in France. Wars, ongoing economic problems, and opposition by supporters of the overthrown monarchy resulted in a plot against the government in 1799. The people, however, were tired of conflict and violence. Finally, a popular general seized control of the government and ended the revolution. His name was Napoleon Bonaparte.

The Outcome

Despite its violence, the French revolution produced major positive social and political changes. The aristocracy and monarchy no longer controlled the society economically, politically, and culturally. France had become a free, unified society with a strong central government that was now dominated by landowners and the middle class. Representative government was established, and the common people could now influence their own destiny.

Sources: Information from *Encyclopedia Britannica, World Book*

SAMPLE NOTES

1. Why was the French Revolution a time bomb waiting to explode? (Title question)
   - Fr. Rev. 1789–99 ⟶ imprtnt evnt Euro. hstry
   - Financial crisis ⟶ radical chngs Fr. soc. & govt.
   - Rule king ends
   - mid. clss rghts strngthnd
   - soc. condit. peasants imprvd
   - Democrt. ideals encrgzd

2. What factors led to the overthrow of the monarchy? (Subtitle question)
   - Mny theories: poltcl & econ. prblms ⟶ revoltn
   - Fr. bnkrupt 1789
   - Strggle pwer Fr. clsses
   - Louis XVI king ⟶ absolute monarch ⟶ divine right (God)

Copy these sample notes on a separate piece of binder paper and continue taking notes on your own. Remember to convert each subtitle into a main idea question by using the appropriate question words. Leave out information you don't think is important, and include the information you think a history instructor would consider important.

When you've completed your notes on the entire article, compare them with those below and add any important information you may have left out. Don't look at the completed sample notes until you've done your own! If you simply copy the notes, you won't learn how to take notes on your own.

COMPLETED MODEL NOTES

1. Why was the French Revolution a time bomb waiting to explode?
   - Fr. Rev. 1789–99 ⟶ imp. evnt Euro. hstry
   - Financial crisis ⟶ radical chnges Fr. socty & govt.
   - Rule king ends
   - mid. clss rghts strngthnd
   - soc. condit. peasants imprvd

- Democrt. ideals encrged

2. What factors led to the overthrow of the monarchy?
   - Mny theories: poltcl & econ. prblms ⟶ revoltn
   - Fr. bnkrupt 1789
   - Strggle pwer Fr. clsses
   - Louis XVI king ⟶ absolute monarch ⟶ divine right (God)
   - $ prob. ⟶ 7 yrs war & fnding Amer. Revoltn (1775–83) ⟶ unrest & riots
   - Breakdown army discipline ⟶ no order
   - Div. Fr. soc. classes ⟶ 1st estate (clergy)/ 2nd est. (nobls)/ 3rd est. peasants (wrking clss, middl clss merchnts, lwyers, gov't offcls)
   - Clergy/Nobles paid few taxes—commn people paid mst
   - Be4 rev. Fr. aristoc. pwerful, influential ⟶ flt Kng ddn't accpt pwr
   - 3rd est. wntd lmit pwer aristoc. ⟶ end systm pwer bsed brth rghts/soc. status ⟶ wnted demcrat. sys. respnd will people

3. Why was it the will of the people to have representative gov't?
   - enorm. debts: King needed $
   - Parliament refsed borrw $ / raise txs unlss meetng Estates General ⟶ rep. all 3 est. ⟶ hdn't met 170 yrs. ⟶ king agrd relctntly
   - 3rd est. wnted equal represent. ⟶ 1 vote each ⟶ king/clrgy/ nbles refsed
   - 1779: 3rd est. declared themselves Nat. Assembl ⟶ wouldn't disband til constit. wrtten
   - Influence Am. Rev. & Bill Rights, philosophers ⟶ Rousseau ⟶ right govrn frm people
   - K. allw 3 est. Nat. Assem. ⟶ K plots agnst 3 est w. troops
   - 3rd est. stormed/captured Bastille 7/14/89 ⟶ massive peasnt revlt ⟶ ctzns frmed revoltnry cty gov't Paris
   - Nbles fearfl ⟶ fled
   - Pop. uprising success ⟶ saved Nat. Assembly

4. What were the profound changes in French society?
   - Aug. 1789: Nat. Assem. ⟶ Declar. Rights of Man & of Citizen ⟶ liberty/property/ security/resist.

oppression/rprsntative gov't $\longrightarrow$ clrgy & nbls pay txes $\longrightarrow$ some feudal dues elimin.

- Constitut. drafted $\longrightarrow$ monarch. limtd 83 regions/depart-ments created $\longrightarrow$ local gov't
- Rght vote/ hold pub. offce $\longrightarrow$ pay txes
- Cath. chrch lands seized/sold to mid. clss pay debts
- Priests/bishops elcted
- Convnts/monsteries closed
- Judges elcted
- Nat. Assembly $\longrightarrow$ Legislative Assembly
- Govrnng body mainly mddle clss
- Louis XVI still oppsed rev. $\longrightarrow$ plotted
- Pub. opin. divided $\longrightarrow$ sme oppsed measures against Chrch $\longrightarrow$ othrs wnted harsher measures against rev. oppnnts
- Foreign threats $\longrightarrow$ Fr. army defeats $\longrightarrow$ invsion
- K. wanted invadrs to win $\longrightarrow$ infuriated people $\longrightarrow$ K dethrnd & imprisnd 1792
- 9/21/92 $\longrightarrow$ Nat. conven. $\longrightarrow$ Fr. republic (Liberty, Equality, Fraternity)
- Shpkprs, peasnts, wrk run poltcl systm.
- Pub. assis. poor $\longrightarrow$ free elem. ed. $\longrightarrow$ price cntrls
- infltion $\longrightarrow$ tx refrms $\longrightarrow$ aboltn slv colnies
- Nw citzen army $\longrightarrow$ repell forgn enmies

5. What was the Reign of Terror?
   - K. execvtd/hlping enmies
   - Rev. more radicl/violnt
   - 18,000 execvtd
   - Robespierre (early leader) rev. excvted 1794
   - New dem. constit. 1795 $\longrightarrow$ still turmoil & discontent
   - Wars/hard tmes $\longrightarrow$ plot agnst gov't 1799
   - People tired cnflict/violnce
   - Napoleon Bonaparte seized gov't $\longrightarrow$ ended rev.

6. What was the outcome?
   - Revltn $\longrightarrow$ violence but postv soc. & polit. chnges
   - Aristoc & Monarch no longer contrlld soc.
   - Free, unfied soc/ strng cen. gov't run by lndwners + mddle clss
   - Repre. gov't $\longrightarrow$ commn people influence own destiny

Answering Essay Questions

It's time to complete the next step of the chewing-up information method.

Step 5: Using the space below, *answer the subtitle questions.* Write strong, powerful sentences that summarize the information in your notes. Use your notes to answer the questions.

Before you begin writing, examine the following information about topic sentences and concluding sentences.

TOPIC SENTENCES

When writing an essay on a test or for homework, make certain you begin with a first-rate topic (introductory) sentence that is thoughtful, comprehensive, forceful, and well-written. The topic sentence should engage the interest of the person reading your essay and cause him or her to "sit up and take notice." You may use the sample topic sentence below to answer the first question, or you may prefer to make up your own topic sentence.

> **Sample topic sentence:** The French Revolution, which began in 1789 and lasted until 1799, produced profound changes in French society.

CONCLUDING SENTENCES

When writing an essay on a test or for homework, it's vital to summarize your points or your position on an issue with a first-rate concluding sentence. After writing the important information, you must end your essay with a thoughtful, comprehensive, forceful, and well-written final sentence that "ties everything together." This sentence should succinctly summarize the key information you included in the body of your essay. A sample concluding sentence is shown below. You may use this sample or write your own.

> **Sample concluding sentence:** By ending the monarchy, controlling the influence of the nobility, and creating a democratic constitution that gave power to the workers and middle class, the French Revolution forever altered the course of French society.

Answering the Subtitle Questions

It's now time to answer the subtitle questions.
Subtitle Questions:

1. *What factors led to the overthrow of the monarchy?*

_____

_____

_____

_____

_____

_____

2. *Why was it the will of the people to have a representative government?*

_____

_____

_____

_____

_____

_____

3. *What were the profound changes in French society?*

_____

_____

_____

_____

_____

_____

4. *What was the Reign of Terror?*

_____

_____

_____

_____

_____

_____

5. *What was the outcome?*

_____

_____

_____

_____

_____

_____

Answering the Title Question

Step 6: Now answer the *title* question: *Why was the French Revolution a time bomb waiting to explode?* Your answer should be in the form of a short essay. You want to demonstrate to your instructor that you understand the article.

You may use your notes to answer the question, or you may want to see how well you can do without using your notes. If this were a test, the teacher would probably not allow students to use notes. You would have to include as much as you could remember from having studied and reviewed your notes. As a general rule, an essay that answers a title question should be longer than an essay that answers a subtitle question.

Before you begin writing, review the following information about "thumbnail" outlines.

WRITING A THUMB-NAIL OUTLINE
WHEN TAKING ESSAY TESTS

Before beginning to answer an essay question on a test, it's a good idea to jot down quickly—using abbreviations you can decipher to save time—the important information you want to include and the important points you want to make. You can write this mini-outline, which is often referred to as a **thumb-nail outline,** in pencil in the corner of your test paper (and erase it before handing it in) or you can write it on a separate piece of paper. Your outline should be *very* brief and take no more than a minute or two to complete.

Essay Test Question: *Why was the French Revolution a time bomb waiting to explode?*

Sample thumbnail outline:

Rev. 1789—99
Financial cris/polit strug/clss strug
K. absolute pwer—div. right
7 yrs war
weak army
3 estat—clrgy, nbles, wrkers, peasants, mid. clss ⟶
unfair txes
Aristrcy. wnted contrl over K.
Influence Amer. Revol. (1775), Constit./ Bill of Rights/
philosph. (Rousseau: rght govrn frm people—not divine)
3rd est. wnted democ. syst respond their will
K. tried disbnd Nat. Assemb./plotted/wnted invdrs to win

Your thumbnail outline will help you remember and organize the key information you want to include when answering an essay test question. You want to convince your instructors that you've understood and mastered the content of the assigned material. Because they have to read and evaluate many essays, they obviously want clear, well-organized essays that present the important information persuasively.

ANSWERING AN ESSAY TEST QUESTION

For practice, pretend this is actually a test question and assume you have 15 minutes to write your essay answer. Use the space below or a separate sheet of paper. Include all of the information your instructor is likely to consider important. Organize the information so that it makes sense and "flows." Your goal is to impress your teacher with how much you know about the French Revolution and why it was such an important event. Remember to begin with a powerful topic sentence. A slightly different sample topic sentence follows. Use it if you want, or make up your own topic sentence.

> **Sample topic sentence:** The French Revolution, which began in 1789 and ended in 1799, was one of the most important events in European history.

Remember: When you finish your essay, make certain that your essay contains the key information and that you have tied everything together with a powerful concluding sentence. When you've finished writing, compare your essay with the model that follows. Your essay will, of course, be different because you've conveyed the information and expressed your ideas and insights in your own words. **Don't look at the model essay until you've completed writing your own.** Once you've compared your work with the model, feel free to make changes.

To write first-rate essays, you must be self-critical. Your mind-set must be: "How can I present my ideas most effectively, and how can I make this read better?" Improving your writing skills is an ongoing process that requires practice, sustained effort, multiple drafts and revisions, and careful proofreading! Of course, you do not have enough time to do multiple drafts and revisions on an essay test, but you can do so when writing essays that are assigned for homework.

Your Answer to the Title Question:

Model Essays

(continued)

SUBTITLE QUESTIONS

1. *What factors led to the overthrow of the monarchy?*

France was bankrupt in 1789 after seven years of war and having provided financial support for the American Revolution (1775). There were also serious political problems, and the social classes that comprised French society were struggling for power. The financial crisis led to unrest and riots. Because the army was weak, it couldn't control the revolutionaries.

France was divided into three estates. The *first estate* (the clergy) and the *second estate* (the nobility) paid few taxes. The *third estate* (the workers, peasants, and middle class) paid most of the taxes. King Louis XVI was an absolute monarch who believed he ruled by divine right. Although the nobility had great influence, they felt the King was not responsive to their desires. The common people wanted to limit the aristocracy's influence and end a system where power was based on social status. They wanted a more democratic system that would respond to the will of the people. These conflicts and problems set the stage for the revolution.

2. *Why was it the will of the people to have representative government?*

Because of France's enormous debts, King Louis XVI had to raise money. The Parliament refused to let the King borrow or raise taxes unless he called a meeting of representatives of all three estates. This group hadn't met in over 170 years. The King agreed reluctantly.

The third estate wanted equal representation. The nobility and the clergy refused. The third estate then declared themselves the National Assembly and refused to disband until there was a written constitution. French philosophers and events in America (the American Revolution, Constitution, and the Bill of Rights) clearly played a major role in influencing the desire of the third estate to establish a democratic form of government.

Although the King allowed the third estate to create a national assembly, he was gathering troops to overthrow the assembly. The people of Paris learned of his plot and stormed the Bastille on July 14, 1789. The peasants also revolted. Because they were fearful, many nobles fled France. The uprising was successful and the National Assembly was saved.

3. *What were the profound changes in French society?*

In August 1789, the National Assembly wrote a Declaration of the Rights of Man and the Citizen. They decreed the rights of liberty, property ownership, resistance to oppression, and representative government. The clergy and nobility would pay taxes, and some feudal dues were eliminated. A constitution was drafted, and the King's power was limited. The country was divided into 83 departments. Citizens could vote and hold public office if they paid taxes. Church lands were sold to the middle class to pay the country's debts. Priests, bishops, and judges were elected. Convents and monasteries were closed. The country would now be governed mainly by the middle class, peasants, and workers.

When France was invaded, the King wanted France's enemies to win. The people were very angry. They dethroned the King and later executed him. A French Republic was formed based upon liberty, equality, and fraternity. There was welfare for the poor, free elementary education, price controls, and tax reforms. Slavery was abolished in the colonies, and a new citizen army was created to fight France's enemies.

4. *What was the Reign of Terror?*

King Louis XVI was executed for helping France's enemies. The revolution became more radical and violent, and 18,000 people were executed by the guillotine. Robespierre, a leader of the revolution, was also beheaded.

Although a new and more democratic constitution was written in 1795, there was still turmoil and unhappiness. Wars and hard times led to a plot against the government in 1799. By now, the people were tired of violence and conflict. A general named Napoleon

(continued)

Model Essays, Continued.

Bonaparte seized the government in 1799 and ended the revolution.

5. What was the outcome of the French Revolution?

Although there had been much violence and turmoil during the revolution, positive social and political changes occurred. The monarchy, the church, and the aristocracy no longer controlled France. A free and unified society had been created with a strong central government run by the landowners and the middle class. Because there was representative government, the common people at last had control over their own destiny.

TITLE QUESTION

Why was the French Revolution a time bomb waiting to explode?

The French Revolution, which began in 1789 and ended in 1799, was one of the most important events in European history. The revolution resulted from a financial crisis, a political struggle, and a class struggle.

King Louis XVI was an absolute monarch who ruled by divine right. Years of war had caused France to become bankrupt. The weak army could not control the people. Each of the three estates (clergy; aristocracy; and workers, peasants, and middle class) wanted more power and influence. The third estate (the common people) wanted a democratic system, and they wanted fair taxation. To protect the Crown and the rights of the nobility, the King plotted to undermine the citizens' attempt to establish a representative government.

The French people were undoubtedly influenced by the American Revolution, Constitution, and Bill of Rights. They were also influenced by philosophers who said the power to rule comes from the people and not from God.

The time bomb finally exploded when in 1789 the people stormed the Bastille, a fortress in Paris. The peasants in the countryside also revolted. Thousands of France's "enemies" were executed. The King was dethroned and ultimately executed because the people believed he had helped France's enemies. When the violence finally ended, France was a democratic republic whose government was controlled by the people.

Essay Writing Methods

Most American students write traditional essays that use a **deductive format.** They begin with a topic sentence, substantiate their position with relevant facts, and finish with a powerful and persuasive concluding statement. This method is introduced in elementary school, and students repeatedly practice the format throughout middle school and high school. There are, however, several alternatives for writing effective essays.

DEDUCTIVE METHOD

The preceding model essays employ a deductive format. The author writes a **topic sentence** that encapsulates the **point** being made and then *substantiates the point with facts and information.* The better the substantiation, the more persuasive the essay, and the better the grade.

The deductive method can be represented by a triangle (see Figure 7.1). The topic sentence (or point) is the tip of the triangle. Layers of substantiating facts and information follow, with the concluding sentence at the base of the triangle.

FIGURE 7.1   *Graphic representation of the deductive method.*

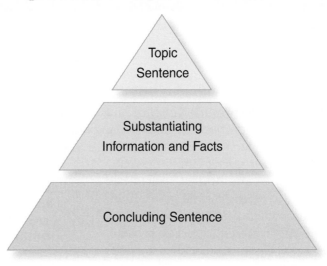

INDUCTIVE METHOD

In the inductive method, the author arrives at a conclusion based on the facts and data that precede the conclusion. If the essay is successful, *the facts and data should lead inescapably to the conclusion that is presented in the last sentence.* This **concluding sentence** is the **point of the essay.** The inductive method is usually considered more challenging than the deductive method because the author must present the information very logically, systematically, and sequentially. The content of the essay must be structured very carefully.

The inductive method can be best represented by an inverted triangle or pyramid (see Figure 7.2). The tip at the bottom of the triangle represents the *point* that the author is making in the essay.

FIGURE 7.2   *Graphic representation of the inductive method.*

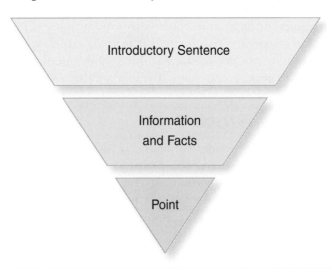

Using the Inductive Method to Answer the Title Question

Why was the French Revolution a time bomb waiting to explode?

King Louis XVI was an absolute monarch who ruled by divine right. Years of war had caused France to become bankrupt. The weak army could not control the people. Each of the three estates (clergy; aristocracy; and workers, peasants, and middle class) wanted more power and influence. The third estate (the common people) wanted a democratic system, and they wanted fair taxation.

The French people were undoubtedly influenced by the American Revolution, the Constitution, and the Bill of Rights. The people were also influenced by philosophers who said the power to rule comes from the people and not from God.

The King plotted against the attempts by the people to establish representative government. He was ultimately dethroned and later executed.

The time bomb finally exploded when, in 1789, the people stormed the Bastille, a fortress in Paris. The peasants in the countryside also revolted. Thousands of France's enemies were executed. When the violence finally ended, France was a democratic republic whose government was controlled by the people.

The French Revolution was the result of a financial crisis, a political struggle, and a class struggle. The revolution, which began in 1789 and ended in 1799, spelled the end of monarchy in France and served notice on the other governments of Europe that the people would tolerate only so much injustice and inequity before they would rise up, overthrow their oppressors, and demand democratic reforms.

The French Revolution, a time bomb that had been waiting to explode, was one of the most important events in European history. The reverberations from the explosion had a profound and lasting impact not only on French society, but also on European society and Western Civilization.

The inductive method can be very persuasive. If this style appeals to you, you may want to experiment with the method. For practice, you might convert the model essays (pages 152–153) into inductive essays using the sample above as a guide. *Remember:* your *point* should be the inescapable conclusion that is drawn from the data you present.

HEGELIAN DIALECTIC

Another powerful and persuasive expository technique can be used to present information when you're writing an essay. This method, called Hegelian dialectic, is named after the German philosopher Hegel. When you use the dialectic method, you state a reasonable position (**thesis**), and a reasonable alternative position (**antithesis**), and then establish a reasonable compromise between the two positions (**synthesis**). This format, which might also be viewed as presenting the *pros* and the *cons* of an argument, can be a highly effective tool for writing a convincing essay because it acknowledges that there are often two ways to perceive an issue. By combining the best points of each argument, the dialectic presents a well-balanced and well-reasoned conclusion.

Let's explore how the dialectic method might be used to present the important issues discussed in the passage "Insanity and the Law" that you read in Chapter 5. Assume that the following question appears on a test: **Discuss the legal and psychological issues involved in the "sane versus insane" controversy.** Although you don't have to reread the article,

Essay Following the Hegelian Dialectic Method

THESIS

The criminal justice system has a legitimate and justifiably narrow legal definition of sanity. The courts in many states consider the accused person to be sane if mental health professionals determine—and the court concurs—that the accused knew *right* from *wrong* at the time the crime was committed. In some states, another ill-conceived criterion for determining sanity is used: the defendant could have *controlled* his or her actions. The origins of this debate about the definition of insanity can be traced to England. In 1843, Daniel M'Naghten shot and killed the English prime minister. M'Naghten pleaded innocent by reason of insanity and claimed that he didn't understand the difference between right and wrong. The jury accepted this plea and judged him not guilty, and U. S. courts have been struggling under the burden of this misguided decision ever since.

ANTITHESIS

The standard for the insanity defense was exceedingly simplistic: The court must be convinced that the defendant could not distinguish right from wrong. This standard does take into consideration the possibility that the defendant might have known his conduct was wrong but was *powerless* to control that conduct because of a mental disease or defect. Some states have recognized this flaw and have wisely added a second criterion: the capacity to exert self-control. If it's determined that a mental disorder compelled a person to commit a crime, he should legitimately be judged insane.

SYNTHESIS

The key issue in the sane versus insane debate is whether insanity should be allowed as a defense and whether those who are classified as "mad" should be treated differently from others who commit crimes. Determining whether a defendant truly understood right and wrong and could have controlled his or her conduct calls for a subjective opinion. Mental health professionals frequently do not agree about what actually constitutes sanity and insanity, and they frequently do not agree about whether or not a particular defendant could have controlled his or her actions. Consequently, a judge or a jury must attempt to make this often complex and difficult determination. Given the differences in interpretation of the true definition of insanity, justice requires that the legal and psychological professions resolve their differences and create standards of mental responsibility that are uniform and fair both to the accused and to society.

carefully examine the dialectic essay example above and note how the essay is formatted and structured.

Practice Using the Dialectic Method

Reread the short entry about Native Americans on page 107. Using the preceding dialectic essay as a model, apply the Hegelian method and examine the issue of resettling Indians on reservations. Although you may feel very strongly about a particular position (the *thesis* or the *antithesis*), make every effort to argue both positions persuasively. Then, *synthesize* the two polarized positions (i.e., combine the best points of each argument) into a balanced assessment of this highly controversial historical event.

THESIS

_____

_____

_____

_____

_____

ANTITHESIS

_____

_____

_____

_____

_____

_____

_____

SYNTHESIS

_____

_____

_____

_____

_____

_____

_____

Distinguishing Main Ideas from Details

L et's now return to the issue of note taking. You have completed taking notes, and you have answered the subtitle and main idea questions. Before taking a test, carefully review your notes (and mindmaps) at least once. _To help you review, read through your notes and highlight the main idea information in one color and detail information in another color._ For example: "strggle pwer Fr. clsses" is a main idea. It's a main idea because the revolution was largely caused by this class struggle. Examples of details would be: "Fr. Rev. 1789-99." "18000 excted." You might also want to write key facts on index cards that you can review on the bus, between classes, or while you are eating dinner.

When you take notes, use one specific color to indicate details and another to indicate main ideas. By using these colors consistently in all subjects, you can train your mind to make an automatic association with, for example, yellow for details, and blue for main ideas. The technique may also help you recall the information. If you prefer, you may want to use a pencil for details and a pen for main ideas.

To review the study techniques that you have learned so far, take a few moments to complete the following questionnaire.

Reviewing What You've Learned

QUESTIONS ABOUT NOTE TAKING

True False

○ ○ 1. Turn the title into a question before reading the material.

○ ○ 2. Turn each subtitle into a question before reading the material.

○ ○ 3. Answer the title question before reading the material.

○ ○ 4. Answer the subtitle questions before taking notes.

○ ○ 5. Speed-read the material after taking notes.

○ ○ 6. When speed-reading, read every word very carefully.

○ ○ 7. After speed-reading, read the material again more carefully.

○ ○ 8. Write down key information in note form while reading carefully.

○ ○ 9. Include words such as "the," "a," and "of" in notes.

○ ○ 10. Avoid using abbreviations.

○ ○ 11. Highlight or underline textbooks.

○ ○ 12. When reviewing, consistently use one color to highlight details and another color to highlight main ideas.

QUESTIONS ABOUT ANSWERING ESSAY QUESTIONS

True False

○ ○ 1. After taking notes, answer the main idea title question first with an essay.

○ ○ 2. After taking notes, answer each subtitle question with a short essay.

○ ○ 3. The last step in the note-taking process is to answer the title question.

○ ○ 4. Before writing an essay on a test, make a quick thumbnail outline to help organize the key information and to make certain that you include everything you know about the subject.

Answers to the questionnaire:

T T F F F T T F F T T F T T T

For Your Information

S tudents who have difficulty identifying, understanding, and recalling important information when they read and study are destined to struggle academically. For these students, studying may translate into little more than simply rereading the assigned unit and quickly leafing through lecture notes before a test. The consequences of this ineffectual study procedure include:

- **Passive learning.** Students are primarily concerned about getting the job done as quickly as possible and not with content mastery.
- **Poor study habits.** Student have difficulty with planning, goal setting, establishing priorities, time management, and organization.
- **Poor comprehension.** Students have difficulty identifying, digesting, and recalling important information; differentiating main ideas and details; and linking facts and concepts.
- **Poor test preparation.** Students have difficulty identifying information that their instructor is likely to consider important. They do not make up and answer practice questions while studying and have not developed effective methods for memorizing key information (see Chapters 8 and 9).

These nonproductive behaviors are avoidable. A far more effective alternative is for students to train themselves to:

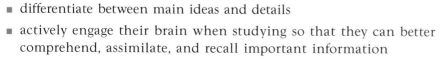

- ask penetrating questions that will help them understand the material they are studying and make the material more relevant and meaningful
- identify and record important information in their notes
- differentiate between main ideas and details
- actively engage their brain when studying so that they can better comprehend, assimilate, and recall important information
- develop and utilize effective memorization techniques
- prepare strategically for tests and anticipate what their instructors are likely to ask

Good notes help you understand and remember what you are studying and help you link what you are currently learning to what you have already learned. Clearly, methodical note taking initially requires extra time, but the procedure can actually *reduce* your total study time. Instead of having to reread an entire unit for a test, you can review your notes.

TAKING NOTES FROM LECTURES

OBJECTIVES

- Taking effective lecture notes
- Using lecture notes productively when studying

Holding onto the Gems

Despite having mentally prepared himself for an hour of frustration, it still took a great deal of self-discipline for Ken to enter the science classroom. It wasn't that he disliked biology. The problem was that the instructor spoke so quickly that Ken found it impossible to listen to the information and take notes at the same time.

Ken confronted the same dilemma with every class in which his instructors lectured. Should he listen and try to make sense out of what they were saying, or should he write down as much information as possible? He also faced the added challenge of deciding what was important and what was unimportant. In most of his classes, everything the instructor said seemed significant. How could he possibly write it all down? His hand and his brain couldn't move fast enough.

Having to take notes interfered with Ken's thinking, and if he were given the choice, he would much rather listen, digest the content, and not take notes. Because he couldn't decide what to write down and couldn't write fast enough, he ended up recording very little. All he could do was hope that he would somehow remember enough to pass the next test. As he looked around the room, he could see the other students writing furiously, and this made him feel all the more anxious and insecure.

When Ken left class on Thursday, he felt especially discouraged. The problem seemed insurmountable. If he didn't figure out how to solve it, he was certain that he would do poorly on the final exam, and get a D in the course or perhaps even flunk. In desperation, he decided to ask his friend Tasha if he could borrow her lecture notes for a couple of hours, promising to return them later that afternoon. When Ken went to the library and compared his notes with Tasha's, he became even more despondent. "No wonder I got a D on the last test!" he thought.

Ken began to copy Tasha's notes, but he knew that this wasn't a long-term solution to the problem. He couldn't ask Tasha to lend him her notes after every lecture. They were both English majors, but Ken realized that they wouldn't always be taking the same courses.

After some hesitation, Ken decided to tell Tasha about his dilemma. She was a straight-A student, and they had gone to the same high school.

Ken: I'm at the end of my rope. I'm really having a terrible time taking notes in Dr. Porter's class, and I think it could cause me to flunk the final. I have to get at least a C in this class. How do you get everything down? He speaks so quickly. I don't know whether to listen to what he's saying or to just write frantically.

Tasha: He really does talk fast. I just write down what I think is important and sort it out when I'm studying. It's sort of like being a court stenographer. You write furiously because you want to get the key information down on paper. By the end of class, my hand is totally cramped. Listen, I have an idea. Let's do a practice run. I'll pretend I'm Dr. Porter, and I'll give a lecture on the nuclear energy unit we just covered. I'll use my textbook notes. I'll intentionally speak quickly, and you take down what you think is important. After a few minutes, I'll stop, and we'll look over your notes. Pay attention to the tone of my voice and any hand gestures I use. You must also pay particular attention if I repeat something. Instructors usually signal in some way what's important. I make sure I record this information because they almost always ask questions about it on tests.

Ken: Let's give it a shot.

Later that evening, they met at Tasha's house, and she gave her "lecture." When Ken fell behind or omitted something important, she signaled for him to record what she was saying by pointing at Ken's notebook. After five minutes, she stopped lecturing, and they examined what Ken had written. They discussed what he had left out and why particular information was important. They also discussed why some of the facts and comments he wrote down were *not* important and could be eliminated. Tasha reminded Ken that he could save time and write quicker if he abbreviated as many words as possible, just as he did when he was taking textbook notes.

Tasha began to lecture again, and Ken found it easier this time to identify what should be recorded. Using abbreviations helped him save time and energy. Again they examined what he recorded, and they evaluated what Ken omitted and what he included. By the time they finished, Ken felt more confident. Tasha no longer had to indicate with her finger what he should be writing down, and Ken discovered to his delight that he had recorded everything Tasha would have noted.

When Ken and Tasha compared their notes after the next science lecture, the notes were almost identical. They discussed certain information Ken didn't write down, and Tasha explained why she felt this information was important: She was certain that the instructor would include at least one or two questions about this information on the next test.

Ken felt relieved. He was convinced that Tasha helped him resolve his note-taking problem. Just to be sure, he decided to continue comparing notes for another week.

zooming in on the issues

Recording Pearls of Wisdom

Tasha helped Ken devise a creative solution to his note-taking dilemma. Her idea is based on the principle that mastering a new skill requires practice.

Evaluate the effectiveness of Tasha's solution.

1	2	3	4	5	6	7	8	9	10
ineffective				fairly effective					very effective

Why did you make this evaluation? _____

_____

_____

Evaluate the practicality of the solution.

1	2	3	4	5	6	7	8	9	10
impractical				fairly practical					very practical

Why did you make this evaluation?

Can you think of any other possible solutions to Ken's note-taking predicament?

Alternative solution #1:

Evaluate the practicality of your proposed solution.

1	2	3	4	5	6	7	8	9	10

impractical   fairly practical   very practical

Alternative solution #2:

Evaluate the practicality of your proposed solution.

1	2	3	4	5	6	7	8	9	10

impractical   fairly practical   very practical

Alternative solution #3:

1	2	3	4	5	6	7	8	9	10

impractical   fairly practical   very practical

Perhaps one of your alternative solutions involves listening in class and then borrowing a classmate's notes and copying those notes after class every day. List the potential advantages and disadvantages of this method.

ADVANTAGES:

1.

2.

3.

DISADVANTAGES:

1.

2.

3.

Another possible solution is to take a cassette recorder to class and tape the lectures (with the instructor's permission, of course). List the potential advantages and disadvantages of this solution.

ADVANTAGES:

1. _____

2. _____

3. _____

DISADVANTAGES:

1. _____

2. _____

3. _____

A third alternative is to write furiously while the instructor is speaking and record as much as possible. After class, Ken could review the notes and make sense out of them by comparing the notes to a classmate's notes and correlating the lecture information with the corresponding textbook chapter. List the possible advantages and disadvantages of this solution.

ADVANTAGES:

1. _____

2. _____

3. _____

DISADVANTAGES:

1. _____

2. _____

3. _____

A fourth alternative is to sit next to a good student. Whenever that student records something, Ken could do the same. List the possible advantages and disadvantages of this solution.

ADVANTAGES:

1. _____

2. _____

3. _____

DISADVANTAGES:

1. _____

2. _____

3. _____

Drawing a Conclusion from the Evidence

Having read about Ken's predicament, what specific conclusion can you draw from the information in the story? Using the *inductive method*, express in a well-crafted sentence what you have concluded. *Remember:* You are summarizing the **point** of the story.

The point of Ken's story: _____

_____

_____

_____

_____

zooming out on the issues

Different Learning Preferences

The introductory case study reaffirms something you learned in Chapter 1: Students learn differently. Ken's preference is to listen in class, strongly suggesting that his dominant learning modality is *auditory*. Tasha's preference is to get the important information down on paper so that she can look at it. This strongly suggests that her dominant learning modality is *visual*.

Despite his preference, Ken is smart enough to recognize that to improve his grades, he must learn how to take effective class notes. With Tasha's help, he develops a creative strategy for improving this critically important skill.

Trying to listen, understand, and write at the same time can be difficult for some students and relatively easy for others. One student may only feel secure when he has written down virtually everything the instructor says, and he may prefer to think about and digest the information *after* class. Another may believe that having to record an endless stream of data during a lecture is a distraction that prevents her from listening carefully and comprehending the content. This student prefers to think about the information *while it is being presented*.

Instructors use lectures to identify, clarify, and amplify important material. Their lectures are intended to *supplement and explain* information in the textbook or required reading list. Some of the lecture content may come directly from these sources. Other information is derived from sources that students are not required to read.

The advantages of having good lecture notes are self-evident. These notes give students immediate access to key content when they review and study for tests. When used in tandem with good textbook notes, class notes provide a powerful resource for effective studying.

In some upper-level college courses, there are no assigned textbooks. The instructor may supply handouts and an extensive reading list of required and suggested source material (i.e., books and articles written by authorities on the subject). Your grade in the course, to a large extent, hinges on how well you assimilate the information in the reading list and how well you record, understand, and recall the information your instructor presents in class. (There is, of course, another key factor that obviously affects your grade—your actual test-taking skills. Test taking is examined in Chapter 9.)

Instructors intentionally use lectures to shape, "color," and organize subject matter and to put their individual "stamp" and "slant" on the course they are teaching. Because they obviously consider their lectures to be a vital component of the instructional process, most instructors spend a great deal of time preparing the material they present in class. Strategically minded students realize that they must carefully study what has been emphasized during lectures if they want to get a good grade in the course. They also realize that their class notes are an invaluable resource for helping them understand and master the course content and for reviewing before exams.

Using DIBS

Pretend that you are Ken. You recognize your note-taking deficiencies, and with your friend's help, you've improved your skills. Nonetheless, you are carrying a D– average going into the final, and you have to score at least a C+ on the final to get a C– in the course. If you can get a C–, you can graduate with the 3.2 G.P.A. necessary to transfer into a good four-year college. You have negative expectations about how you will do on the exam, in as much as you've received Ds on all of your previous tests. Use DIBS to find a solution to your problem. Remember to use "I" messages.

Define:
_____

Investigate:
_____
_____
_____

Brainstorm:
_____
_____
_____
_____

Select:
_____
_____

Assess the likelihood that the selected solution will resolve the problem.

| 1 | 2 | 3 | 4 | 5 | 6 | 7 | 8 | 9 | 10 |

unlikely   fairly likely   very likely

Thirteen Steps for Taking Good Lecture Notes

1. Locate. Consider sitting next to a good student in class. When this person writes something down, you probably should also.

2. Prepare. Review any handouts the instructor provides *before* the next class. Read assigned textbook pages *before* the lecture and take notes on this material using either a mind-map or standard note taking. The more you understand *in advance* about the content of the lecture, the easier it is to understand what the instructor is saying.

3. Focus. Concentrate during lectures and deliberately push nonrelevant thoughts from your mind. Use relaxation techniques to help you become "centered" (see Chapter 4). Consider sitting in the first row to minimize visual and auditory distractions. This should improve your concentration, especially if you have difficulty paying attention.

4. Be alert. Look for "signals" and "flags" that the instructor uses to indicate important information. These signals may include repeating certain facts and data, or statements such as *in conclusion*. When the instructor writes information on the chalkboard or uses an overhead projector, he or she is clearly flagging something important. The instructor's intonation may change, or he or she may punctuate key information with a hand gesture. Pay particular attention if there is a lecture summation. Instructors often recap the main points and key facts during the last few minutes of class.

5. Abbreviate. To help you to write more quickly, consistently use abbreviations you can understand.

6. Speed-think. As you take notes, don't spend excessive time trying to digest everything the instructor says. Digest the content of the lecture after class.

7. Speed-write. Get the information down quickly.

8. Evaluate. Some instructors want you to analyze, link, and think critically about what's presented in the lecture. In this case, you'll have to adjust your note-taking procedures accordingly. You should be able to assess your instructor's priorities relatively quickly. If he or she asks many questions when lecturing, the instructor expects you to think about the lecture content *as it's presented*. If you're confused about your instructor's priorities, ask for clarification. Also ask other students who are doing well in the course about what they believe the priorities are.

9. Question. If you don't understand something that is said in class, ask for clarification at *appropriate* points during the lecture. Do this selectively and use your discretion about the timing of your questions.

10. Compare. If your note-taking skills are weak, compare your notes to those of a classmate who is doing well in the course. Use your classmate's notes as a model. Add any important information you've omitted and delete information you now believe is superfluous. Analyze why you left out important data and attempt to include this type of information the next time you take notes. Also, analyze what you included that was not important and try to exclude this type of extraneous information the next time you take notes.

11. Practice. If you're having difficulty taking lecture notes, consider having a few practice note-taking sessions with a classmate. Have your friend pretend to be an instructor and give a mini-lecture while you take notes to improve your skills.

12. Pretend. Practice giving lectures covering the material you're learning to an imaginary audience. Someone doesn't actually have to hear your lecture. You can deliver the lecture in the privacy of your room. Use your class notes and textbook notes. This procedure should make you more aware of what ought to be included in your class notes, what's missing, what you understand, and what you haven't fully comprehended and mastered. By lecturing to your imaginary "students," you'll discover an added benefit: You'll understand the material better, and you'll probably have an easier time recalling the information when taking the test. Although the primary function of your notes is to record important facts and data, equally important functions are to help you comprehend the underlying issues and provide an *overview* of the course content. The better you understand what you're studying, the more likely you are to recall it and do well on tests.

13. Organize. When you review your lecture notes after class, make certain that you understand the information. You may have to organize, reorganize, revise, or amplify (by comparing the lecture information with information in your textbook or other sources) certain sections that are confusing. You may also have to recopy sections that are sloppy or difficult to read.

POWERHOUSE THINKING

Good Lecture and Textbook Notes

- Encapsulate important information.
- Underscore what the instructor considers important.
- Provide quick access to significant facts.
- Correlate textbook content with lecture content.
- Save time when reviewing for tests.
- Organize key data.

Maximizing the Value of Lecture Notes

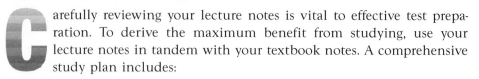arefully reviewing your lecture notes is vital to effective test preparation. To derive the maximum benefit from studying, use your lecture notes in tandem with your textbook notes. A comprehensive study plan includes:

- highlighting key information in your textbooks

- mind-mapping (optional but recommended)

- highlighting textbook notes using different colored markers to indicate main ideas and details

- highlighting lecture notes using different colored markers to indicate and differentiate main ideas and details

- highlighting handouts to indicate main ideas and details

- reviewing previous tests and exams to identify the type of test the instructor gives and to help identify your knowledge deficit areas

- confirming (using your course syllabus and assignment sheet) that you have studied the assigned material

- developing practice tests and answering the questions

Just as you highlighted your textbook notes to indicate main ideas and details, you should use the same procedure with your lecture notes and handouts. Get into the habit of consistently using a specific color to highlight the main ideas and another color to highlight details. Make note if your instructor's lectures primarily emphasize facts and details or concepts and the application of information. This will suggest the types of material the instructor considers important.

You can often determine your instructor's orientation by reviewing previous tests and exams. This review may indicate that you are expected to assimilate not only facts (e.g., the process of photosynthesis), but also concepts (e.g., the photosynthetic consequences of massive deforestation) and concrete applications (e.g., intentionally building parks and planting trees and shrubs in polluted urban areas). Adjusting your study methods so that you learn what the instructor considers important is clearly an example of sound, strategic thinking.

For Your Information

lass notes are a critically important resource. These notes can significantly improve your test performance and provide you with a distinct competitive advantage in courses in which you are expected to assimilate and recall a great deal of information. In these classes, your notes are likely to play a pivotal role in determining your grade. Although you may prefer classes that emphasize class discussions, you must be able to take good notes when your instructors use lectures to provide students with vital information.

To take effective notes, you must be capable of juggling several balls at once. You must be able to listen, assimilate information, and write at the same time. If you have difficulty with this juggling act, compare your notes with those of academically successful classmates and identify any key data that you've omitted and any unimportant data that you've included. Other techniques for improving your note-taking skills include looking for clues that indicate what your instructors consider important and using comprehensible abbreviations to improve your note-taking speed. The goal is to figure out what's not working and to make tactical adjustments in your methodology.

Getting good grades is not all that mysterious. You must be able to:

- record important information in class
- record important information that appears in your textbooks
- understand the information in your notes
- identify main ideas and details
- link the information in your lecture notes with the information in your textbook notes
- identify and capitalize on your preferred learning modality
- use multiple learning modalities when appropriate
- memorize key facts and data (see Chapter 9)
- anticipate what might be asked on a test

Your capacity to perform these functions will improve with effort and practice. Before long, you'll discover that you are running through the steps automatically. The payoffs for this diligence are better comprehension and recall, improved grades, pride, and expanded academic and vocational options when you complete your studies.

Students who think strategically achieve academic success because they're resourceful. They recognize that the more effective their study tools, the better their academic performance. These strategic and resourceful students are prepared to do whatever is necessary to get the job done successfully.

TAKING TESTS

OBJECTIVES

- Personalizing your studying procedures
- Studying effectively for objective tests
- Studying effectively for subjective tests
- Making up practice tests
- Learning how to memorize information
- Dealing with test anxiety

What to Study and How to Study

The countdown for the history chapter test had begun. Tyisha wanted at least a B+ on the test, and she was determined to use all of the study skills methods she had learned. If she could get a B+, or ideally an A–, she had a shot at getting an A– in the course, assuming she did well on the final exam.

Tyisha's instructor announced that the test would be on Friday and would cover the French Revolution. Although she had already taken standard notes from her textbook, she decided to spend some extra time mind-mapping the unit as an additional review.

It was now Monday, and Tyisha only had four days to prepare for the test. The time had come to put her study strategy into high gear. Monday night, she reviewed her notes and wrote short essays to answer the subtitle questions from the chapter. Then, she answered the main idea question about the chapter title. She made sure her practice essays were well-organized with powerful topic and concluding sentences. She also made sure she included all of the key information from her notes.

Tuesday night, Tyisha reviewed her notes again, using two different colored highlight pens. She marked the main ideas in yellow and the details in blue. Using the same two colors, she followed the same highlighting procedure with her lecture notes.

On Wednesday, Tyisha used a new memory technique she had learned (this technique is examined later in this chapter). She wrote the key facts on index cards and carefully applied the three steps of the visualization method as she memorized the important names, facts, and dates identified in her notes.

It was now time for the final effort. Thursday evening, Tyisha used her "test radar" to predict the types of questions her instructor might ask. She made up practice multiple-choice and short-answer questions about the unit and made sure she could answer them. She then drove to her friend's house, and Tyisha and Rashad spent an hour and a half asking each other questions. When they couldn't answer a particular question, they referred to their notes. After completing this final step, Tyisha felt confident she had done everything she could to prepare. She believed she was as ready as she could possibly be!

zooming in
on the issues

The Nuts and Bolts of Test Preparation

Tyisha had a comprehensive strategy for preparing for the history exam. Go back into the story and underline and number each of her procedures.

Evaluate the effectiveness of Tyisha's overall study strategy.

1	2	3	4	5	6	7	8	9	10
ineffective				fairly effective					very effective

Why did you make this evaluation?

Evaluate the practicality of Tyisha implementing this comprehensive study plan.

1	2	3	4	5	6	7	8	9	10

impractical   fairly practical   very practical

Why did you make this evaluation?

Evaluate the likelihood of Tyisha achieving her targeted objective—a B+ or an A– on the exam.

1	2	3	4	5	6	7	8	9	10

unlikely   fairly likely   very likely

Why did you make this evaluation?

Can you think of any other effective study methods that she might have used? If so, list them below.

1.

2.

3.

4.

Drawing a Conclusion from the Evidence

Having read a description of Tyisha's study strategy, what specific conclusion can you draw from the information in the story? Using the *inductive method*, express in a well-crafted sentence what you have concluded. *Remember:* You are summarizing the **point** of the story.

The point of Tyisha's story:

A Holistic Study Strategy

Your final test preparation procedures can make the difference between getting a good grade, a mediocre grade, or a poor grade. Let's review the eight methods you already know about studying smart. You've learned how to:

1. speed-read

2. mind-map

3. ask title and subtitle questions

4. take good textbook notes

5. answer questions about the title and subtitles

6. take good lecture notes

7. identify, differentiate, and highlight main ideas and details in textbooks and notes

8. identify and capitalize on your preferred learning modality

The preceding list comprises the nuts and bolts of a comprehensive and effective test preparation procedure. To transform yourself into a superior student, you must bolt this hardware together and create a *personalized study platform* that works best for you. By so doing, you create a *custom-fitted test preparation system* that can consistently produce good grades. Once the assembly is completed, you have to attach another critically important component to your study platform. This component is incorporated in **Method #9:** *Develop individualized techniques for memorizing and retaining key information.* This method is introduced later in this chapter.

Tailoring Your Study Procedures

nstructors give tests for a very basic reason: to determine how much of the assigned material you understand and remember. Students who can demonstrate that they have mastered what their instructors consider important are rewarded with good grades. (Reports, essays, homework assignments, and term papers, of course, represent other criteria that instructors use to evaluate your skills and your mastery of the course content.)

Instructors generally use two basic testing methods to evaluate what you have learned and assimilated: *objective tests* and *subjective tests*. Learning how to adjust your study procedure so that you can study effectively for each test type is vital.

Objective Tests

any instructors believe that they can most effectively assess your knowledge by giving multiple-choice and short-answer tests. These tests, which are described as **objective tests** because the grader does not have to interpret whether the answers are correct, primarily emphasize the recall and application of factual information. The grader simply requires an answer key. The answers are either right or wrong. Typical objective test formats include a mix of multiple-choice, true–false, and short-answer questions.

In addition to gauging your retention of details and facts, well-designed objective tests can assess your knowledge of course content and your in-depth comprehension and insight. To evaluate your mastery of the subject matter, instructors ask probing and challenging questions. Not knowing the assigned material "backward and forward" and not memorizing the key facts is a prescription for disaster. One particular word embedded in a test question or in one of the answers on a multiple-choice test can alter the meaning, and if you do not meticulously examine the questions and answers, you can easily make a mistake. Because the questions are often "tricky," answering them correctly requires careful deliberation, and you must discipline your-self to examine all of the choices carefully before selecting one. By eliminating obviously erroneous answers, you can significantly improve the odds of selecting the correct answer if you are forced to guess. For example, if there are five choices, and you can rule out three, you have increased the odds from a 20 percent chance of guessing correctly to a 50 percent chance of guessing correctly.

CHARACTERISTICS OF OBJECTIVE TESTS

- assess knowledge of facts, details, and concepts
- require answers that are either right or wrong
- are easy to grade
- are often "tricky"

POWERHOUSE THINKING

Keys to Getting a Good Grade on an Objective Test

- Demonstrate that you understand the obvious and underlying issues.
- Recall facts and details that your instructor considers important.
- Recognize subtle contradictions, inaccuracies, and fallacies that are intention-ally built into the test questions and answers.
- Increase your odds by eliminating obviously incorrect answers.

If an instructor typically gives multiple-choice, short-answer, and/or true–false tests, strategic students focus on identifying, learning, and mem-orizing key details and facts from textbook and lecture notes when they study. These students realize that recording important information on index cards and memorizing this information can be time-consuming, but they also realize that this meticulous procedure can be pivotal in producing bet-ter grades. Conscientious, goal-directed students are willing to invest the required time and effort because they know that the payoffs more than jus-tify the investment.

Many students find multiple-choice, true–false, and short-answer ques-tions challenging because instructors must ask thought-provoking questions to gauge whether students have truly understood and learned the information. From the instructor's perspective, there is, of course, another obvious advantage to objective tests. The answer is either right or wrong, and the person grading the tests does not have to go through a laborious process of subjectively assessing each answer. Many instructors who teach 200 students each week find this feature particularly appealing.

A history instructor who wants you to learn important facts and details about the French Revolution might ask the following types of questions on a multiple-choice or short-answer test:

- When did the French Revolution begin?
- What was the first estate?
- When did the people of Paris storm the Bastille?
- Who was the French philosopher whose ideas stimulated the Revolution?

The correct answer to a particular question on a short-answer or multiple-choice test may be obvious (e.g., the date when the French Revolution began), especially if you've learned and memorized the specific information that the question addresses. In other cases, the choices listed under a particular question may *reframe* (present a slightly different slant on) the information just enough to create doubt and confusion when you attempt to select the correct answer. An example of such a question might be:

The primary motivation for the third estate to attack the first and second estates was to:

A. limit the aristocracy's power.

B. have equal representation.

C. end a system that awarded power on the basis of inherited birth rights and social status.

D. place restraints on the Church.

E. all of the above.

STUDYING FOR OBJECTIVE TESTS

When you take an objective exam, you are engaged in an intellectual chess game with your instructor. You can expect multiple-choice, short-answer, and true–false questions that are intentionally designed to be thought provoking and, perhaps, crafty. The attitude of most instructors is "I've got to make this test tough if I want to differentiate those who truly know the material from those who do not." As you study, you must figure out what you have to learn, and when you take the test, you must be able to demonstrate that you have mastered the information that your instructor considers important.

As you search for the correct answer to a multiple-choice question, you may conclude that answers "A" *and* "B" are both plausible, but after a careful analysis, you may decide that answer "A" is better than "B" or that "all of the above" is actually the best answer. This process can produce anxiety, especially when you are aware that the question may be deceiving and that the clock is ticking. In some instances, you may immediately realize that three out of four choices are obviously wrong because they contain blatantly inaccurate information. Obviously, these are the easiest questions to answer.

An objective test often offers choices that contain *subtle* or *camouflaged* inaccuracies that challenge your analytical skills and attention to details. At first glance, an answer may appear correct, but upon careful scrutiny, it may actually be wrong. For this reason, it is important to look carefully at *all* the answers before choosing one. If you assume that the instructor has deliberately included difficult questions that are designed to *probe* your insight, *test* your recall, and *challenge* your knowledge, you will be more alert and cautious. This can reduce the risk of responding impulsively and selecting the wrong answer. Sometimes, however, too much deliberation can cause problems. You may be so intent on looking for tricks that you reject your initial instincts on a particular question, and these instincts may be correct. This is an inherent predicament that all students face when taking multiple-choice tests: *Too little deliberation can be bad, and too much deliberation can sometimes also be bad.*

POWERHOUSE THINKING

Practical Guidelines When Preparing for an Objective Test

- Identify key information in textbooks, textbook notes, and class notes.
- Link main ideas and concepts with key facts and details.
- Review previous tests to determine the types of questions the instructor typically asks.
- Review the instructor's clues about what will be covered on the test.
- Predict questions the instructor is likely to ask and be prepared to answer them.
- Develop an effective procedure for memorizing key information.
- Make up practice test questions.
- Review with a conscientious classmate and ask each other questions.

Your test preparation "radar" is acquired through experience with a particular instructor, keen observations about the types of information he or she emphasizes, clues provided in class indicating what is likely be covered on the test, an analysis of previous tests, and an assessment of your past performance. If your "radar" is operating effectively, you can better understand how your instructor thinks and what your instructor values, and it is easier for you to identify what you are expected to learn. Be alert to verbal clues (e.g., "This is an important point."). Make note of statements that are repeated by the instructor during a lecture. Also be alert to nonverbal clues that may involve facial expressions (e.g., nodding and pursing lips or furrowed brow) or hand gestures (e.g., pointing repeatedly to particular information written on the chalkboard). When you identify something important in your textbook or your class notes, you will find yourself automatically saying, "I'm sure she'll ask about this on the test." Sometimes you'll be wrong, but more often than not, you will become increasingly accurate at anticipating the content of your instructor's tests.

STRATEGIC PROCEDURES FOR TAKING OBJECTIVE TESTS

As previously stated, *eliminating clearly erroneous choices significantly improves the chance of selecting the right answer.* Once you've rejected the obviously wrong answers, you can focus on examining the remaining choices. Be on the lookout for subtle inaccuracies that can help you rule out other incorrect answers. Ideally, this methodical analysis will lead to the correct answer. Of course, you face another major challenge: *You are working under time pressure, and you must evaluate each question relatively quickly.* For this reason, skip the especially difficult questions that require extra deliberation, and return to these questions after you have answered the easier questions. You don't want to run out of time before you've answered the "cinch" questions.

POWERHOUSE THINKING

Practical Guidelines When Taking an Objective Test

- Scan the test quickly before answering any questions.
- Remain calm even if the test appears to be difficult.
- Budget your time so that you can answer all of the questions.
- Answer the easy questions first.
- Apply logic and rule out implausible answers to "increase the odds."
- Discipline yourself not to respond impulsively.
- Be on the lookout for "tricky" or "loaded" questions.
- Look for errors in small details and subtle flaws in logic that the instructor has intentionally planted in the choices.

ARGUMENTS AGAINST OBJECTIVE TESTS

1. **Facts and data are usually quickly forgotten after the test has been given.** Most physicians, lawyers, and accountants admit that they quickly forgot as much as 50 percent of the information they crammed into their heads to pass their licensing exam.

2. **Memorizing information and being able to answer "tricky" questions does not necessarily demonstrate that a student has acquired an overview of the material, understood the key concepts, assimilated key facts, and properly applied the information.** A student may know that the Bastille was a military fortress in Paris that was stormed by the peasants on July 14, 1779, but he or she may not grasp the underlying class and church–state issues that inspired this monumental social upheaval. The student may not

recognize the important parallels between the French and the Soviet Revolution that occurred 138 years later.

3. **Acquiring in-depth knowledge and content mastery demands that students be able to analyze, evaluate, distill, and synthesize information and express their insights.** This knowledge can best be documented by requiring students to write essays that encapsulate their understanding of the key issues. Memorizing data and learning how to detect tricky questions does not necessarily indicate mastery of concepts and ideas.

ARGUMENTS IN FAVOR OF OBJECTIVE TESTS

1. **Instructors must have a practical and efficient means for evaluating large numbers of students.**

2. **Well-designed objective tests can effectively assess comprehension of the course content.**

3. **Students must learn how to take standardized exams** (tests administered to thousands of students that produce statistically derived scores) **that employ the multiple-choice format.** These include college and graduate school entrance exams, professional and vocational licensing tests, personality and vocational interest tests, and aptitude tests. Taking multiple-choice tests helps prepare students for these standardized tests.

Subjective Tests

A test that requires you to communicate your ideas, insights, reactions, and impressions about the course content in an essay is referred to as a **subjective test.** Many instructors believe that subjective exams consisting of carefully selected essay questions (or a mix of multiple-choice, short-answer, and essay questions) are the most effective means for determining whether or not you:

- understand key concepts and main ideas
- recall important information
- have mastered the content of the course
- can apply what you have learned

Essay tests are called subjective because the instructor must make a subjective judgment about whether you have mastered the content; have stated your ideas and insights effectively, persuasively, and succinctly; and have substantiated your position with appropriate facts and data. Essay exams typically probe your grasp of both conceptual and factual knowledge.

CHARACTERISTICS OF SUBJECTIVE TESTS

1. Instructors make subjective judgments when selecting questions that can assess mastery of course content.

2. Instructors make subjective assessments about the quality of a student's writing skills when grading the essays.

3. Students subjectively select and interpret relevant information for inclusion in their essays.

4. The grade is determined by the student's substantiation of his or her position and the effectiveness and precision of the student's writing.

5. Essays require more time to grade.

Examples of questions that might be asked on an essay exam include:

- What major social and political issues caused the French third estate to revolt against Louis XVI?

- What were the similarities and differences between the American Revolution and the French Revolution?

To write a first-rate essay in response to either of these questions, you have to incorporate information from multiple sources—your textbook, lecture notes, required and suggested supplemental reading, and in-class discussions. The more comprehensive your essay and the more substantiating data you include, the better your grade. Conversely, the more incomplete your essay and the more lacking it is in supporting facts and details, the lower your grade. Your expository writing skills and organization are also factored into the grading equation. Instructors typically give the best grades to students who can express their ideas and insights effectively and persuasively.

To respond effectively to challenging essay questions, you must usually apply critical-thinking skills and evaluate the relevant information and issues quickly (see the critical thinking discussion in Chapter 5). For example, the second sample essay question asks you to compare and contrast information about two monumentally important historical events: the American Revolution and the French Revolution. To answer this question, you must identify the common threads that connect the two revolutions, as well as the facts and issues that differentiate these two monumental historical events.

A vital prerequisite to comprehensive test preparation for both objective and subjective exams is to identify the important details, facts, concepts, and issues in your textbooks and notes. The next step is to develop effective methods for recalling the key information. Unless you are blessed with exceptional visual memory capabilities, simply looking over index cards with facts written on them is insufficient. (Memorization techniques are presented later in this chapter.)

POWERHOUSE THINKING

Getting a Good Grade on a Subjective Test

- Prove that you have an overview of the subject matter.

- Document your understanding of the obvious underlying issues with concrete information and facts.

- Demonstrate your ability to distill, associate, and apply what you have learned.

- Indicate your ability to think critically about the key issues.

- Address the questions directly and candidly.

- Express your insights using well-organized, well-written, and cogent paragraphs.

STUDYING FOR SUBJECTIVE TESTS

The instructor who reads your essay will grade it based on his or her impressions about its comprehensiveness (i.e., the inclusion of key information and demonstrated understanding of the issues) and the quality of your written language skills (e.g., organization, grammar, syntax). Most instructors have a list of key points that they want students to include. The more of these key points you address and the more convincing your essay, the better your grade.

You must be able to demonstrate in your essay that you understand important concepts and that you can link what you are currently learning with what you have already learned. For example, you may be asked on an English test to write an essay comparing a poem written by T. S. Eliot with one written by D. H. Lawrence that was analyzed in class several months ago. In history, sociology, or political science courses, you must be aware of the relationship between major social movements and key historical events. In a psychology course, you might be asked to compare and contrast the different perspectives and criteria for identifying, understanding, and classifying specific emotional problems. You may also be asked to explain in your essay how these perspectives have led to different philosophies about effective treatment.

The key to doing well on essays is to demonstrate your ability to *zoom in* and minutely analyze both the obvious and underlying issues (this procedure is often referred to as a *microanalysis*) and your ability to *zoom out*, analyze the far-reaching implications of the issues, and present a cohesive overview of the subject (this procedure is often referred to as a *macroanalysis*). You must also be able to clearly substantiate your conclusion with facts, and you must organize the data so that the essay flows logically. Your language, grammar, spelling, punctuation use, and neatness may also affect the grade you receive. Although the content is critically important, instructors are far more likely to evaluate favorably writing that is engaging and interesting. A well-written essay that contains all of the important information may receive an A, whereas a poorly written essay that contains the same information could receive a B.

POWERHOUSE THINKING

Practical Study Guidelines When Preparing for Essay Tests

- Make every effort to get on the same "wavelength" as your instructor so that you can anticipate the types of questions that are likely to be asked.

- Carefully consider clues given in class by the instructor about what is likely to be covered on the test.

- Carefully review previous tests to get a sense of the instructor's priorities.

- Gear your test preparation to the questions you expect to be asked.

- Write practice essays that answer title and subtitle questions in your notes.

STRATEGIC PROCEDURES FOR TAKING A SUBJECTIVE TEST

For an essay answer to be considered well-written, organized, and persuasive, instructors expect you to summarize succinctly the important facts and demonstrate your understanding of these facts. They also expect you to be able to delve beneath the surface and get to the core issue. For example, an essay test question about the French Revolution might ask you to examine the similarities and differences between the French Revolution and the American Civil Rights Movement. Your essay should reflect your subjective interpretation of the issues and historical facts and your ability to select and incorporate relevant data from textbooks, class lectures, and reading lists. You also want to document that you are capable of *thinking critically* about the subject.

POWERHOUSE THINKING

Practical Guidelines for Taking Essay Tests

- Scan all questions on the test quickly before beginning to write.
- Decide what key information you want to include in your essay.
- Organize the important information in your head.
- Make a thumbnail outline (see Chapter 7) before you begin to write.
- Decide whether you prefer the deductive, inductive, or Hegelian method.
- Be conscious of writing clearly, simply, incisively, and persuasively.
- Use a powerful topic sentence and concluding sentence.
- Avoid long, complex sentences.
- Make your points convincingly.
- Write plausible essays that contain substantiated arguments clearly reflecting your understanding of the issues.
- Demonstrate critical intelligence in evaluating the issues.
- If you have time, proofread to eliminate grammar and spelling errors.
- Work efficiently and quickly. Be aware of the clock.
- Leave the hardest essays until last.

ARGUMENTS AGAINST SUBJECTIVE TESTS

Several key points are usually made when arguing against the use of subjective exams to gauge mastery of course content, namely:

1. An instructor's personal biases influence the questions that are asked, the criteria for what should be included, and the grades that are given.
2. Students who have mastered the material may receive a poor grade because they lack good writing skills.
3. If the instructor uses readers to grade exams, their evaluative skills and grading criteria may vary considerably.

4. If the perspectives of the student and instructor differ significantly, the student may receive a low grade despite having written a well-documented, factually based essay.

ARGUMENTS IN FAVOR OF SUBJECTIVE TESTS

1. Facts and details are generally forgotten, but ideas and concepts are generally retained and applied.

2. Distilling information and communicating ideas and key points persuasively in an essay is a superior measure of what was truly understood and assimilated.

3. The world is perceived both objectively and subjectively. To de-emphasize students' subjective impressions negates an important component of the content mastery and assimilation.

4. Good instructors can apply objective criteria (i.e., the inclusion of specific key facts and details) when grading a student's essay.

5. Effective expository writing skills are a key indication of being well-educated.

Although many of the tests and exams you will take in college will be objective, you can also expect to take subjective essay exams, particularly in English and history courses. It is smart and strategic to develop an effective methodology for preparing for these types of tests.

Improving the Odds of Getting Good Grades

Students who think and act strategically are pragmatists. They want to get good grades because a good G.P.A. can open doors to opportunities in life. They also want to get their studying done efficiently and with a minimum amount of pain and grief. They certainly don't want to waste time and effort studying the wrong material or studying in the wrong way.

Good students gear their test preparation strategy to the material they're expected to learn and to the type of test they're likely to be given. They study differently for a test that is likely to emphasize details than for a test that is likely to emphasize concepts. They also study differently for a multiple-choice test than they do for an essay test.

Two practical test-preparation procedures can improve your test performance:

1. **Devote extra time to reviewing and memorizing information your instructor would probably consider important.** Look for "flags" that signal important information in your class notes and in hand-outs. If an instructor repeats certain information or says, "This is important," you obviously must learn this material.

2. **Make up practice tests.** If previous tests or other clues from your instructor indicate that you can expect a multiple-choice or short-answer test, create your own practice test that asks these types of questions about the assigned material. Then, make sure you can answer your questions! Use the same procedure if you are preparing for an essay test. Studying with a classmate and asking each other test questions is also a highly effective test-preparation procedure.

Thinking Like an Instructor:
Short-Answer Questions

Review the exercise in Chapter 7 entitled "Mastery: More Practice Taking Notes." Make up 10 short-answer detail questions from the French Revolution article. For example: When did the citizens of Paris storm the Bastille?

SHORT-ANSWER QUESTIONS

1. _____
2. _____
3. _____
4. _____
5. _____
6. _____
7. _____
8. _____
9. _____
10. _____

Now, answer your own questions!

ANSWERS

1. _____
2. _____
3. _____
4. _____
5. _____
6. _____
7. _____
8. _____
9. _____
10. _____

Thinking Like an Instructor:
True–False Questions

For practice, make up 10 true–false questions from the French Revolution article. To make this process easier, you can make minor alterations in the short-answer questions to change them to true–false. For example: The people of Paris stormed the Bastille in 1779.　○ True　○ False

TRUE–FALSE QUESTIONS

1. _____   ○ True ○ False

2. _____   ○ True ○ False

3. _____   ○ True ○ False

4. _____   ○ True ○ False

5. _____   ○ True ○ False

6. _____   ○ True ○ False

7. _____   ○ True ○ False

8. _____   ○ True ○ False

9. _____   ○ True ○ False

10. _____   ○ True ○ False

Now, answer your questions by marking the correct response.

Thinking Like an Instructor: Multiple-Choice Questions

Now, practice making up 10 multiple-choice questions from information in the French Revolution article. For example:

Louis XVI was the King of France because he:

A. had the approval of Parliament

B. was a member of the first estate

C. was a member of the nobility

D. was supposedly ordained by God to be King

MULTIPLE-CHOICE QUESTIONS

1. _____

    A. _____

    B. _____

    C. _____

    D. _____

2. _____

    A. _____

    B. _____

    C. _____

    D. _____

3. _____

   A. _____

   B. _____

   C. _____

   D. _____

4. _____

   A. _____

   B. _____

   C. _____

   D. _____

5. _____

   A. _____

   B. _____

   C. _____

   D. _____

6. _____

   A. _____

   B. _____

   C. _____

   D. _____

7. _____

   A. _____

   B. _____

   C. _____

   D. _____

8. _____

   A. _____

   B. _____

   C. _____

   D. _____

9. _____

    A. _____

    B. _____

    C. _____

    D. _____

10. _____

    A. _____

    B. _____

    C. _____

    D. _____

Now, answer your multiple-choice questions!

Thinking Like an Instructor: Essay Questions

Making up essay questions should be a "piece of cake" because you converted the chapter headings and subtitles into questions when you mind-mapped and practiced the chewing-up information method. For example, in the science article about nuclear energy, you converted the unit heading, "Nuclear Energy: Harnessing the Atom," into a main idea question: *"How was the atom harnessed to produce nuclear energy?"* You also converted the subtitles into questions, such as: *"What are the pluses and minuses of nuclear energy?"* These are the types of essay questions that an instructor might ask on an exam.

Your instructors will undoubtedly make up essay questions that do not come directly from the title and subtitles in your textbooks. Nonetheless, you can significantly improve your chances of being able to answer *any* question if you take the time to answer the essay questions you pose when you convert titles and subtitles into questions. Be prepared, however, for your instructors to make the essay questions difficult. This is done to challenge you intellectually and to probe the depth of your understanding of the issues. When studying, make note of what your instructors stressed in their lectures. Many are likely to ask essay questions that directly relate to the information they emphasized in class.

If you learn from experience that a particular instructor doesn't ask essay questions, it is strategic to spend most of your study time preparing for multiple-choice, short-answer, and true–false questions. *Smart students identify and analyze their instructor's testing "style" and adjust their study procedures accordingly.* Sometimes, however, instructors can fool you! They might change their testing style from time to time because they don't want their students to study on "auto-pilot." This can be unsettling for students who crave predictability. It's smart to be prepared to answer *anything* your instructor might "throw at you." If you misjudge, analyze what went wrong and learn from your miscalculation. Don't make the same preparation miscalculation the next time you study for this instructor's test.

How Instructors Design Tests

You may think that designing a test is easy. Actually, developing a fair test that covers a history or science unit requires a great deal of time and thought. Issues that instructors consider when designing a test include:

1. What information is important in this chapter?
2. What do I want my students to understand and remember?
3. How do I determine if my students have understood and retained the key information?
4. What questions are intellectually challenging and differentiate the superior students who have studied diligently and comprehend the course content?

Training yourself to think like your instructors when you study gives you a significant advantage over students who don't identify important information when they study. Unless the semester has just started, *you probably already know quite a bit about how your instructors think!* You've taken their tests, and you've spent many hours together in class. By reviewing the types of questions your history instructor asked on previous tests and the information emphasized in class, you can increase the likelihood of anticipating the questions correctly.

You've already made up objective questions about the French Revolution. On a separate piece of paper, use these questions to create a practice *objective* test consisting of 25 questions. Select questions you think an instructor would be likely to ask on a unit test. Your test should incorporate the three different types of objective questions (see the examples below).

Practice Test Questions

1. What were the dates of the French Revolution? _____

2. Describe the three estates.

   _____

   _____

   _____

3. King Louis XVI wanted the people to have a National Assembly.
   ○ True   ○ False

4. How many people were executed during the French Revolution?
   A. 1,200
   B. 1,800
   C. 10,000
   D. 18,000

5. The Bastille was another name for the French parliament.
   ○ True   ○ False

Use these questions as a model, and create your own test. Your ability to design tests will improve with practice! As you create your test, consider what your instructor might want you to know and remember.

THE BENEFITS OF THINKING LIKE AN INSTRUCTOR

When instructors design tests, they go through essentially the same procedure that you just completed. They determine what information is important and what they want and expect you to know about the assigned material. Instructors, however, have their own biases and priorities. Some are detail- and fact-oriented. Others are concept-oriented. If you get in the habit of considering in advance what each instructor probably considers important and create practice tests, your grades should improve.

Of course, you may be surprised and discover questions on a test that you *didn't* anticipate. This can be upsetting, especially if you did poorly on the test, but you can learn from the negative experience. Try to figure out *why* your instructor considered particular information important enough to include. The next time you study for this instructor's test, incorporate what you've learned about his or her testing style, make adjustments, and fine-tune your test-preparation "radar." Smart students are rarely surprised when they take a test. Because they prepare strategically and methodically, they often know many of the questions in advance.

How Memory Works

Have you ever thought about all of the information you've memorized in your life? Most of us take the huge amounts of data stored in our memory for granted. Let's look at some basic examples of information you've imprinted in your mind that you can recall without even thinking:

Your address	Your telephone number
Your ZIP code	Your PIN code
The number of states in the Union	Your social security number
The words to many of your favorite songs	The Pledge of Allegiance
The date Columbus landed in North America	The spelling of the word "through"
The name of the first U. S. president	The multiplication tables

You may not realize that you're continually memorizing information. As a child, you probably memorized the alphabet, addition and subtraction number facts, your teacher's name, the "Star Spangled Banner," and the dates of your birthday and major holidays. As an adult, you've memorized your work telephone number, the date of your anniversary (if you're married), your best friend's telephone number, and perhaps even the numbers and letters on your license plate.

Most people memorize information through repetition and association. In some cases, the imprinting is all but indelible. For example, you may only have to hear the words: "I pledge" and you can immediately complete the rest. Perhaps you actually see yourself as a child reciting the pledge in class or at a Brownie, Cub Scout, Girl Scout, or Boy Scout meeting.

Much of the information you've memorized, however, is not as accessible as the Pledge of Allegiance or the date that Columbus "discovered" the New World. You forget this information because you don't use it very often or because it is not especially relevant or important to your life. Unlike the important number fact 5 x 5 = 25, you don't have to recall the distance separating the earth and the moon (254,000 miles) unless you are an astronomy student or a science teacher. Chances are if you memorize this data, you will forget it unless you use it.

Some people have a greater capacity to remember information than others do. These are the people who answer trivia questions with ease. Although this capacity can certainly be an asset, it does not indicate that they are necessarily more intelligent than people with less exceptional memories. Nor does their recall ability suggest that they have greater insight or understanding. Being able to remember data, however, can be a distinct advantage in school, especially in courses that require you to assimilate a great deal of details and facts.

It makes sense to develop your retention and to learn how to apply methods that can enhance your memory. Even though you may not have to *remember* that the moon is 254,000 miles from the earth, you might have to *know* this fact if you take a science test.

There are two primary types of memory: *long-term* and *short-term*. The Pledge of Allegiance is imprinted in your long-term memory, as is your social security number, your aunt's name, and the name of your best childhood friend. The current win–loss record of your local professional football team and the first name of the person who was your waitress two days ago are stored in short-term memory (assuming you even bother to remember this data).

In most cases, the quality of your recall is linked to the significance and relevance of the material you are memorizing. If you consider this material to be important, you are more motivated to learn and remember it. Strategic students are practical. They commit to memory any material that they believe will improve their grade, and when doing so, they deliberately capitalize on their preferred learning modality.

If you're planning on majoring in history in college, going to graduate school, and teaching at the high school or college level, you have an incentive to remember information about the French Revolution. If you are planning to become a veterinarian, an engineer, or a court stenographer, you have less incentive. Clearly, your motives play a key role. A strategically minded engineering student would undoubtedly be willing to memorize information about the French Revolution if her goal is to get a good grade in her history course. It is likely, however, that she will forget many of the details once she completes the course.

IMPROVING YOUR MEMORY

Students do not memorize information in the same way. The dynamics of memorization, however, share three common denominators. You must:

1. **Input** information into your brain.
2. **Imprint** the information in memory.
3. **Access** the imprinted information stored in memory.

COMMON MEMORIZATION TECHNIQUES

1. *Writing information over and over until you memorize it.*

2. *Saying information aloud over and over until you memorize it.*

3. *Reading something over and over until you memorize it.*

4. *Making a picture or word association with the information.*

5. *Categorizing.* You could categorize the types of materials used to produce electricity (e.g., burning fossil fuel such as coal, hydroelectric power from dams, nuclear energy, wind turbines, waves from the ocean, solar power generators).

6. *Clustering.* You could create a constellation of information that relates to a particular issue (e.g., the negative social and economic forces that triggered the French Revolution). This clustering is a natural application of mind-mapping in which you visually link information in clusters.

7. *Chaining.* You might lay a "track" or a "timeline" of information that leads to or from a key issue you are studying (e.g., the evolution of nuclear energy from the early discovery of radioactivity, to the dropping of nuclear bombs, to the emergence of nuclear reactors, to the proliferation of such reactors). You would include relevant facts, dates etc. in the chain.

8. *Cue–response.* You might use a main idea or issue (cue) and repeatedly practice associating everything you know about the issue (response) until you've memorized these associations (e.g., causes of the French Revolution, types of nuclear power, etc.)

9. *Mnemonics.* You could use or create a formula or acronym to remember information (e.g., use the acronym DIBS to remember the steps of the problem-solving method or the trigonometry acronym SOHCAHTOA to remember sine = opposite over the hypotenuse, cosine = adjacent over hypotenuse, tangent = opposite over adjacent).

You've undoubtedly already used the first three methods when studying for tests. Let's take a look at the fourth technique: making a picture or word association. This method (i.e., linking what you have to learn with something you already know) is a very valuable study tool when you have to memorize vocabulary words, chemical symbols, foreign language conjugations, or facts from textbooks or notes. For example, you may link your best friend's birthday with Christmas plus three (December 28th). In the following section, you'll learn how to use this basic tool with great effectiveness.

MAKING POWERFUL ASSOCIATIONS

Look at the following definitions and sample sentences:

- **hedonist:** one who holds that pleasure is the chief good
  The man's wealth permitted him to be a *hedonist* and indulge himself in every extravagance.

- **miscible:** capable of being mixed
  She discovered in the laboratory that the two chemicals were *miscible*.

- **mitigate:** to make or become less severe or intense

  The defense attorney argued that her client had never before committed a crime and that this should *mitigate* the sentence.

- **narcolepsy:** a condition marked by sudden, uncontrollable, and usually brief attacks of deep sleep

  His *narcolepsy* was unpredictable and when sleep suddenly overcame him, he was often injured.

- **alacrity:** cheerful willingness and speed

  She was delighted to be invited to the party, and she answered her friend's invitation with *alacrity*.

- **patina:** a thin layer of usually brown or green corrosion that appears on copper or bronze as the result of natural or artificial oxidation

  The *patina* on the statue made it look like an antique and added immensely to its beauty.

- **confluence:** coming together

  After many adventures, the explorers finally arrived at the *confluence* of the two rivers.

- **clandestine:** hidden or secret

  The captain didn't realize that the crew had drawn up a *clandestine* plan to seize the ship.

An effective method for memorizing the definitions of these words is to form a vivid visual association between the word and its meaning and see the word, the definition, and the association "in your mind." This process of forming a mental pictorial construct is described as the **association–visualization method.**

The Association–Visualization Method

Using words from the preceding list, complete the following exercise.

Step 1: Write the words and their definitions on index cards or pieces of paper. Put only one word and definition on each card. Write each word using a different color felt pen or pencil. Write the definition in another color.

Step 2: After writing the words and definitions, create a picture in your mind that uses the word. *See* this image clearly. For example, you might be learning the word *hedonist*. You might visualize someone driving a white or black Rolls Royce convertible. Or you might visualize a hedonist in an elegant shop buying a blue silk shirt. (Choose any color you want!) In your mind, *see* the person trying on the shirt in front of a mirror. *See* him playing with the collar and trying to look very chic. Choose a *powerful* image to help you "take a picture" of the scene and help you remember the meaning of the word. Follow the same procedure with the next word, *miscible*. After writing the word and its definition, you might visualize a student in a white lab coat mixing blue and green chemicals in a flask held above a Bunsen burner.

Step 3: Keep looking at the card until you can imprint in your mind the word and its written definition in the color you've selected. Then, close your eyes and **visualize** the image you associated with the word (e.g., the *hedonist* flaunting his gold chains and opulent home). Then, **visualize** the written definition in color projected onto the *inside of your eyelids.* If you can't recall it, open your eyes and study it again. When you're ready, try to see the word and definition. When you can, write them on a piece of paper. Use the same procedure with the next word and definition. Holding the index card slightly above your head helps you use the visualization technique. (When your eyes look up, even behind closed lids, you're putting your brain into a visual mode.) Experiment with taping or tacking the card with the word slightly to the left or the right of your nose above eye level. Determine whether it's more comfortable looking up to the right or the left. The position that feels best will help you memorize most effectively.

Seeing a familiar image in your mind—perhaps from a movie or a personal experience—is a highly effective memory stimulus. The more powerful your associations or links, the easier it is to recall the information. For example, when memorizing the definition of *confluence*, you might visualize two bearded explorers wearing buckskin clothes sitting in a canoe and gazing in wonderment at the spot where two major rivers join. This association technique can be especially useful when learning foreign languages, vocabulary definitions, or historical information.

Use these three steps to learn the eight vocabulary words on the preceding pages. Once you can see the words and their definitions in your mind and access your visual associations, write the words on a piece of paper. Then, write the definitions of the words and use the words in a sentence. This final procedure will reinforce mastery.

A PHOTOGRAPHIC MEMORY

You've probably heard the expression "She has a photographic memory." The term is usually used to describe good students who have inherited a remarkable capacity to remember virtually everything they read or see. This analogy with photography and the idea that the eyes and brain function as a camera are actually very accurate. For most people, however, the visual imprinting procedure does not occur automatically. Although there are actually very few people who have a photographic memory, some students have a greater natural facility than others for imprinting visual information and remembering what they see. You may not have been born with this "natural" talent, but you can certainly improve your ability to take visual pictures, make visual associations, and imprint information in your mind.

Thinking of your eyes as the lens of a camera and your brain as a roll of film onto which you imprint images and information is consistent with the principles of the association–visualization method. The process of intentionally and systematically linking information (e.g., definitions, dates, spelling words, symbols) with images and colors and seeing these images and colors in your mind works with most visual information you have to memorize. Always choose colors you like! When studying vocabulary definitions or a foreign language, use sentences that incorporate the words or grammar, and then link this information with images that you can see vividly in your mind. You might even incorporate several words or facts you are learning into one image.

Examples of this picture-linking process might include visualizing a mountain climber *enveloped* in swirling snow and slowly *ascending* a *sheer* cliff face, or imagining yourself in a foreign country greeting someone, offering your hand, and saying, *"Me llamo Paul."*—"My name is Paul." In this latter example, you are actually combining both visual and auditory associations.

Certain material may not easily lend itself to forming vivid mental pictures. For example, the chemical symbol *Na* represents sodium. You could visualize a white powder, but you can't actually distinguish one white powder from another. In this case, it might be more productive to imprint the letters of the symbol *Na* and see the word sodium in your "mind's eye" with or without forming a visual picture of the chemical. In the case of H_2SO_4 (sulfuric acid), you can actually visualize the "bubbling" chemical in a flask being poured onto some paper on which the formula and the words "sulfuric acid" are written, and you could then visualize the paper disintegrating.

Mastery: Practice Forming Visual Associations

As an experiment, use the visual imprinting procedure to learn the following chemical symbols. After you've used the method and feel you've learned the symbols, test yourself to see how well you remembered them.

H_2O = water	H = hydrogen
Mg = magnesium	Pb = lead
CO = carbon monoxide	Na = sodium
CO_2 = carbon dioxide	Cl = chlorine
Fe = iron	He = helium
N = nitrogen	H_2SO_4 = sulfuric acid
HCl = hydrochloric acid	NaCl = salt

You can also use the visual imprinting procedure to remember math facts. Look at the math facts below and after studying each one, close your eyes and see it in color in your mind. Use the color imprinting technique to help you remember the following multiplication facts.

11 x 11 = 121	16 x 16 = 256
12 x 12 = 144	17 x 17 = 309
13 x 13 = 169	18 x 18 = 324
14 x 14 = 196	19 x 19 = 361
15 x 15 = 225	21 x 21 = 441

Now, use the same method to memorize the spelling of the following words:

prerogative	sergeant
losing	colonel
flammable	buoyant
lieutenant	delectable
circuitry	deleterious
misspell	miscreant

Practicing Additional Memorization Techniques

There are five other methods for memorizing and learning material: *categorizing*, *clustering*, *chaining*, *cue–response*, and *mnemonics*. All of these procedures, which are described on page 193, can be enhanced when used in conjunction with the association–visualization method. By *seeing* in your mind the particular cluster, chain, or acronym you've created, you can make the linkage all the more concrete.

As an experiment and for practice, select a subtitle section from either the nuclear energy or the French Revolution article, and use one of the five methods to memorize key information. Use the facts and details you included and color coded in your notes. If appropriate, combine the method with the association–visualization method to enhance the memorization procedure. Then, select another subtitle section and use another of the memorization techniques. Use all five methods and see which method, or combination of methods, works best for you.

Once you've practiced all of the methods, you may want to modify them so that they are tailored to how you recall information most effectively. Your goal is to develop your own *personalized* memorization system.

Final Test Preparation Checklist

As you prepare for a test, you might want to use the following checklist to verify that you have completed the steps that increase the likelihood of getting a good grade. These steps clearly require extra time and effort, but the rewards justify the additional labor. Each time you use the methods, the studying procedure will become easier. As you become increasingly adept at studying effectively, your performance will improve and your pride and self-confidence will soar.

Some of the statements in the checklist do not apply to all courses. Check only those that are relevant to the subject matter and the exam you are about to take.

Test Preparation Checklist

YES NO

○ ○ 1. I have identified what is likely to be covered on the test.
○ ○ 2. I have asked main idea and subtitle questions.
○ ○ 3. I have speed-read the material at least once.
○ ○ 4. I have either mind-mapped or taken traditional notes.
○ ○ 5. I have answered the subtitle and main idea questions.
○ ○ 6. I have identified the main ideas and details in my textbook and lecture notes.
○ ○ 7. I have used an effective memorization technique to recall important data.
○ ○ 8. When appropriate, I have used the association–visualization method.
○ ○ 9. I have reviewed previous quizzes, tests, and exams.

YES NO

○ ○ 10. I have used a study schedule.

○ ○ 11. I have allowed enough time to study and review adequately.

○ ○ 12. I have made sure I can answer any questions I missed on previous tests.

○ ○ 13. I have geared my study procedures to the type of test I expect.

○ ○ 14. I have made up practice tests.

○ ○ 15. I have studied with a friend or friends if appropriate.

If you completed all of the steps on this checklist, pat yourself on the back. You have done a first-rate job of preparation, and you have studied strategically! If you're disappointed by your grade on a test, analyze what went wrong. Perhaps you didn't understand the material. Perhaps you had test anxiety. Perhaps you misjudged what the instructor wanted you to learn. The setback will, of course, be disappointing. Don't give up! If you cannot figure out what went wrong, talk with your instructor. Discuss what you did to prepare and ask for suggestions about how to adjust your study strategy. Most instructors will respect your attitude, effort, motivation, and diligence.

Being Calm When Taking Tests

Some students do a first-rate job preparing for a test, but panic when taking the test. Despite having studied diligently, their anxiety undermines their performance and may even cause them to fail. Although the grade they receive might suggest that they didn't study effectively and didn't comprehend the assigned material, these students were, in fact, highly focused and conscientious when they studied the material and fully understood the content.

Taking tests can generate anxiety for anyone. The stress can be all the more debilitating when students desperately want to do well but have doubts about their abilities. Those who have a poor academic track record are often convinced in advance that they will do poorly, and their negative expectations are frequently self-fulfilling. As they wait for the test to be handed out, they become increasingly nervous and frightened. By the time they finally look over the test, they are a "basket case." Although they may know the material "backward and forward," they panic. The questions that are asked may be slightly different from those they expected, and because of their panic, they may not be able to recall the information they knew that morning. As their anxiety mounts, they decide that the test questions cover material that they never studied, and they "clutch" and forget everything they learned.

If you are one of those who panic when you take an exam, you know from first-hand experience the effects of test anxiety. Being convinced in advance that you'll get a bad grade can generate a debilitating apprehension that undermines performance and reinforces the belief that you are "dumb." Feelings of hopelessness can make you nonfunctional in testing situations, despite the fact that you are capable of succeeding academically.

If you go into a panic mode when taking tests, you can proactively respond to this predicament, analyze the situation, and think logically about finding a solution. DIBS is clearly an effective resource, and you can use it to define, investigate, brainstorm, and solve the predicament. Let's see how DIBS can help you achieve this objective.

Define: I become terrified when I take tests, and I forget what I've studied.

Investigate: I want to do well, but I get stressed and anxious.

I fear that if I don't do well, it will prove I am dumb.

I fear that if I don't do well, my parents (significant other or friends) will be disappointed in me.

I worry so much in advance that I become a nervous wreck.

I expect a disaster to happen, and it usually does.

I lack confidence when taking tests because I never do well.

Brainstorm: I could take a few deep breaths while waiting for the test to be handed out, close my eyes, intentionally relax my body, and feel myself becoming calm.

If I begin to panic when I look at the test, I could close my eyes and reassure myself that I studied conscientiously and know the material.

I could visualize myself getting a good grade on the test before I take it.

Select: I'll take a few deep breaths as I am waiting for the test to be handed out, close my eyes, intentionally relax my body, and feel myself becoming calm.

METHODS FOR DEALING WITH TEST ANXIETY

You may want to experiment with the following relaxation and anxiety-reducing techniques. If a particular technique doesn't work for you, try another. You may also want to combine the techniques and develop an individualized, tailor-made strategy for dealing with your test anxiety.

TEST RELAXATION TECHNIQUES

1. Close your eyes and *slowly* take several deep breaths while waiting for the test to be handed out. (Do not take more than three or four breaths as this could cause you to hyperventilate and become dizzy.)

2. Keep your eyes closed and form a picture in your mind of you looking at the questions, knowing the answers, taking the test, feeling confident, doing well, and feeling proud.

3. Silently recite and repeat positive statements about doing well while you are studying and when you are waiting for the test to be handed out.

4. With your eyes closed, feel your body relax and feel the fear and stress flowing out. Imagine that your stress is localized in a particular place in your body—your chest, your throat, or your stomach. Focus on this spot and imagine the anxiety ebbing away.

5. Select an easy question to answer first.

As you probably know, many professional actors and actresses experience severe stage fright before the curtain rises. Realizing that they must somehow conquer their fear, most figure out a personal system that helps them cope with their anxiety and go on with the show. In most cases, the stage fright quickly dissipates as the play progresses. The same is true about test anxiety. Once you begin to answer the questions and discover that you can answer them, your anxiety will lessen.

The described relaxation techniques are intended to allow you to maximize your test performance. If you experience chronic test anxiety, make it a habit to go through these steps when you take tests. As your grades improve as a result of your new study skills, you will discover that your anticipatory stress and fear are less debilitating.

For Your Information

f you want to prepare strategically for tests, you must do more than read your textbooks, take notes, understand what you're studying, and identify important information. Certainly, these are critically important steps in the preparation process, *but they are not enough*. If you want good grades, you must also develop an effective method for recalling key information, and you must be able to anticipate what questions are likely to be asked on an exam. By the time you finish studying, you must be certain that you can answer these anticipated questions.

Strategic students get into the habit of thinking like an instructor when they study. If they conclude that their instructor is detail-oriented, they study accordingly and memorize the key data. If they conclude that their instructor is concept-oriented, they focus on main ideas and spend less time memorizing the details. If they conclude that their instructor stresses facts *and* concepts, they "cover all the bases." They realize that their grade in a course may hinge on their ability to determine their instructor's orientation and adjust their study procedures accordingly.

Because many instructors require that you assimilate and memorize historical dates, chemical formulas, math formulas, vocabulary definitions, and idiomatic expressions in a foreign language, you must acquire effective memorization skills. Some students have a "natural" ability to memorize information they read or hear. If you do not possess this natural ability, you must learn how to compensate. You may be as bright or brighter than those classmates who have little difficulty memorizing data, but you may get lower grades because you struggle to remember information that may not appear particularly relevant to your life. An example is memorizing the phyla in a biology course if you are not majoring in science. Despite the seeming irrelevance of certain material that your instructors require you to learn, you must retain the information if you want to get a good grade on the next test. Strategic students recognize the facts of life, and they figure out how to get the job done as painlessly as possible.

Students who think smart make every effort to capitalize on their natural learning style and preferred learning modality when they study and memorize. If they are visual learners, they write down important information and reread the data until they have committed it to memory. If they are auditory learners, they recite information aloud and perhaps, if permitted, tape class lectures so that they can review them at home. Asking and answering questions about what they are studying is, of course, critical to both types of learning. Smart students realize that to get good grades on tests, they must not only remember key information, they must also understand it!

Whatever your "natural" learning style, you will encounter countless academic situations that require you to assimilate vast amounts of visual information. The key to improving your visual memory is to learn how to imprint pictures in your mind so that you can *see* the pictures and readily access the imprinted information.

Strategically minded students intentionally and systematically develop a wide range of study and learning resources. Imagine, for example, that you're preparing for a Spanish test. To help make the vocabulary, idiomatic expressions, and regular and irregular verb conjugations more relevant and to motivate yourself to master the material, you might create imaginary scenarios in which you visualize and hear yourself speaking Spanish in Mexico or Spain. You can either verbalize aloud or hear the words in your mind as you speak to a waiter using the verbs, idiomatic expressions, and vocabulary. To enhance your recall, you would also try to *see* the vocabulary words and their definitions in your mind, and you would reinforce this association by intentionally repeating the words. This procedure of using your preferred (and when appropriate nonpreferred) learning modalities makes the material you are studying more meaningful. Using creative methods for improving your recall and actively and creatively engaging yourself in the learning process can dramatically improve the likelihood that you will master the material and receive a good grade on the next test!

SECTION THREE

Applying Strategic Intelligence

GETTING WHAT YOU WANT, NEED, AND DESERVE

10

GOALS AND PRIORITIES

CHAPTER 10

OBJECTIVES

- Establishing goals
- Using goals as an academic and career-enhancing tool
- Breaking down challenges into manageable parts
- Using goal setting as a problem-solving resource
- Establishing priorities
- Using priorities to create better organization
- Linking priorities and goals

Getting There Through Goal Setting

When Kelsey first decided to go back to school, she planned to become a court stenographer. As she began taking courses, her ambitions expanded, and she realized that she actually wanted to become an attorney. She liked the law, and she could imagine herself someday being a district attorney or trial lawyer. At times, she fantasized about becoming a judge. She could see herself sitting on the bench in her black robe with the attorneys arguing their case in front of her and awaiting her ruling on a point of law.

After analyzing her situation objectively, she concluded that her ambitions were not very realistic. As a widow and the mother of two young children, her immediate goal was to make a good income as quickly as possible so she could support her family. After her husband died, Kelsey invested the life insurance money in certificates of deposit. She soon discovered that the interest was not enough to cover her expenses. Reluctantly, she had begun to tap into the principal. Going back to school and getting a well-paying job was now an absolute necessity. She was very aware that the insurance money wouldn't last forever.

Kelsey had borrowed $5,000 from her parents to help with her expenses—books, school charges, car insurance, childcare, and a used computer. Whenever she thought about how much getting a law degree would cost and about the required time and effort commitments, she became depressed. "This whole idea about going to law school is stupid!" she fumed.

Becoming a court stenographer was clearly a far more practical goal. The job paid well. There was always a demand for stenographers, and the work was secure. "Why am I so unwilling to settle for this?" she asked herself. She knew it would take a minimum of seven years to get a law degree even if she went to school full-time and studied every free moment. This schedule would leave her virtually no time to spend with her kids. And, of course, there was the worry about not having enough money to complete school. "Give it up!" she would grumble when she felt particularly discouraged. To justify her decision to abandon her goal, she rationalized that she probably wouldn't even earn a good income as a lawyer. "Lawyers are a dime a dozen," she thought. "Why go to school for eight years and make tremendous sacrifices to earn maybe $50,000 a year?"

When Kelsey looked at the formidable challenges that lay ahead, her reasons for taking the path of least resistance seemed logical. But in her heart, she still wanted to be an attorney. Although she didn't think it would make a difference, she decided to make an appointment to speak with an academic advisor.

Together she and the advisor examined the pluses and minuses of being a 30-year-old reentry student who had to support a family on her own while aiming for a law career. The counselor brought up some issues that hadn't occurred to Kelsey.

Counselor: I believe people should pursue their dreams, but I also believe people must be realistic about the challenges. I could make a good argument for advising you not to spend the next eight years studying to become a lawyer. The reasons are obvious. At the same time, I think that establishing challenging personal goals and attaining them after a hard struggle is one of life's most gratifying experiences. The rewards help us appreciate our abilities and develop respect for ourselves. It's like running a marathon. You're dead tired when you cross the finish line, but you feel an indescribable exhilaration.

Kelsey: How can I possibly stay in school on a fixed income of $18,000 a year? Every year, this income is less because I'm being forced to use my savings, and this reduces the interest. I don't qualify for welfare because of the insurance money. Even with food stamps and student loans, I don't see how I can do it. I am continually borrowing money from my parents. And then, I wonder if it's fair to my kids. We'd have to live in poverty for eight years. I know I could just use up all of the insurance money and hope I make it through an A.A. degree, college, law school, and the bar exam, and can find a decent-paying job. But it's so risky, and if I don't make it, we'll be broke.

Counselor: There's another option. You could complete the court stenography program, work part-time, and earn a good hourly salary while going to school part-time. You may only be able to take one or two course per semester. It might take 10 years to finish the entire process, and you may be tempted to give up along the way, but at least you'll be on a track leading to a law degree. The stenography courses and the practical courtroom experience will help you decide if you really want to make the sacrifices. As a "practicing" court stenographer, you may discover you really don't like the law.

Kelsey: It makes sense, I guess.

Counselor: Let's do some testing and find out what your interests and preferred learning style are. You might also take an aptitude test and a vocational interests test to see if you can realistically handle the demands of law school. I suspect you can, but you may want more data before making your decision.

The advisor urged Kelsey to think carefully about the issues they had discussed. She told her that if she still wanted to become a lawyer after having analyzed the test results and having carefully considered the required academic obligations and personal sacrifices, she would need to develop an effective and focused long-range strategy. The advisor suggested that the plan should be in writing and should include the specific required steps to attain her objectives. She recommended that Kelsey first establish specific goals and then set her priorities. She explained that these priorities should be placed in a logical order to allow her to proceed from point A to point B to point C. They decided to meet again in one week.

After doing research at the library and reviewing some law school catalogues, Kelsey defined her goals and a sequenced list of priorities. She developed the following plan:

STRATEGY FOR BECOMING AN ATTORNEY

1. Take required courses for the court stenography certificate.
2. Take required courses and earn a degree in Criminal Justice.
3. Take pre-law classes.

4. Get good grades and a G.P.A. of at least 3.4.

5. Get a part-time job as a court stenographer.

6. Transfer into a local four-year state college.

7. Earn a scholarship.

8. Complete my B.A. degree.

9. Complete law school.

10. Pass the bar exam.

11. Become an assistant district attorney.

During the next week, Kelsey continued to wrestle with her decision. Realizing she was at an important crossroad in her life, she was eager to meet again with her advisor.

After examining Kelsey's plan, the counselor asked several questions about the details. She then showed Kelsey a worksheet with an easy-to-follow system for developing a personal strategy. The worksheet, which contained eight sections, asked her to:

1. Define her long-term goal (in specific terms).

2. Indicate what she has learned from life experiences about making the plan work.

3. Prioritize specific short-term goals (interim steps) that will permit her to achieve her objective.

4. Identify possible problems, challenges, or obstacles.

5. Identify resources that can provide help if it's needed.

6. Identify any additional factors that could affect the outcome.

7. Calculate the odds of success.

8. Make strategic adjustments and modifications to improve the odds of success.

Kelsey took the worksheet home and completed it. Once she "had it down on paper," she felt better. The challenges she faced seemed awesome, but, at least, she now had a strategy and long- and short-term goals. Kelsey felt that she had a decent chance of attaining her objective if she kept to her plan. She decided that whenever she felt overwhelmed or discouraged, she could counteract the negative thoughts by visualizing herself in court, smartly dressed, confidently presenting her case, and dazzling the jurors with her legal talents. She hoped that this image would inspire her to keep on working.

on the issues

Confronting Major Obstacles

Kelsey was understandably demoralized by the challenges she faced. Carefully examine Kelsey's story and underline and number each obstacle. You should find at least eight. List each obstacle and assess its seriousness.

Obstacle #1. _____

_____

Evaluate this obstacle.

1	2	3	4	5	6	7	8	9	10

not serious   fairly serious   very serious

Obstacle #2. _____

_____

Evaluate the obstacle.

1	2	3	4	5	6	7	8	9	10

not serious   fairly serious   very serious

Obstacle #3. _____

_____

Evaluate the obstacle.

1	2	3	4	5	6	7	8	9	10

not serious   fairly serious   very serious

Obstacle #4. _____

_____

Evaluate the obstacle.

1	2	3	4	5	6	7	8	9	10

not serious   fairly serious   very serious

Obstacle #5. _____

_____

Evaluate the obstacle.

1	2	3	4	5	6	7	8	9	10

not serious   fairly serious   very serious

Obstacle #6. _____

_____

Evaluate the obstacle.

1	2	3	4	5	6	7	8	9	10

not serious   fairly serious   very serious

Obstacle #7. _____

_____

Evaluate the obstacle.

1	2	3	4	5	6	7	8	9	10

not serious   fairly serious   very serious

Obstacle #8.

Evaluate the obstacle.

1	2	3	4	5	6	7	8	9	10

not serious   fairly serious   very serious

Although convinced that she could not achieve her goal, Kelsey decided to discuss her predicament with her academic advisor.

Evaluate the wisdom of this decision.

1	2	3	4	5	6	7	8	9	10

not smart   fairly smart   very smart

Go back to the story and underline and number each of the advisor's suggestions. You should be able to identify at least six specific recommendations.

How do you rate the advisor's recommendations?

1	2	3	4	5	6	7	8	9	10

poor   fairly good   very good

How do you rate Kelsey's response to her advisor's recommendations?

1	2	3	4	5	6	7	8	9	10

not smart   fairly smart   very smart

How do you rate Kelsey's motivation?

1	2	3	4	5	6	7	8	9	10

poor   fairly good   very good

How do you rate Kelsey's judgment?

1	2	3	4	5	6	7	8	9	10

poor   fairly good   very good

Why did you make this assessment?

How do you rate Kelsey's chances of attaining her goal and becoming a lawyer?

1	2	3	4	5	6	7	8	9	10

poor   fairly good   very good

Why did you make this assessment?

Drawing a Conclusion from the Evidence

Having read about and carefully examined Kelsey's dilemma, what specific conclusion can you draw from the information presented in the story? Using the *inductive method*, express in a well-crafted sentence what you have concluded. *Remember:* You are summarizing the **point** of the story.

The point of Kelsey's story:

_____

_____

_____

_____

zooming out  on the issues

Using Goal Setting to Handle Challenges

Kelsey discovered that discussing a problem with someone she trusts and respects can provide a different perspective on a seemingly monumental dilemma. Because this person is not emotionally entangled in the problem, he or she may be able to help examine the issues more objectively and see the situation more clearly and less emotionally.

Kelsey also learned from her counselor that the process of systematically establishing specific long-term and short-term goals and setting priorities makes seemingly unsolvable problems less overwhelming. The "divide and conquer" process (discussed later in this chapter) breaks the predicament into smaller and more manageable pieces that can be handled one step at a time.

As you read about the obstacles Kelsey faced, you may have thought of another equally reasonable and effective solution. For example, instead of studying court stenography, she could take as many pre-law courses as possible, and rather than transferring immediately into a four-year college pre-law program after earning her A.A. degree, she could take a year off and work as a receptionist or clerk in a law office. The two advantages of this plan are that she would get more exposure to what it is like to be an attorney and she would also earn a living. The two disadvantages are that it would take her one more year to attain her goal and she probably wouldn't earn a great salary right out of college with just an A.A. degree.

Alternative Solution to Kelsey's Predicament

_____

_____

_____

Major advantage(s):

_____

_____

Major disadvantage(s): _____

_____

_____

If you can think of another reasonable and practical alternative solution to Kelsey's problem, list it below. Then indicate the *major advantages* and *major disadvantages* (if there are any) to your proposed solution.

_____

_____

_____

_____

APPLYING THE GOAL-SETTING METHOD

You have already learned an extremely powerful problem-solving method called DIBS. Although DIBS is a highly effective resource, there is another equally powerful problem-solving tool. It is called the **goal-setting method,** and you may prefer to use it in certain situations.

As Kelsey learned, the procedure of establishing specific long-term and short-term goals can be a potent resource for dealing with challenges and predicaments. By defining goals that address and resolve a particular problem, you can focus your physical and mental energy on solution-oriented procedures. The goal and priority-setting process is not only effective in school, it is also effective in the world outside school. For example, let's say that a major league baseball player finds out that he is being sent down to the minors because his hitting is inconsistent. Rather than becoming demoralized, he decides he will make it back up to the majors within one year. *This is his long-term goal.* To achieve this goal, he realizes that he must improve his hitting. *This is a short-term goal.* When he arrives at the new club, he discusses his problem with the manager and the batting coach. He asks them to help him analyze what he's doing wrong. They pinpoint the problem and make constructive suggestions. The player decides to practice what they have taught him for an extra hour every day before the team takes the field. Changing his batting stance and swing and spending extra time practicing his hitting every day become *additional short-term goals* designed to help him attain his long-term goal—making it back to the majors.

Mastery: Practice Using Goals to Neutralize Challenges

List one or two goals that might solve each of the following problems:

1. Your English instructor is lowering your grades on essays and reports because you're making too many spelling and grammar mistakes (e.g., run-on sentences, nonparallel construction).

   Long-term goal(s):

   a. _____

   b. _____

Short-term goal(s) (be specific):

a. _____

b. _____

MODEL APPLICATION:

Long-term goal(s):   Reduce careless spelling and grammar mistakes.

Improve my grade on essays and reports.

Short-term goal(s):   Use word processor in learning lab.

Use spell check and grammar check.

Slowly and carefully read over and edit what I write.

Ask someone to proofread my work.

2. You have to get your car tuned so it can pass an emissions test. You can't register it without the certificate. Unfortunately, you're short on money.

Long-term goal(s):

a. _____

b. _____

Short-term goal(s) (be specific):

a. _____

b. _____

3. You're paying service charges because you've been paying your bills late.

Long-term goal(s):

a. _____

b. _____

Short-term goal(s) (be specific):

a. _____

b. _____

4. You have to take three major exams in one week. You're feeling overwhelmed by all of the studying you must do.

Long-term goal(s):

a. _____

b. _____

Short-term goal(s) (be specific):

a. _____

b. _____

5. Your kids (roommates, housemates, brothers, sisters) are making too much noise at home when you're studying.

Long-term goal(s):

a. _____

b. _____

Short-term goal(s) (be specific):

a. _____

b. _____

DEFINING YOUR PERSONAL GOALS

You've undoubtedly given some thought to what you want to do when you finish school. As you well know, going to college represents a major time commitment and financial sacrifice. If you're attending full-time, your income is likely to be reduced or eliminated. If you're attending part-time, you have to devote most of your free time to studying.

Personal long-term goals serve an essential function: They provide you with a sense of direction and purpose. As an adult, you may have very practical goals, including earning a degree, procuring a rewarding job, achieving job security, and earning more money. You may want to become an engineer, a physician, or an attorney. Once you define your goals, you can then focus your physical, emotional, and mental energy on attaining the desired payoff.

To avoid unnecessary frustration and demoralization, it makes sense to establish *realistic* short-term and long-term goals. For example, let's say that you're working hard in your algebra class. The semester is half over, and you're carrying a C average. It might not be very reasonable or realistic for you to establish a goal of getting an A– in the course (although this might be possible if you got straight A's on all of your remaining tests and an A on the final exam). Targeting a B or B– in the course represents a more realistic goal. The same principle applies in other areas of your life. If you are overweight, it isn't realistic to go on a diet and set a goal to lose 10 pounds the first week. If you establish an unreasonable goal, you are setting yourself up to fail. Losing two pounds the first week is far more realistic.

Establishing goals can be a double-edged sword. Goals can motivate you, but if you aim too high you can become discouraged and give up. It is far more strategic to establish goals that you can reasonably achieve and then aim higher after you've attained the initial objective. For example, if you are struggling in physics, aiming for an A on your midterm could be tantamount to setting yourself up for a disappointment. It's for you to decide objectively whether an A is realistic. You should certainly have a fall-back position—perhaps a B or B– on the midterm and a B or B– in the course.

Take a few minutes to list your personal goals below.

My Goals

DATE: _____

1. _____

2. _____

3. _____

4. _____

5. _____

6. _____

7. _____

8. _____

When you define your goals and develop a plan for attaining the objectives, you are creating a *strategy*. (Later in this chapter, you will practice creating strategies.)

GOALS ARE NOT SET IN CEMENT

You have every right to change your goals when they no longer meet your needs. For example, you may enter school thinking that you want to earn a degree in biology and work in a hospital lab. You may subsequently decide that you prefer to study criminal justice with the goals of ultimately getting a B.A., going to law school, and becoming an FBI agent. Altering your career course may represent a well-reasoned choice. You may have taken one or two science courses, and you may have concluded that you do not have a natural science aptitude or that you are not sufficiently interested in biology to continue majoring in it. A course in criminal justice may convince you that you are far more suited to a career in federal law enforcement.

Let's assume you're wrestling with the situation just described (i.e., becoming a biologist versus becoming an FBI agent). You may begin to have a dialogue in your mind about the wisdom of changing course, and you may find yourself becoming confused and paralyzed by doubts. To help make the right choice, you list the pluses and minuses of continuing on a track that leads to a career in biology and the pluses and minuses of pursuing a track that leads to a job in federal law enforcement. You may conclude that one of the pluses of working for the FBI is a better salary. Another plus might be the prestige associated with being a special agent. Minuses might include the possibility of being transferred to another area of the country and having to get an advanced degree, especially if you are not particularly interested in law or accounting (FBI agents must have a graduate degree either in law or in accounting). An example of a plus for seeking a job in biology might be remaining in your community where you have family and friends. A possible minus is that to advance your career in science, you must have at least a master's degree. As best you can, continue listing the pluses and minuses of pursuing a degree in biology versus pursuing a degree in criminal justice. Think of as many logical pros and cons as you can.

Weighing the Pros and Cons and Making a Difficult Choice

PURSUING A CAREER IN BIOLOGY

PLUSES:

1. _____

2. _____

3. _____

4. _____

5. _____

6. _____

MINUSES:

1. _____
2. _____
3. _____
4. _____
5. _____
6. _____

PURSUING A CAREER IN FEDERAL LAW ENFORCEMENT

PLUSES:

1. _____
2. _____
3. _____
4. _____
5. _____
6. _____

MINUSES:

1. _____
2. _____
3. _____
4. _____
5. _____
6. _____

GAINING PERSPECTIVE

For most students, attending college involves practical considerations. You want to make a better life for yourself (and for your family if you are married) and acquire new skills. As you progress through the semester, you may decide to change your goals and redirect your efforts. There are risks, however, in doing so, especially when you abandon a cherished goal simply because you encounter challenges or problems. If you're working hard, making major sacrifices, trying to juggle multiple responsibilities, and feeling overwhelmed, you can lose your focus when you encounter major obstacles. Attaining a long-term objective such as a college degree or specialized certification may begin to seem like an impossible dream, particularly if you're experiencing academic or financial difficulty. Because you are emotionally vulnerable, abandoning your goals, simplifying your life, and resigning yourself to lesser achievement may appear to be an appealing solution to the dilemma.

If you begin to believe that the struggle is endless and the problems are insurmountable, you can become demoralized and lose your sense of direction. You may become resentful of the amount of time, energy, and money required to get where you want to go. You may become discouraged by the seemingly endless academic challenges and impatient with your progress. In response, you may choose the path of least resistance and abandon your goals.

If you find yourself at a critical, potentially life-altering crossroad, it is vital that you not make an irrational decision that you may regret for the rest of your life. Key decisions should never be made when you are feeling frustrated, discouraged, or despondent. Having someone whose judgment you trust and respect help you objectively evaluate your options and carefully examine the ramifications of your choices is critically important.

To help you sort out your options, make an appointment with your academic advisor or a counselor. This person can help you assess the situation clearly and forge solutions to those problems and challenges that may appear overwhelming and insurmountable. Another option is to talk with the instructor of any course in which you're having problems. Instructors have a great deal of experience helping students who have faced similar dilemmas. It's also smart and strategic to take advantage of the learning assistance and counseling resources available at your school and to use these resources to help you over the rough spots!

Going to school, being retrained in a new field, or deciding to earn a degree demands courage and commitment. An A.A. degree can require from 18 months to three or more years to complete, depending on how many credits you take each semester. If you are in a B.A. program, you may have to spend from four to eight years in school, again depending on the number of credits you take each semester. The sacrifices can be enormous, especially if you have a family to support. To save money, you may have to sacrifice vacations. Instead of watching TV or going to a movie, you'll have to discipline yourself to study. You'll have less time to spend with your friends and your family. But when looking back after attaining your goal, these sacrifices will seem inconsequential. The *price of victory* may be expensive and demanding, but the *taste of victory* can usually erase a multitude of unpleasant memories.

POWERHOUSE THINKING

Key Issues to Consider Before Abandoning a Goal

- Am I abandoning this goal because I am convinced that another goal would better serve me?
- Have I discovered issues about myself that have caused me to reassess my talents, interests, and objectives?
- Am I abandoning this goal because I have run into a glitch and I want to take the easy way out?
- Am I making this decision when I am feeling frustrated and discouraged?
- Can I overcome the glitch with extra effort and attain my original goal?
- Have I taken advantage of the available resources?
- Am I likely to regret this decision?

TARGETING WHAT YOU WANT IN WRITING

Becoming discouraged when the road ahead seems long and difficult is a very human response. To counteract these negative emotions, it is helpful to remind yourself periodically *why* you've chosen a particular path and *why* you've decided to make the associated sacrifices. The following self-directed memo may help you sustain your focus. Complete it using the goals you listed on page 214. Then, put the memo in a desk drawer or tape it on the wall where you study. When you need reassurance, refer to it. It will help you remember what you want to achieve in school and in life.

Should you become discouraged, lose steam, and start procrastinating, *reread your memo*. Remind yourself that you *deserve* the goals you have targeted. Reviewing your personal goals will motivate you to overcome the obstacles and make the sacrifices seem less painful!

Memo to Myself

TO WHOM IT MAY CONCERN:

I am recording my personal long-term and short-term goals. I realize that I may become discouraged by the amount of time, effort, and sacrifice required to get what I want. This memo will remind me of my objectives and my reasons for making these sacrifices.

Whenever I'm tempted to abandon a major goal or lower my standards, I'll reread the memo. I'll take it a day at a time, prioritize my obligations, plan carefully, examine my mistakes and setbacks, and pat myself on the back for what I've already achieved. By working efficiently and planning strategically, I am certain that I can ultimately attain my goals. These goals are realistic. I *deserve* to achieve what I want in life, and I'm *determined* to make it happen.

My Long-Term Goals

1. _____
2. _____
3. _____
4. _____
5. _____

My Short-Term Goals

1. _____
2. _____
3. _____
4. _____
5. _____
6. _____
7. _____
8. _____

My Specific Short-Term Academic Goals

Subject	Most Recent Semester Grades (if available)	Grades Desired Next Semester

Other Personal Short-Term Goals

1. _____
2. _____
3. _____
4. _____
5. _____
6. _____
7. _____
8. _____
9. _____
10. _____

Signed: _____   Date: _____

Experiment: Using Goal Setting to Improve Your Grades

To demonstrate how goal setting is a key academic success tool, do the following experiment. For each of the next two weeks, choose a specific academic short-term goal (e.g., at least a B on your weekly English essay) and record the weekly goals on the following forms. Then, list several specific short-term goals for each day of each week (e.g., a B+ on your Spanish vocabulary quiz). At the end of each day, check "yes" or "no" to indicate whether you achieved your daily goals. On Friday, check "yes" or "no" to indicate whether you've attained your weekly goal.

WEEK #1

Achieved

Yes   No

WEEKLY GOAL: _____   ○   ○

Daily Goals:

Mon. _____   ○   ○
_____   ○   ○
_____   ○   ○
_____   ○   ○

Tues. _____   ○   ○
_____   ○   ○
_____   ○   ○
_____   ○   ○

Wed. _____   ○   ○
_____   ○   ○
_____   ○   ○
_____   ○   ○

Thur. _____   ○   ○
_____   ○   ○
_____   ○   ○
_____   ○   ○

Fri. _____   ○   ○
_____   ○   ○
_____   ○   ○
_____   ○   ○

WEEK #2

Achieved

Yes   No

WEEKLY GOAL: _____   ○   ○

Daily Goals:

Mon. _____   ○   ○
_____   ○   ○
_____   ○   ○
_____   ○   ○

	Yes	No
Tues. _____	○	○
_____	○	○
_____	○	○
_____	○	○
Wed. _____	○	○
_____	○	○
_____	○	○
_____	○	○
Thur. _____	○	○
_____	○	○
_____	○	○
_____	○	○
Fri. _____	○	○
_____	○	○
_____	○	○
_____	○	○

As a student, you have undoubtedly faced an all-too-common dilemma: too many obligations and too little time. To your dismay, you have probably found yourself being pulled in several directions at the same time. You may have an important English paper due the same day that a chapter test in geology is scheduled. An effective antidote for this predicament is to have a specific short-term goal you want to attain each day of each week.

If you find that recording your daily and weekly goals focuses your efforts, motivates you, and produces positive payoffs, continue to record your goals for the rest of the school year. Feel free to modify the recording form to include as many daily and weekly goals as you want.

Goals: A Four-Step Problem-Solving System

As previously stated, goal setting can be a powerful problem-solving tool. Let's examine how you can use, as an alternative to DIBS, a simple *four-step problem-solving system*. (*Please note:* You may be very happy with DIBS, but give this alternative method a try.)

Situation: Before she lost her job and returned to school, Sarah promised her kids that she would take them to Disneyland during their summer vacation. Now that she was a student, Sarah was overwhelmed by the amount of studying she had to do and the expenses she faced. She was a single mother who was determined not to be on welfare for the rest of her life. Despite the challenges she was facing, she knew she would feel guilty if she had to cancel the trip and disappoint her children. She was determined to figure out how to keep her promise.

Applying the Four-Step Problem-Solving System

Step 1:

Challenge: Figure out how to juggle finances, studying, and school schedule so that she can take her kids on the promised trip to Disneyland.

Step 2:

Long-term goals: Save $1,000.00 by summer.

Take my kids to Disneyland this summer as promised.

Step 3:

Short-term goals: 1. Examine school schedule and plan trip during semester break.

2. Create a budget.

3. Offer to do baby-sitting at night while studying.

4. Save $50.00 each week for the trip.

5. Find out least expensive way to get to Los Angeles.

6. Write chamber of commerce for a list of inexpensive hotels.

Step 4:

Specifics: 1. Put up notices at school that I'm available to baby-sit.

2. Put up notices at laundromats and supermarkets.

3. Take lunch to school to save money.

4. Buy advance-purchase discount bus tickets to Disneyland.

5. Ask kids to find jobs they can do in neighborhood to earn money.

6. Spend 50 percent less on Christmas and birthday presents.

Many problems can be solved when you analyze the problem carefully and establish specific short-term and long-term solution-oriented goals. If applied systematically, the procedure neutralizes obstacles and helps you overcome barriers that stand in your way.

Mastery: Practicing the Four-Step System to Solve Problems

Use the four-step problem-solving system to solve any *two* of the following problems:

1. You have to spend three days rebuilding the engine in your wife's car so she can get to work. You want to persuade your instructor to let you hand your paper in late.

2. Your wife (husband, boyfriend, girlfriend, best friend) is upset because you're spending all of your time studying and not spending enough time together.

3. You're trying to go to school part-time and hold down a full-time job. Your boss complains that you appear tired and that the quality of your work has slipped.

4. You're doing the best you can in your English class, but your grades are terrible.

5. You'd like to get a B.A. degree, but you don't know how you can possibly spend four years in college without having a steady income.

6. You're concerned that you won't be able to find a job after completing your degree.

SELECTED PROBLEM # _____

Step 1:

Challenge: _____

_____

Step 2:

Long-term goals: _____

_____

_____

Step 3:

Short-term goals: _____

_____

_____

_____

_____

_____

Step 4:

Specifics: _____

_____

_____

_____

_____

_____

SELECTED PROBLEM # _____

Step 1:

Challenge: _____

_____

Step 2:

Long-term goals: _____

_____

Step 3:

Short-term goals: _____

_____

_____

_____

_____

_____

_____

Step 4:

Specifics: _____

_____

_____

_____

_____

_____

_____

USING GOAL SETTING WITH A PERSONAL PROBLEM

As previously stated, *Study Wise* presents various ways to handle an issue. The program encourages you to experiment with the different techniques and select those that work best for you. You may also prefer to "borrow" components of certain methods and combine them with components of other methods to create your own personalized system.

In keeping with the suggestion that you *experiment* until you find what *works best for you*, use the four-step problem-solving system to solve a personal problem. To derive benefit from this exercise, do not select an intimate problem that you are embarrassed to discuss in class. Choose a problem that matters to you, but not one that makes you feel uncomfortable.

After doing the following exercise, you may conclude that you prefer either the DIBS problem-solving method or the four-step system. You may also conclude that you prefer to use one method in certain situations and the other method in other situations.

Briefly describe your personal problem:

_____

_____

_____

_____

_____

Using the Four-Step System to Solve a Personal Problem

Step 1:

Challenge:

_____

_____

Step 2:

Long-term goals:

_____

_____

Step 3:

Short-term goals:

_____

_____

_____

_____

_____

_____

_____

Step 4:

Specifics:

_____

_____

_____

_____

_____

_____

_____

Prioritizing the Steps
for Getting the Job Done

Evan felt like he was drowning. When he thought about all he had to do during the next 10 days, his anxiety became palpable. It was already Tuesday, and his Administration of Justice term paper was due on Friday. He had a math midterm the following Monday, and an important English essay was due in two weeks. He had to submit his algebra homework on Thursday, and he had to take notes on two chapters in his computer technology textbook.

There were also plenty of non–school-related tasks that Evan had to take care of during the next two weeks. Somehow, he had to find the time to replace the carburetor in his 12-year-old car that was continually stalling. The car was now so unreliable that if he didn't fix it, he would have to start taking the bus to school. This would add 30 minutes each way to his commute time. Evan had also promised to referee two basketball games each week at the community center, and on Wednesday and Friday afternoons, he had to drive his mother to her physical therapy appointment. He had no idea how he was going to do all of this.

Although initially supportive of his decision to go back to school, Evan's girlfriend was becoming increasingly upset with him. She continually complained that they weren't spending enough time together and that they never went dancing, to the movies, or out to dinner anymore. Natalie was right, of course. But Evan could barely keep up with his schoolwork as it was, and he was drowning in debt. Now that he was going to school full-time, he really had no money for entertainment. His rent and the last tuition bill had consumed more than half of his savings, and because he wasn't working, he had no income. This reality was causing him to consider looking for a part-time job.

As he looked at what seemed to be an impossible situation, Evan became depressed. Maybe going back to school really wasn't worth it after all. The challenges seemed staggering. This was compounded by the fact that he found studying difficult. Because his academic skills were weak, he had to spend at least four hours doing homework every evening, and he studied at least 10 hours over each weekend. There just didn't seem to be any solution. Evan certainly didn't want to lose Natalie. And he didn't want to flunk out of school. He had to figure out how to handle his obligations.

A METHOD FOR ESTABLISHING PRIORITIES

Feeling like you're drowning is a common reaction when you have too many things to do and too little time get them done. You may conclude the situation is hopeless and give up, or you may rush around feeling anxious and stressed and accomplish very little.

Too many responsibilities may also cause you to become emotionally paralyzed. To avoid having to deal with your obligations, your unconscious mind may pretend that they don't exist, and you may escape by watching TV, talking on the phone, or playing with your dog. This coping behavior, which is often referred to as *"being in denial,"* provides only a temporary reprieve. At some point, you must get the work done or suffer the consequences.

Determining your priorities (i.e., a logical order of what's most important and should get done first) can save your sanity when you feel overwhelmed. Some simple guidelines can help you create this logical order.

Three Basic Steps for Establishing Priorities

1. Write down all responsibilities, obligations, assignments, projects, tasks, items, or issues that have to be handled.
2. Number the list in order of importance or necessity. (The most essential, important, or immediate obligations should be at the top.)
3. If you're pressed for time, eliminate (or put off till later) those obligations, tasks, or items that are less essential or urgent.

For practice, use these three steps to prioritize Evan's obligations. Reread his story carefully; underline each of his tasks, projects, and responsibilities; and then list them below. Do not worry about the order—you will prioritize them after you complete the list.

EVAN'S LIST OF RESPONSIBILITIES, TASKS, AND PROJECTS

_____

_____

_____

_____

_____

_____

_____

_____

_____

_____

_____

_____

_____

_____

Now, number the list in order of importance or urgency. You may decide to place Evan's academic responsibilities at the top of the list, or you may choose to place his obligation to drive his mother to her physical therapy appointment at the top. You may decide to rank his desire to make his girlfriend happy at or near the top, in the middle, or at the bottom of the list.

As you can see, the process of ranking Evan's obligations is *subjective* and reflects your perspective, attitudes, and value system. Evan clearly has to make some important decisions, and he has to decide on and rank what he considers most important. He might juggle his time and attempt to do everything on the list, or he may be forced to choose between being successful in school and maintaining his relationship with his girlfriend. If he decides that earning as much money as possible while attending school is critical, he will make this his top priority. He may have to take fewer credits and allow more time to get his degree.

To make reasonable and strategic choices, Evan has to create a hierarchy of importance. *But before he can do this, he must define his long-term goal.* This will make the decision making, planning, and prioritizing process less confusing. If Evan's most important goal is to earn a degree, he may conclude that he cannot referee the basketball games or that he has to place Natalie's needs and desires lower on his priority list. He may also conclude that by working more efficiently and managing his time more effectively, he can attain his objective and, at the same time, satisfy Natalie's needs (see Chapter 2 for time-management skills).

Review Evan's responsibilities and eliminate at least *three* obligations that you believe are the least important, urgent, or critical. This requires value judgments, and not everyone will agree on what should be eliminated.

DIVIDE-AND-CONQUER PRINCIPLE

Defining goals, establishing priorities, recording deadlines, and ranking tasks and obligations in order of importance or urgency makes complex and seemingly impossible projects and challenges more manageable. The "divide-and-conquer" procedure—breaking big undertakings into smaller units and prioritizing the units—helps you handle complicated assignments that involve many steps and details. For example, let's say the instructor of your government class assigns a term paper. She tells the class that the paper counts for 40 percent of the course grade. After adding up your previous grades on quizzes, tests, and homework assignments, you realize you can get a B in the course if you get a B on the term paper and at least a B– on the final exam. To avoid wasted effort, you decide to prioritize the required steps. You create a list of the specific tasks necessary to complete the assignment successfully and get a good grade.

Let's say that you have written down the tasks listed below. To practice prioritizing, number the list in a logical order that allows you to complete the assignment efficiently. Use a pencil so you can erase and make changes.

Steps for Writing a First-Rate Term Paper

____ Write down quotations

____ Go to the library

____ Review specific instructions for writing paper

____ Edit second draft

____ Write the final draft

____ Choose a topic

____ Check for spelling and grammar mistakes

____ Have friend proofread final draft

____ Create schedule for completing project on time

_____ Check out the necessary books

_____ Write notes on index cards

_____ Ask the librarian for assistance

_____ Print out (or type) copy to be submitted

_____ Make up a bibliography

_____ Write second draft

_____ Turn in the report on time

_____ Organize information on index cards

_____ Edit first draft

_____ Consult with your teacher about the topic you've selected

_____ Read material about subject in the encyclopedia

_____ Write first draft

_____ Organize index cards to correspond with how you want to present information

_____ Do a computer search for articles about the subject in magazines or newspapers

If you were to compare your ordering system with that of a classmate, you may discover that you each ordered the list slightly differently. For example, you may prefer to create your bibliography *after* writing the final draft, and your classmate may prefer to do it *before* writing the final draft. Both procedures are acceptable. The key is to consider—before beginning the project—the most logical sequence for doing the steps so you can complete the assignment with a minimum amount of grief.

POWERHOUSE THINKING

Divide-and-Conquer Principle

- Break major projects into smaller manageable units or tasks.
- Create a logical order for handling the tasks based on urgency, importance, or appropriate sequence.
- Schedule a realistic completion date for each task.

SETTING YOUR PRIORITIES AND ORGANIZING YOUR LIFE

In the space below, write down all of your important obligations, projects, and deadlines for this semester. **Priority List 1** should focus exclusively on *school responsibilities* and should include studying for tests in specific courses, completing specific homework assignments, reports, and so on. Obviously, there will be homework and projects that haven't yet been assigned. List only those obligations you already know about or can anticipate with certainty. Don't worry about listing your responsibilities in order. You'll prioritize your list later.

School Obligations, Tasks, and Projects

_____

_____

_____

_____

_____

_____

_____

_____

_____

_____

_____

_____

_____

Now, go back and prioritize the list. If possible, eliminate at least three of the less important, urgent, or critical obligations. Of course, eliminating school obligations may not be realistic. For example, you cannot simply cross off studying for your Spanish midterm or writing up your chemistry experiments in your lab book. These responsibilities must obviously remain on your list.

Priority List 2 should focus on your _personal obligations_. Include commitments to your family and chores you have to do around the house.

Personal Responsibilities, Tasks, and Projects

_____

_____

_____

_____

_____

_____

_____

_____

_____

_____

_____

_____

It's now time to prioritize your list. For practice, eliminate (if possible) at least three of the less important, urgent, or critical personal obligations. Eliminate more than three if feasible.

Mastery: Practice Establishing Priorities

You may prefer to keep your academic and personal priority lists separate. For now, however, combine both lists into one master list of obligations and priorities. At the top of your list, indicate your long-term goal or goals. For example, you may decide that your most important long-term goal is to complete your degree in Criminal Justice within two years.

COMBINED PRIORITY LIST OF PERSONAL AND SCHOOL RESPONSIBILITIES

Long-term goal(s):

_____

_____

_____

_____

_____

_____

_____

_____

_____

_____

_____

_____

_____

_____

_____

Before prioritizing your list, eliminate, if possible, at least three of the less important, urgent, or critical obligations.

Using DIBS

Let's say that there's an obligation that you are convinced you *must* somehow eliminate. For example, you may have to do a great deal of schoolwork during the Thanksgiving break. You may have an English essay due the following week, and you may also have to study for a sociology midterm. You want to prioritize these responsibilities, but unfortunately, your husband (wife, girlfriend, boyfriend, best friend) wants you to go to his (her) parents' home for the holiday. They live 300 miles away. You are expected to spend at least two nights at their home and will spend six hours driving each way.

Your dilemma is how to meet your school obligations without offending people and without causing your "significant other" to be angry at you. What can you do? Well, you can use either the four-step problem-solving system or DIBS to help you handle the problem. Because you've already practiced the four-step problem-solving system in this chapter, use DIBS here.

Define: _____

Investigate: _____

_____

_____

_____

Brainstorm: _____

_____

_____

_____

Select: _____

_____

Following is an example of how DIBS might be applied to your dilemma. Your DIBS application may differ, and may be as good as or better than the one modeled.

APPLYING DIBS

Define: I have to study over the holiday and I don't have the time to go away.

Investigate: I don't want to offend or upset people.

I want good grades this semester.

If I don't get my work done, I'll have major problems.

I prioritized a list of important goals. This trip will undermine my plans.

Brainstorm: I could explain the situation and hope that people understand why

I can't go.

I could take my books with me and explain that I have to spend

at least six hours studying and writing my report.

We could leave very early Thursday morning, get there by 2:30 P.M.,

have dinner, spend the night, and return the next day. This will

leave Saturday and Sunday for schoolwork.

Select: We'll leave early Thursday and return Friday.

For Your Information

A key characteristic distinguishes students who think strategically from those who do not: *Strategic students recognize the direct cause-and-effect link between establishing personal goals and achievement.* These students consistently define their objectives, formulate a practical plan for attaining their goals, and focus their intellectual, physical, and emotional energy on achieving the payoff they desire.

Once you learn how to use goal setting as a planning and problem-solving tool, you will become the equivalent of a heat-seeking missile. Whether your target is short-range (a B+ on the next biology test) or long-range (a college scholarship and a B.A. degree), you will be able to vector for a bull's-eye. The payoffs and pride you'll derive from your accomplishments will more than compensate you for your hard work.

Figuring out the most effective way to get the job done is the essence of *thinking smart.* As you define and attain your long- and short-term goals, your self-confidence will improve, and you will be motivated to establish new personal objectives to replace those you've already achieved.

The process of setting priorities plays an equally pivotal role in the academic success equation. To get from point A to point B to point C, you must rank your responsibilities, tasks, desires, and needs in order of importance and urgency and in a logical sequence. You have to recognize that there are steps to completing challenging projects and that you must do steps one and two before you begin step three.

For some students, establishing priorities is a reflex. Because they automatically create a progression or hierarchy of importance in their head without writing down an actual list, they may not be consciously aware that they are setting priorities.

Whether you prioritize automatically or as a result of deliberate conscious effort, you will accrue monumental benefits in terms of efficiency, time management, and organization from your planning and tactical thinking. You will also discover that consistent prioritizing helps you avoid becoming overwhelmed and discouraged when you are confronted with complex challenges.

Determining what you have to do and developing a sequential, ordered, and logical plan for completing the tasks and meeting the obligations is directly linked to being aware of what's most compelling and urgent. You must realize that studying for tomorrow's science exam is more important than going to a movie with friends. If you have defined your goals and you are thinking smart, you will prioritize studying over entertainment. You will recognize that the payoff for doing well on an exam is greater than any immediate gratification you might derive from seeing a movie.

Intentionally creating order in your life, defining what counts, and figuring out a logical order for doing what has to be done allows you to work more productively. Rather than wasting time going in several directions at once, procrastinating, and feeling stressed, you use your time wisely and complete your work as efficiently and painlessly as possible.

As you begin to think more strategically and plan more effectively, your capacity to handle the challenges you encounter in school and at work will provide you with a significant competitive advantage. You will become more efficient, productive, self-reliant, and self-confident. The ultimate goal is for you to apply planning and goal-setting methods consistently, making these procedures an integral part of your personal *modus operandi.*

MOTIVATION

Strategic, goal-oriented students are propelled by a powerful fuel called **motivation** that is supercharged with a performance-enhancing additive called **zest.** If you add motivation and zest to your tank, your engine will produce enhanced power and torque. You'll zip along the straightaways, climb hills with RPM to spare, negotiate hairpin turns deftly, and maneuver safely around road debris.

Non-strategic, non–goal-oriented students have a different propulsion system. Floating through school and life in cerebral neutral, these students run on low-octane fuel. This weak petrol produces predictable consequences: Their motor generates fewer RPM and less torque. They chug along the straightaways at a snail's pace, stall as they climb hills, fishtail around hairpin turns, and repeatedly crash into barriers.

Motivation is not mysterious. Observe people who are doing something they enjoy or find stimulating, challenging, and rewarding. Their level of enthusiasm and motivation is directly linked to the pleasure and sense of accomplishment they derive from their participation.

Most people are motivated when they believe their efforts will produce positive results. The formula is very basic: Motivation and effort produce success, and success, in turn, produces motivation and effort. There is, however, an inherent irony in this formula. To be successful and motivated, you must feel good about yourself and have confidence in your abilities. But to have good feelings and confidence, you must experience success and be motivated. This is a classic Catch-22.

If you find yourself enmeshed in a non-success loop, there is a solution: *You must deliberately and strategically engineer opportunities for achievement.* These achievements do not have to be monumental at first. A success may simply involve establishing the goal of getting a B on the next Spanish quiz and then studying hard and attaining the objective.

Intention and effort are powerful antidotes for marginal achievement. With success comes enhanced self-confidence and self-appreciation—soon you will discover that you have extricated yourself from the non-success loop.

Winning in school is akin to eating pistachio nuts or popcorn. Once you start, if you are like many people, you find it hard to stop. The pleasure you derive from winning generates the desire to win again because you want to reexperience the pleasure. This recycling success loop is represented graphically in Figure 10.1.

If you are having difficulty extricating yourself from a non-success loop, you may be tempted to give up, shut down, and accept marginal performance as your fate in life. To break free from this negativity, you must intentionally, consistently, and strategically apply the specific, practical, success-oriented skills you have learned in this program. This deliberate smart thinking (i.e., *applied intelligence*) will help you attain your goals. Your achievements will produce tangible evidence that you are making progress and that you are in control of your own destiny.

Success–motivation cycle.   **FIGURE 10.1**

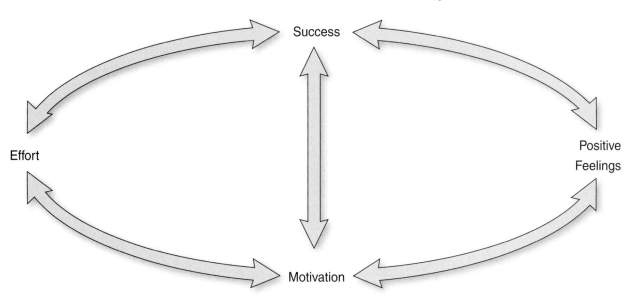

The antithesis of this loop is graphically represented in Figure 10.2.

Non-success–low motivation cycle.   **FIGURE 10.2**

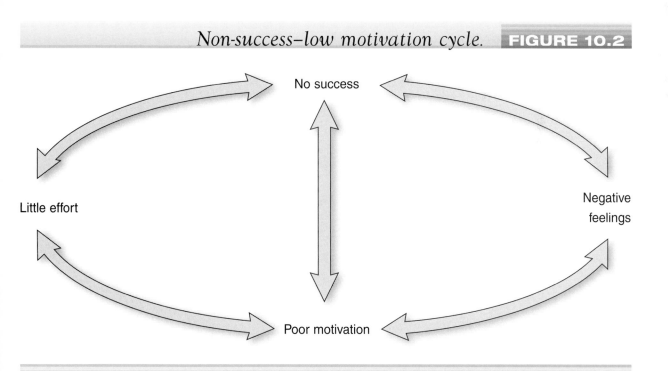

Note that the arrows in the two cycles *point in both directions.* Positive feelings produce success, and success, in turn, produces positive feelings. Conversely, negative feelings produce poor motivation that, in turn, produces lack of success and additional negative feelings.

If, despite your best efforts, you conclude that you cannot extricate yourself from a non-success loop on your own, seek out someone who can help you assess the situation objectively. This person might be an instructor, an academic advisor, a counselor, or a wise friend. Acknowledging that you can't solve the problem yourself and asking for assistance indicate that you are *thinking and acting smart.* Smart people ultimately prevail!

DEVELOPING A PERSONAL STRATEGY

OBJECTIVES

- Utilizing strategies and tactics
- Developing a plan to attain goals
- Creating a personal educational plan
- Making strategic adjustments when study procedures are not working

Giving It Your Best Shot

Martin was determined to get an A– on the chemistry final. The exam would account for 35 percent of the semester grade. Because he was carrying a B+ in the course, his grade on the final was critically important. If he could get an A– on the final and an A on his report, he would have a lock on an A– for the semester. This would raise his G.P.A. to 3.2. Not bad for someone who had barely graduated high school and joined the Army at eighteen.

Because he was working full-time and taking eight units, Martin had begun to prepare two weeks in advance. He had made up a study schedule, and he had kept to it. He carefully reread the assigned chapters and reviewed his class and textbook notes several times, using two different colored highlighters to identify the important information and differentiate key facts from concepts. Because the final would cover the entire semester, he carefully reviewed his previous quizzes and midterm, and he made sure he could answer all of the questions correctly. If there was information he didn't know, he went back to his notes and textbook to find it. He drew a mind-map to help him remember key facts and represent how the information was linked. Then, he put the facts and formulas on index cards and reviewed the cards until he had memorized the data.

To help him recall formulas and scientific symbols, Martin used a study technique his friend had taught him. He closed his eyes and pretended that his eyes were the lens of a camera and that his brain was a roll of film. He then took a mental picture of the information and imprinted the "pictures" in his mind in vivid colors.

The final step in his test preparation was a three-hour marathon study session with two classmates who were A and B+ students. As they plowed through the material, they asked each other questions and made up practice test questions. Basing the questions on the types of questions their instructor had asked on previous tests, they tried to anticipate what was likely to be on the exam.

Martin spent a total of 12 hours studying for the final. Over the two-week period, this translated into an average of less than one hour per evening. If he could get the A– he had targeted, the time investment would certainly have been worthwhile.

When he completed his study plan, Martin felt that he was as prepared for the final as he could be. He wasn't overly confident, but he felt he could get a decent grade, assuming, of course, that he didn't panic and forget everything.

Despite his preparation, Martin was nervous on the day of the exam. To reduce his test anxiety while waiting for the instructor to hand out the exam, he closed his eyes and took several deep breaths. He visualized himself looking at the test, reading the questions, and confidently answering them.

When he finally received his copy of the test, Martin quickly scanned the questions and breathed a sigh of relief. He knew he would be able to answer all of the questions. He had to remind himself not to feel too confident. If he did, he might get careless and make silly mistakes.

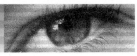

zooming in on the issues

Having a Game Plan

Martin's comprehensive study strategy consisted of at least 12 specific steps. Go back to the story and underline and number each step in Martin's study strategy. Then, underline twice and number each of the steps Martin took to relax, reduce his anxiety, and build his confidence while he waited for the exam to be handed out.

Evaluate Martin's motivation.

1	2	3	4	5	6	7	8	9	10
poor				fair					excellent

Evaluate Martin's effort.

1	2	3	4	5	6	7	8	9	10
poor				fair					excellent

Predict Martin's grade on the final exam.

1	2	3	4	5	6	7	8	9	10
poor				fair					excellent

Predict the likelihood that Martin will earn his degree.

1	2	3	4	5	6	7	8	9	10
poor				fair					excellent

Evaluate the overall effectiveness of Martin's study strategy.

1	2	3	4	5	6	7	8	9	10
poor				fair					excellent

Can you think of any other steps that Martin could have taken to improve his test performance? For example, you might suggest that he study in the library if it's noisy at home or that he use a tape recorder to help him recall important information. (This can be especially valuable if he is an auditory learner.) After mentally reviewing the smart studying techniques that you've practiced, list any additional steps that might be applicable.

ADDITIONAL STEPS:

Step 1: _____

Step 2: _____

Step 3: _____

Step 4: _____

Step 5: _____

Drawing a Conclusion from the Evidence

Having read about Martin's strategy, what specific conclusion can you draw from the information in the story? Using the *inductive method*, express in a well-crafted sentence what you have concluded. *Remember:* You are summarizing the **point** of the story.

The point of Martin's story:

_____

_____

_____

_____

_____

zooming out on the issues

Linking Tactics and Strategies

The expression "the whole is the sum of its parts" is useful in understanding the relationship between tactics and strategies in the planning process. A military example illustrates this link. A general commanding soldiers in battle has to develop specific **tactics** to neutralize snipers and land mines. To defeat the enemy, he also has to develop a comprehensive battle **strategy.** Whereas the tactics focus on the microcosmic (small and limited) issues, a strategy addresses the macrocosmic (larger and more expansive) issues.

Tactics: Specific techniques for attaining a limited and immediate goal.

Strategy: An overall plan for attaining a long-term goal that involves interim steps (short-term goals) and incorporates specific tactics.

You will discover that to handle life's demands and challenges, you have to develop both strategies and tactics. For example, one of your strategies may be to buy a fixer-upper home and trade up to a better fixer-upper until you ultimately own the home of your dreams. Your *tactics* may include reducing your living expenses, saving money, and making improvements in each property so that you can sell it for more than you paid. These tactics allow you to maximize the return on your investments, implement your strategy, and attain your long-term objective.

From personal observations and experiences, you may have discovered that *few of life's most desirable payoffs come easily.* The rewards you covet might include earning a college degree, advancing your career, owning an expensive German sports car, and buying a home overlooking the ocean. To attain these rewards, you must be motivated, conscientious, and diligent. You have to plan strategically. You have to figure out how to get around roadblocks, handle setbacks, learn from mistakes, and bounce back from failures. You have to persist when you experience a glitch or run into a wall. It doesn't matter whether you are playing professional basketball, writing a book, flying a jet fighter, or creating a marketing campaign for a new product. To do a first-rate job, you must have a plan in place and a well-conceived strategy for getting from point A to point B to point C. This strategic thinking is a requisite to success in any challenging endeavor.

Creating a Personal Strategy

ome people fall into a perfect situation with little conscious planning. It seems to happen serendipitously. A famous actor being
interviewed by a reporter might describe how he never thought
about a career in acting. One day, quite by chance, he happened to
be wandering past the theater arts building on campus. He was drawn inside
for reasons he can't explain, and he stumbled on a play rehearsal. He found
himself fascinated and became engrossed in the rehearsal. To his surprise,
the director walked over to him and asked if he would be interested in a one-
line walk-on role in the second act. He agreed, and that was the beginning
of a long, productive, and satisfying career.

In reality, careers are seldom launched by accident. Most actors are
drawn to the theater as children. They try out for every school play. They
major in drama in college and take acting lessons after college. They try out
for any part that is available, and they do everything they can to interest an
agent in representing them. In most instances, each step is carefully
planned. They play in small regional theaters and in summer stock. They
may decide that they must move to California to be close to the heart of
the film industry or to New York to be close to off-Broadway and Broadway
productions. They select the best acting coaches and the best theater training companies. Their plan to attain their objective is well-researched,
methodical, and deliberate.

Unless you have a remarkable natural talent, and you are lucky to boot,
assume that you won't fall into a rewarding career serendipitously. You have
to work hard and plan. You have to define your short- and long-term goals
and develop strategies and tactics to attain them. You have to have a **personal strategy.** Let's review what you have already learned.

Personal strategy: A
carefully conceived, sys-
tematic plan for attaining
clearly defined and per-
sonally significant
objectives. The steps are
highly focused, practical,
logical, and deliberately
designed to improve the
likelihood of success.

List three benefits of defining long-term goals:

1. _____

2. _____

3. _____

List three benefits of defining short-term goals:

1. _____

2. _____

3. _____

List three benefits of creating a personal strategy:

1. _____

2. _____

3. _____

POWERHOUSE THINKING

Key Principles for Developing a Strategy

- Figure out what matters to you and what you want.
- Create a plan that addresses precisely defined objectives.
- Assess rationally the challenges that you might encounter.
- Develop tactics for neutralizing the obstacles.
- Methodically implement the components of your plan.

A Strategy That Failed

Manuel had been thinking about opening his own store for three years. He wanted a shop that specialized in providing kitchen items specifically for men who like to cook. Manuel was an excellent chef who loved to BBQ and make creative sauces for pasta. His wife and kids loved his homemade salad dressings and ravioli stuffed with mozzarella cheese and Italian sausage.

Manuel's plan was to quit his job as a bus driver and find a small shopping center where he would open his store "There's a MAN in the Kitchen!" Although he and his wife, Carmen, had saved more than $15,000, he knew he would need at least another $15,000 to open the business, make the renovations he wanted, order supplies, pay the first and last month's rent, install a phone, and pay for newspaper and radio ads. With reluctance, he went to Carmen's parents to ask about borrowing the necessary funds. Carmen's dad was a retired electrician, and Manuel knew he had a considerable amount of money sitting in a savings account.

Because he had never borrowed this much money before, Manuel felt very uneasy. After Carmen's parents agreed to lend him the money, Manuel insisted on signing a promissory note to repay the loan. Once he had the money, Manuel quit his job and began looking for a store location. He found a very attractive small shopping center in a wealthy community. Although the rent was considerably higher than he expected, he signed the lease within two days. He then hired the best contractor he could find to install the shelves and displays. Manuel wanted everything to be top-of-the-line. He hired an electrician and a plumber to make major renovations so that he could give daily cooking demonstrations.

Manuel had budgeted $5,000 for alterations, but the final bill was $9,700. Getting the store ready took four weeks longer than he expected. Because he wanted to sell only the finest products and ingredients—utensils, spices, BBQs, stainless steel pots and pans, aprons, chef hats, towels, cookbooks—stocking the store with inventory required $5,000 more than he had planned.

Because the store was new and had no credit rating, Manuel had to pay cash for everything. The quantities he bought were relatively small, so he did not receive the same discount that larger stores were able to negotiate. Other unanticipated expenses were also much more than Manuel had budgeted. He needed a lawyer to set up the company and an accountant to set up the books. He also had to procure a business license. He needed to have a multi-line phone installed. He also had to buy a fax for phone orders and a computer for his webpage and online orders. The ad in the Yellow Pages was three times as expensive as anticipated because he had to advertise in several different phone books to reach his potential customers. Then, he had to pay to turn on the electricity and water, print business cards, and hire a sign painter.

The store wasn't ready to open until December 1st, and, much to his dismay, Manuel discovered that he had missed an important part of the Christmas selling season. He realized he should have signed the lease and started renovating the store at least six weeks earlier than he did. After paying all of his bills, Manuel found that he had only $1,500 left in his account. He used most of this money to run three small ads in the local newspaper. The results from the advertising were negligible.

Although the shopping center was attractive, foot traffic was much less than Manuel expected. When he discussed his concerns with other store owners, he learned that the traffic was poor because the center did not have a major department store as a draw for customers. There was also another major drawback. Because the center was not enclosed, people shopped elsewhere whenever it rained, snowed, or was very hot.

After six months, Manuel realized that he might have to close his shop. Although he had some loyal customers, he couldn't compete with the discount stores and the national chain stores. He had no money left to advertise.

When Manuel realized he couldn't pay July's rent, he had to decide whether he wanted to ask Carmen's parents to lend him more money. It was a heart-wrenching decision. Business was poor, and the local economy was depressed. If he borrowed more money and business didn't improve, he might have to declare bankruptcy. After many sleepless nights, he and Carmen decided to close the shop. The venture had been a financial disaster, and they were now more than $23,000 in debt, excluding the $7,000 they owed on their credit cards. The challenge Manuel now faced was figuring out how to get himself out of the hole he had dug.

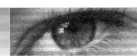

zooming in on the issues

Analyzing a Debacle

As you read about Manuel's ill-fated business venture, you may have identified several key decision points. These decisions clearly affected the outcome. Go through the story carefully and number each decision in order (e.g., hiring the best contractor). Then, write each decision below and evaluate the wisdom of this decision.

Manuel's decisions:

#1. _____

| 1 | 2 | 3 | 4 | 5 | 6 | 7 | 8 | 9 | 10 |

not smart   fairly smart   very smart

#2. _____

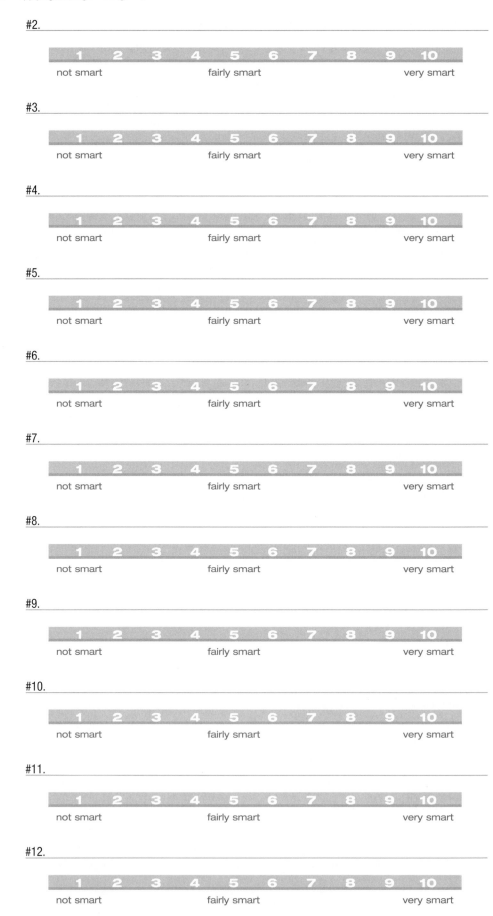

| 1 | 2 | 3 | 4 | 5 | 6 | 7 | 8 | 9 | 10 |
| not smart | | | | fairly smart | | | | | very smart |

#3. _____

| 1 | 2 | 3 | 4 | 5 | 6 | 7 | 8 | 9 | 10 |
| not smart | | | | fairly smart | | | | | very smart |

#4. _____

| 1 | 2 | 3 | 4 | 5 | 6 | 7 | 8 | 9 | 10 |
| not smart | | | | fairly smart | | | | | very smart |

#5. _____

| 1 | 2 | 3 | 4 | 5 | 6 | 7 | 8 | 9 | 10 |
| not smart | | | | fairly smart | | | | | very smart |

#6. _____

| 1 | 2 | 3 | 4 | 5 | 6 | 7 | 8 | 9 | 10 |
| not smart | | | | fairly smart | | | | | very smart |

#7. _____

| 1 | 2 | 3 | 4 | 5 | 6 | 7 | 8 | 9 | 10 |
| not smart | | | | fairly smart | | | | | very smart |

#8. _____

| 1 | 2 | 3 | 4 | 5 | 6 | 7 | 8 | 9 | 10 |
| not smart | | | | fairly smart | | | | | very smart |

#9. _____

| 1 | 2 | 3 | 4 | 5 | 6 | 7 | 8 | 9 | 10 |
| not smart | | | | fairly smart | | | | | very smart |

#10. _____

| 1 | 2 | 3 | 4 | 5 | 6 | 7 | 8 | 9 | 10 |
| not smart | | | | fairly smart | | | | | very smart |

#11. _____

| 1 | 2 | 3 | 4 | 5 | 6 | 7 | 8 | 9 | 10 |
| not smart | | | | fairly smart | | | | | very smart |

#12. _____

| 1 | 2 | 3 | 4 | 5 | 6 | 7 | 8 | 9 | 10 |
| not smart | | | | fairly smart | | | | | very smart |

Overall, how would you rate Manuel's strategy?

1	2	3	4	5	6	7	8	9	10

not smart　　　　　　　　fairly smart　　　　　　　　very smart

Assume that before launching his business, Manuel asked you to be his partner, and you agreed. What specific things would you have done differently to change the outcome?

1. _____

2. _____

3. _____

4. _____

5. _____

6. _____

7. _____

8. _____

9. _____

10. _____

If Manuel had developed a more realistic strategy, carefully analyzed the capital requirements (i.e., the money necessary to finance the venture adequately), and incorporated contingency plans (i.e., a strategy for dealing with miscalculations and setbacks) *before* opening his store, do you think this venture might have turned out differently?

○ yes　　　　○ no　　　　○ perhaps

Modifying Your Study Procedures

The ability to make tactical adjustments in your strategy when it's clear that your current plan is not working is essential to success in school and in life. This ability to make adjustments differentiates smart students from not-so-smart students.

You've probably heard the expression "If it ain't broke, don't fix it." This advice is wise in situations where continual tampering and tweaking might be counterproductive. There should, however, be an addendum: *"When it is broken and you have to use it, you must either figure out how to fix it or you must replace it."*

The student who continues to use a flawed methodology is destined to experience failure, frustration, and demoralization. Smart students analyze what has gone wrong. They identify the problem and modify the plan so that it works.

STUDY SKILLS: RED FLAGS AND STRATEGIC ADJUSTMENTS

- **You're studying diligently, but your grades are not up to your expectations.**

  Strategic adjustments: Objectively analyze and evaluate your study methods, use alternative study methods, talk with your instructor, talk with your advisor, ask a classmate who is doing well what techniques he or she is using.

- **You can't find the time to do all of your work.**

  Strategic adjustments: Review time-management procedures, establish a personal study schedule, review and evaluate your priorities, consider taking fewer units.

- **You study conscientiously but forget what you've studied.**

  Strategic adjustments: Learn visualization techniques to improve your memory, use mind-mapping and effective note-taking methods.

- **You don't understand the material you're studying.**

  Strategic adjustments: Review and use mind-mapping and effective note-taking procedures, discuss the problem with your instructor, study with a classmate who understands the material, request information from the college counseling office about being assessed for a possible learning disability, determine whether you qualify for tutorial assistance.

- **You have difficulty understanding your instructor's lectures.**

  Strategic adjustments: Discuss the problem with your instructor, read and review *before class* the relevant material in your textbook that your instructor will cover in class, review class notes *after* the lecture, reread and compare the textbook content with the material covered in class, ask someone who is doing well in the course to help you, ask the course instructor for suggestions, ask the college learning assistance lab if you qualify for tutorial help or diagnostic testing.

- **You lack motivation.**

  Strategic adjustments: Review your goals and priorities, review your personal educational plan, talk with your advisor.

- **You procrastinate.**

  Strategic adjustments: Set up a personal time-management program, establish specific short-term goals each day, review your long-term goals and priorities, visualize yourself attaining your goals and recall the image whenever you begin to procrastinate.

- **You're disorganized and waste time looking for things you need.**

  Strategic adjustments: Apply organizational principles and use appropriate organizational checklists to pinpoint specific deficits.

- **You can't concentrate.**

  Strategic adjustments: Review relaxation techniques, review goals and priorities, set up a time-management program with clearly defined periods for studying, ask an advisor for suggestions, establish specific concentration goals, reexamine your study break formula, discuss with a physician or advisor the advisability of biofeedback training or medication if your focusing problems are chronic.

- **You believe your instructors think you're lazy or have a negative attitude.**

  Strategic adjustments: Talk with your instructors to verify whether your perceptions are accurate, communicate that you are serious about your studies, express a willingness to do extra assignments to improve your skills and grades, ask for suggestions on how to improve your performance, talk to your instructor if you need help understanding the content in your textbook or information presented in class.

- **You make careless mistakes on your assignments.**

  Strategic adjustments: Review your time-management schedule and add additional time for proofreading, checking, and editing; ask a classmate (husband, wife, friend) to proofread or check problems for accuracy; assume there are errors in your work and go through a careful and systematic process of looking for and finding these errors; use a spell check and grammar check program on the computer.

- **You're spending excessive amounts of time on your schoolwork.**

  Strategic adjustments: Identify your academic and study skill deficits using appropriate checklists; review sections in this program that address any specific learning, study, or academic skill deficiencies you might have; go to the learning assistance lab and ask to be evaluated if you suspect you might have a learning disability.

You can also use DIBS to help you develop your own solutions to these problems. Once you've identified the underlying issues, you can brainstorm and experiment with solutions. As an alternative, you can use the four-step problem-solving system to help you define long- and short-term objectives to address the problems.

Mastery: Practice Making Strategic Adjustments

For the examples below, list two possible strategic adjustments.

1. You forgot to do an assignment and got an F on it.

Strategic adjustments: _____

_____

_____

_____

_____

_____

2. You did not learn key information that was covered on a test.

Strategic adjustments: _____

_____

_____

_____

_____

3. You ran out of time while taking an objective test.

Strategic adjustments: _____

_____

_____

_____

_____

4. You misjudged your finances and ran out of money.

Strategic adjustments: _____

_____

_____

_____

_____

5. You got a poor grade on your science lab write-up.

Strategic adjustments: _____

_____

_____

_____

_____

Developing a Personal Educational Plan (PEP)

magine that you are considering starting your own business. You decide to seek some professional advice before launching the business, and you contact a highly recommended business consultant. This person tells you that the first step in starting a successful business is to develop a business plan. In this plan, you define your objectives, examine the risks and opportunities, and present a systematic and sequential strategy for attaining your short- and long-term goals. The plan maps out the specific steps you must take and objectively analyzes key issues such as the amount of capital required, competition, start-up expenses, marketing, and location. You realize that your objective assessment of these critically important issues will determine the success or failure of your venture. Once completed, the plan provides you with a road map to your destination, helps you focus your efforts, and defines the procedures for solidifying and growing your new business.

Just as there is an obvious value to having a road map that can safely guide you through the perilous minefield of establishing a business, so, too, is there value to having a similar road map to guide you safely through the perilous minefield of the academic world. By creating a carefully conceived educational plan, you can significantly increase the likelihood of attaining your academic goals and mastering the skills necessary to launch and sustain your career trajectory. Taking the time to create such a personalized strategy can be one of the wisest time and effort investments you make.

As you develop your educational plan, review and draw on what you have learned and the exercises you have completed. Once your Personal Educational Plan (PEP) is finished, you can refer to it whenever you become sidetracked or thwarted in the pursuit of your educational goals. The plan is concrete, accessible, and utilitarian.

Note that the following PEP is formatted for you—just fill in the relevant information. In some sections, you are asked to write a concise essay that addresses a specific component of the plan.

The basic rationale for the PEP is that knowing *why* you are doing something that requires prodigious effort and multiple sacrifices can significantly enhance your academic performance. Having a clear understanding of your motives for going to college and your strategy for attaining your objective will stimulate your effort and diligence. Your clarity of purpose will propel and sustain you when the going gets rough and you are tempted to give up. The PEP preparation requires *constructive introspection*. This introspection will help you discover *who* you are, *what* you want, and *where* you are headed. The PEP will also help you remember *why* you embarked on the path you have chosen.

Much of the information in the PEP can be derived from the exercises in the earlier chapters. The PEP is formatted so that you can photocopy it or input it onto your computer. Make a copy to leave at home near your desk. Refer to it periodically to make sure you are on track and are working congruently with your stated goals.

If you input the form into your computer, you can update and revise your study schedule each semester so that it is current. At some point, you may want to revise the content of a specific section. (If you wish to redo your PEP, you can find a copy in Appendix 2.)

Whenever you are beset with self-doubt, insecurity, anxiety, or stress, or whenever your motivation begins to flag, refer to the PEP. This document encapsulates your reasons for being in school and the well-conceived strategy you have devised for achieving your goals.

Personal Educational Plan

Developed By: _____

Date: _____

School: _____

Major: _____

Degree/Certification Objective: _____

TABLE OF CONTENTS

CURRENT STATUS SUMMARY

Age: _____   Number of units: _____

Marital status: _____ Number of hours working: _____

Occupation: _____ G.P.A. to date: _____

MISSION STATEMENT

My long-term goals:

Education: _____

_____

_____

Career: _____

_____

_____

Family: _____

_____

_____

Other:
_____

_____

_____

In this section, discuss why you are in school. Include your priorities, values, beliefs, and personal standards.

_____

_____

_____

_____

_____

_____

_____

_____

MY EPITAPH

At the risk of sounding morbid, compose a 10- to 12-word sentence that you would like to be written on your tombstone. This epitaph should succinctly summarize who you were and what you achieved in your life.

_____

_____

_____

_____

PERSONAL PROFILE

In this section, discuss your background, family, temperament, distinctive characteristics, strengths, and weaknesses. Be forthright, objective, and, at the same time, subjective (i.e., express feelings, not just hard data). This is an opportunity for you to be constructively introspective and use your insights about yourself as a reality check and springboard for self-actualization.

_____

_____

_____

_____

_____

_____

_____

IMMEDIATE GOALS AND PRIORITIES

In this section, indicate and prioritize your short-term goals for the current or next semester. You can distill the information you compiled in earlier chapters.

1. _____
2. _____
3. _____
4. _____
5. _____
6. _____
7. _____
8. _____
9. _____
10. _____
11. _____
12. _____
13. _____
14. _____
15. _____

STUDY SCHEDULE FOR THIS SEMESTER

In this section, summarize the scheduling work you did in Chapter 2.

Courses	Time required per week
_____	_____
_____	_____
_____	_____
_____	_____
_____	_____
_____	_____

Hours Allocated for Studying this Semester:

Monday: _____

Tuesday: _____

Wednesday: _____

Thursday: _____

Friday: _____

Saturday: _____

Sunday: _____

MY WEEKLY SCHEDULE

TIME	MON	TUES	WED	THURS	FRI

MY WEEKEND STUDY SCHEDULE

TIME	SAT	SUN

FIXED EXPENSES AND INCOME

This section summarizes the financial planning you will do in Chapter 12. For the time being, you may wish to leave the section blank. You can either enter the appropriate figures now, or you can go back and plug in the numbers later after completing Chapter 12. Once you insert the data and project your total semester expenses and income, you may discover a shortfall (i.e., more expenses than income). You should indicate how you plan to deal with this situation.

PERSONAL BUDGET

Monthly Expenses		**Monthly Income**	
Rent:	$ _____	Part-time work:	$ _____
Car:	$ _____	Pell grant:	$ _____
Gas:	$ _____	SEOG grant:	$ _____
Insurance:	$ _____	Family:	$ _____
Oil & service:	$ _____	State grants:	$ _____
State registration:	$ _____	Disability:	$ _____
Parking fees:	$ _____	Unemployment ins.:	$ _____
Food:	$ _____	Loans:	$ _____
Entertainment:	$ _____	Interest:	$ _____
Personal/misc.:	$ _____	Social Security:	$ _____
Credit card payment:	$ _____		
MONTHLY TOTAL:	$ _____		
9 MONTHS LIVING EXPENSES:	$ _____		
Tuition:	$ _____		
Books/supplies:	$ _____		
Health fees:	$ _____		
Student fees:	$ _____		
Campus vehicle registration:	$ _____		
TOTAL 9 MONTHS	$ _____	(excluding summer school)	

Plan for dealing with a possible financial shortfall:

_____

_____

_____

_____

RISK FACTORS

In this section, list any factors that might interfere with attaining your educational goals. For example, you might list inadequate financial resources, pressure from your spouse or significant other to return to work or work full-time, loss of motivation, and grades. Be forthright.

1. _____

2. _____

3. _____

4. _____

5. _____

6. _____

7. _____

8. _____

9. _____

10. _____

11. _____

12. _____

THE OPPORTUNITY FOR ADVANCEMENT

In this section, discuss how you plan to use your education and degree or certification to avail yourself of specific opportunities in life. If you discontinued your education at some point, you might examine why you did so. You might describe what you've subsequently learned about life, competition, economics, career advancement, learning, and establishing a plan to make your life work.

_____

_____

_____

_____

_____

_____

_____

_____

SUCCESS FACTORS

In this section, discuss personal traits that you recognize and value in yourself that will ensure the attainment of your objectives. For example, you might state that you are tenacious, highly motivated, keenly aware of your obligation to provide more for your family, cognizant of your responsibility to repay loans, or eager to earn the respect of your family and associates.

1. _____

2. _____

3. _____

4. _____

5. _____

6. _____

7. _____

8. _____

9. _____

10. _____

POWERHOUSE THINKING

Key Principles for Academic Achievement

- Create a master plan for your education.
- Review the plan whenever you begin to run out of steam.
- Learn from your experiences (successes, miscalculations, and setbacks).
- Periodically adjust your PEP so that it is current and accurate.

Using DIBS

In your Personal Educational Plan, you listed several "risk factors" that might interfere with attaining your objectives. Select two of these factors or potential problems and use DIBS to solve each.

RISK FACTOR # 1:

Define: _____

Investigate: _____

_____

_____

_____

_____

Brainstorm: _____

_____

_____

_____

Select: _____

_____

RISK FACTOR # 2:

Define: _____

Investigate: _____

_____

_____

_____

_____

Brainstorm:
_____

_____

_____

_____

Select:
_____

_____

For Your Information

There are no magic pills or potions that you can take to transform yourself into a better student. As is the case with professional athletes, you must be prepared to train rigorously and dedicate yourself to attaining your personal goals. You must prioritize, make sacrifices, stretch yourself to the limit, and continually strive to improve and maximize your abilities.

Academic success requires that you learn actively, not passively. You cannot simply _hope_ to be a good student and get good grades. Learning and acquiring new skills must become your paramount preoccupation, and conscientious study must become your personal mantra. You must be prepared to work diligently, think analytically, and act strategically. Certain facts of life are immutable (cannot be altered):

1. The real world is highly competitive and can be very harsh.
2. Education is the key to advancement.
3. Learning can be one of life's most exciting and rewarding experiences.
4. Knowledge is power.
5. Success generates pride and self-confidence.
6. People without first-rate marketable skills are at risk for ending up at the bottom of the food chain.

Motivation is not an external force. Certainly, having the good fortune to take a course from an inspirational and dynamic instructor can enhance your desire to learn, but you should not count on charismatic instructors to motivate you. The desire to acquire knowledge, master new skills, and expand your career options must come from within. You must produce the zeal.

The baseball player racing for a line drive or the basketball player twisting her body to make a difficult lay-up may appear to react effortlessly and automatically. Those watching on the sidelines may not fully appreciate the hours that these athletes spend training their bodies to function efficiently. The casual fan may never fully appreciate the focused effort and intense motivation that drive consummate athletes to test their limits in the quest for excellence.

Most successful students also have to spend countless hours conditioning themselves to function effectively. Just as the serious athlete must continually practice to acquire and maintain a powerful golf swing, volleyball spike, or tennis serve, so, too, must the serious student continually practice to develop and maintain powerful academic skills. In time, the student begins to respond *automatically* when faced with challenges in the academic arena that demand focused planning, analytical thinking, consistent organization, and efficient time management.

As you begin to improve your scholastic performance, your self-confidence will expand commensurately. Your new skills will produce gratifying payoffs, pride, and satisfaction, and before long, you will become "addicted" to achievement. Success will stimulate your desire for more success, not only in school, but in all aspects of your life.

After completing this chapter, do not let your strategic planning skills slip away! Periodically examine and revise your long- and short-term goals, adjust your tactics, and fine-tune your personal strategy. With practice, the planning procedures will become an integral part of your life. Before long, you'll find yourself methodically mapping out projects without even being consciously aware that you are creating a strategy. You will plan *out of habit!*

HANDLING THE EDUCATIONAL SYSTEM AND YOUR FINANCES

OBJECTIVES

- Communicating successfully with instructors and administrators
- Developing strategies to impress instructors
- Responding strategically to mistakes and miscalculations
- Developing coping techniques for challenging situations
- Analyzing and managing personal finances
- Creating a budget

Getting the System to Work for You

Allison knew she had a major problem, and she was at a loss as to how to deal with it. She was carrying a D in her English class and a D in her math class. The realization that she might fail both courses and flunk out of college had thrown her into a depression. Because of the constant stress, she was having difficulty sleeping, and she and her boyfriend were now arguing every time they got together. Frustrated and demoralized, Allison had begun to think about dropping out of school.

School had always been a struggle—she had barely graduated from high school with a 2.1 G.P.A. After graduation, she worked for six months at a fast-food restaurant. Then, she got a job as a childcare worker at a preschool. Although the job was menial—monitoring the playground and supervising the children until their parents picked them up at night—she loved working with kids, and she decided that she wanted to become a kindergarten teacher. Her plan was to get an A.A. degree in child development and transfer to a four-year college to complete her B.A. and get a teaching credential. Her current academic dilemma had put this plan in serious jeopardy.

Allison's situation had become desperate. Despite four hours of studying every evening, she was struggling to comprehend and recall the assigned material. She had had the same problem in high school, and these negative associations with school had initially caused her to reject the idea of going to college. That decision, however, was made before she realized that she wanted to become a kindergarten teacher. Going to college and earning a B.A. degree were now very important to her.

After a great deal of vacillation, Allison finally summoned the courage to talk with her English instructor. When they met in the instructor's office, Allison struggled to find the words to explain her situation and describe her feelings.

Allison: I know I'm doing terribly in your class. You probably think that I'm not trying, but I do all of the assignments, and I spend four hours every evening studying. Reading has always been difficult for me, and I've always had trouble understanding the information in textbooks. I also have problems with writing. The truth is, I barely graduated from high school.

Dr. Logan: Have you discussed the problem with your advisor?

Allison: No.

Dr. Logan: From your description of the difficulties you're experiencing, Allison, I suspect that you may have a learning disability. Did you receive any learning assistance in high school?

Allison: I was in a resource program in elementary and middle school. I finished the program in 8th grade and was mainstreamed into regular classes.

Dr. Logan: Frankly, I don't know that much about learning problems. You need to discuss your situation with someone in the learning assistance center. They should be able to provide you with tutoring help. My course may be too advanced for you, and you may need to take a remedial English class first to help you improve your writing and comprehension skills. As you know, it's technically too late to drop my course because we're in the final four weeks of the semester. The director of the learning assistance program or your advisor, however, might be able to provide authorization for you to drop the course if they can document that you have a learning disability. You could take this class again after you've acquired the necessary basic skills. But you need to act now. If you wait too long and flunk, the F will be recorded on your transcript.

Allison: All I have to do is go to the learning assistance lab and ask to be tested?

Dr. Logan: That's my understanding. You should speak with your advisor first. She can tell you what the exact procedures are.

Allison: I have to do something. I'm beginning to ask myself why I'm banging my head against the wall. Maybe I should drop out. I'm also doing terribly in math, and I'm probably going to fail that course, too.

Dr. Logan: Your academic advisor can tell you about the tutoring and counseling resources available for students. Make an appointment to see her. There are safety nets to assist struggling students with legitimate problems. The key is to find out what help is available, then develop a plan for mastering the skills you need to catch up.

Allison: Well, I'll call my advisor tomorrow. Thanks for your help, Dr. Logan.

Although still discouraged, Allison at least knew that she could take steps to avoid failing her courses. She realized that it would be foolish not to take advantage of the resources at her college, and knew that the next move was up to her.

zooming in on the issues

Asking for Help

Allison's predicament was dire. Realizing that she could fail two courses, she decided to talk with her English instructor about the situation.

Evaluate this decision.

1	2	3	4	5	6	7	8	9	10
not smart			fairly smart					very smart	

Why did you reach this conclusion? _____

_____

_____

Allison's instructor provided her with important information. Go back to the story and underline and number each relevant point Dr. Logan made. (*Hint:* You should be able to find at least seven.)

How do you evaluate the information and recommendations the instructor provided?

1	2	3	4	5	6	7	8	9	10
poor				fair				excellent	

Are you aware of any other information about the learning assistance program that the instructor failed to mention? If so, list this information below.

1. _____

2. _____

3. _____

4. _____

5. _____

Evaluate Allison's conscientiousness.

1	2	3	4	5	6	7	8	9	10
poor				fair					excellent

Why did you reach this conclusion? _____

_____

_____

Predict the likelihood that Allison will ultimately handle her predicament.

1	2	3	4	5	6	7	8	9	10
poor				fair					excellent

Why did you reach this conclusion? _____

_____

_____

Predict the likelihood that Allison will ultimately earn her B.A. degree.

1	2	3	4	5	6	7	8	9	10
poor				fair					excellent

Why did you reach this conclusion? _____

_____

_____

Predict the likelihood that Allison will attain her goal and become a kindergarten teacher.

1	2	3	4	5	6	7	8	9	10
poor				fair					excellent

Why did you reach this conclusion? _____

_____

_____

Drawing a Conclusion from the Evidence

Having read about Allison's predicament, what specific conclusion can you draw from the information in the story? Using the *inductive method*, express in a well-crafted sentence what you have concluded. *Remember:* You are summarizing the **point** of the story.

The point of Allison's story: _____

_____

_____

_____

zooming out on the issues

What Instructors Require

Instructors evaluate and reward performance, and they give top grades to students who are diligent and do first-rate work. In much the same way that a basketball coach is highly critical of those players who do not "hustle" during practice or fail to give 100 percent during a game, instructors are critical of students who try to coast through a course with minimal effort. Strategic students understand the basic realities of the grading system: Instructors do not appreciate sloppy, incomplete, or late assignments; chronic absences; shoddy work; and inattentiveness in class.

Most instructors are generally willing to help conscientious students who are struggling academically and find themselves in a jam. At the same time, these instructors don't want to be manipulated with phony excuses. If asked for an accommodation such as an extension on an assignment, they generally require a legitimate and compelling reason before granting the request.

Your instructor may not be able to help you solve every problem, but he or she can usually point you in the right direction to find the appropriate assistance. The key to enlisting the support of your instructor or academic advisor is to communicate forthrightly, take responsibility for your miscalculations and mistakes, and demonstrate that you are motivated and conscientious.

Your ability to define problems precisely and identify the underlying issues accurately is critically important when conferencing with school personnel. You want to communicate clearly that you are willing to take responsibility for what happened and that you are prepared to assume a proactive role in seeking and implementing solutions to your predicaments.

The following guidelines can facilitate communication with instructors and advisors and increase the likelihood that you will establish good rapport and elicit cooperation and support.

KEYS TO SUCCESSFUL COMMUNICATION WITH COLLEGE PERSONNEL

1. **Be honest and candid.** *Example:* "My child is very sick, and I'm having difficulty concentrating on my schoolwork and completing my assignments on time."

2. **Don't blame others for your problems.** *Example:* "You never told the class that this material would be covered on the test."

3. **Express a genuine willingness to work hard to solve the problem.** *Example:* "I don't understand how to do these chemistry problems. Could I get together with you or your lab assistant this afternoon for some extra help?"

4. **Identify the issues as precisely as possible.** *Example:* "You've indicated that my essays have run-on sentences, nonparallel constructions, and sentence fragments. I'm not sure I understand what that means. Could you spend a few moments going over my last essay with me and explain the mistakes so that I can avoid them on the next essay?"

5. **Ask your instructors and advisor about resources that might be available at your school to help you.** *Example:* "I'm having trouble recalling the information in my textbooks. I read the material over and over, but I still can't seem to comprehend it."

6. **Before speaking with school personnel, carefully plan what you want to say, and express clearly what your difficulties and needs are.** *Example:* "I'll use DIBS to identify the causes and brainstorm some possible solutions to my problems in my criminal justice course before I talk with my instructor."

Using DIBS and the Four-Part Problem Solving System

Situation: Allison follows her instructor's suggestion and requests an evaluation at the learning assistance center. The tests confirm that she has significant reading problems. She signs up for remedial classes and receives an incomplete in her English class with the understanding that she will retake the class at a later date. This reduces the pressure and anxiety, but Allison must still deal with the problem she faces in her math class. Pretend you are Allison and use DIBS to handle this predicament. Remember to use "I" messages.

Define: _____

Investigate: _____

_____

_____

_____

Brainstorm: _____

_____

_____

_____

Select: _____

_____

Now, use the four-part problem-solving system to resolve Allison's problem.

FOUR-PART PROBLEM-SOLVING SYSTEM

Step 1:

Challenge: _____

_____

Step 2:

Long-term goals: _____

_____

Step 3:

Short-term goals: _____

_____

_____

_____

_____

_____

_____

_____

Step 4:

Specifics: _____

_____

_____

_____

_____

_____

_____

_____

Making a Good Impression

In many respects, college instructors and job supervisors perform parallel functions. These functions include:

- assigning tasks
- establishing deadlines
- evaluating your production
- rewarding or penalizing you for the quality of your performance and effort

College instructors have a great deal of control over your destiny. Their assessment of your abilities and work plays a pivotal role in whether you get the job you want after graduation, are admitted into a four-year college, or are accepted to graduate school. Given this impact, it is clearly in your best interests to make a positive impression.

Instructors dedicate their professional life to teaching in their area of specialization. That they have little patience, appreciation, or respect for students who are unmotivated, manipulative, uninterested in learning, and irresponsible is understandable.

Most instructors are quite perceptive about their students' attitude, motivation, and dedication, especially if they have been teaching for many years. If they conclude that a student is serious and conscientious, they are more likely to be supportive and affirming. If, however, they conclude that a student is lazy and irresponsible, they are more likely to be critical and nonsupportive. They are also likely to respond by giving the student poor grades.

Your mastery of the subject matter is the primary litmus test of your capabilities and diligence. You may not realize it, but instructors generally also consider their students' assimilation of the course content to be the primary litmus test of their own teaching efficacy. Most instructors work hard to teach effectively, and, in return, they expect you to work hard.

Strategic students are acutely aware of the benefits of making a positive impression on their instructors. They do everything possible to affirm their diligence and demonstrate on tests, homework assignments, reports, and projects that they have mastered the assigned material. They:

- attend class consistently
- come to class prepared
- review the assigned material before class
- participate in class discussions
- answer questions thoughtfully
- express interest in the course material
- communicate a desire to learn what is being taught
- apply what they have been taught
- follow directions
- complete assignments on time
- proofread their work carefully
- take pride in their accomplishments
- discuss problems and course-related issues with their instructors during office hours
- accept criticism nondefensively
- demonstrate motivation, diligence, and goal-oriented attitudes and behavior

Making a positive impression and communicating that you are intent on learning what your instructor considers important is not only strategic, it is also good psychology. Your attitudes and behaviors can build positive relationships and create allies—this is invaluable if you ever need your instructor's support.

Coping Skills

t's rare when everything in your life is working perfectly and all of the conditions are ideal. More likely than not, something will be amiss at any given time. For example, when you attempt to study, you may have to deal with noisy roommates, a loud TV, a crying infant, or rambunctious children. You may have to cope with the demands of a full-time job while dealing concurrently with the demands of two college courses. In your chemistry class, you may be assigned a lab partner who is lazy or incompetent, and you may have a boss who insists that you work overtime during finals week.

In some situations, problems cannot be totally resolved, and the best you can do is use functional coping skills. This capacity to handle less-than-perfect conditions is essential to survival in the real world. The realities of student life often require that you become a consummate juggler who must keep several balls in the air at the same time—job, school, family, and friends. With practice and focus, this juggling becomes easier and easier.

Brainstorming Practical Coping Mechanisms

Examine the following less-than-ideal situations and brainstorm practical coping mechanisms. The solutions need not be perfect, but they should prevent you from becoming incapacitated. For this exercise, do not use the complete DIBS method. Skip to the brainstorming step.

A. There are a dozen children in your neighborhood who make a great deal of noise when they play on the street. This disturbs you when you're trying to study.

PRACTICAL COPING MECHANISMS:

1. _____

2. _____

3. _____

B. You can't afford the insurance on your car, but you need it to get to school.

PRACTICAL COPING MECHANISMS:

1. _____

2. _____

3. _____

C. You don't get along with the lab assistant in your physics class.

PRACTICAL COPING MECHANISMS:

1. _____

2. _____

3. _____

D. Your Spanish instructor is assigning too much homework for you to complete in the time you've scheduled.

PRACTICAL COPING MECHANISMS:

1. _____

2. _____

3. _____

E. Your computer is broken, and it will take a week to repair it. You desperately need it to do your work.

PRACTICAL COPING MECHANISMS:

1. _____

2. _____

3. _____

F. They've raised the fees at your school. You don't know if you can afford to continue your studies.

PRACTICAL COPING MECHANISMS:

1. _____

2. _____

3. _____

Figuring Out Where You Stand

What are your responses to the following statements?

Winning is everything.   ○ I agree.   ○ I don't agree.   ○ Not sure.

Why did you respond this way?

_____

_____

Life is kill or be killed.   ○ I agree.   ○ I don't agree.   ○ Not sure.

Why did you respond this way?

_____

_____

The ends justify the means.   ○ I agree.   ○ I don't agree.   ○ Not sure.

Why did you respond this way?

_____

_____

Only the tough survive.   ◯ I agree.   ◯ I don't agree.   ◯ Not sure.

Why did you respond this way?

_____

_____

Only the ruthless get ahead.   ◯ I agree.   ◯ I don't agree.   ◯ Not sure.

Why did you respond this way?

_____

_____

To win in life, you've got to cut corners.   ◯ I agree.   ◯ I don't agree.   ◯ Not sure.

Why did you respond this way?

_____

_____

You can be smart and strategic and still be honest, moral, and ethical.

◯ I agree.   ◯ I don't agree.   ◯ Not sure.

Why did you respond this way?

_____

_____

Acting smart *doesn't translate* into being unethical or dishonest. It *doesn't translate* into taking advantage of other people. It *doesn't translate* into being manipulative, deceptive, or self-centered. It *doesn't mean* cutting corners illegally.

Acting smart *does mean* figuring out how to get from point A to point B to point C without getting battered and bloodied. It *does mean* using your head to figure out a practical strategy for getting what you want in school and in life. You can be smart without sacrificing your ethics and values. You can be smart and still have a moral compass that guides you through life.

POWERHOUSE THINKING

Key Principles for Communicating Successfully with Instructors

- Take responsibility for your decisions and actions.
- Demonstrate that you are conscientious and goal directed.
- Communicate forthrightly.
- Identify issues and extenuating circumstances precisely.
- Examine your study procedures critically and make appropriate strategic adjustments.
- Learn from your mistakes.

The "How Do I Pay for School?" Tango

Ricky's future looked bleak Monday afternoon when he went to the bank to check on how much money he had in his checking account after buying his books and paying his tuition. The ATM indicated that his balance was $432.67. This money would have to last for the entire semester. Unfortunately, it was only the second week of the semester.

Ricky realized he was in trouble. His rent was due in six days, and his roommates wouldn't accept any excuses. If he couldn't come up with his share on the day it was due, they would look for another roommate. His car insurance was also due in one week.

When Ricky decided to return to school after working construction for three years, he felt he had saved enough to cover his expenses for two years, assuming he lived frugally. At first, it seemed like everything was OK. But by the end of the first semester, Ricky sensed that he was spending more money than he had planned. He was dating quite a bit, and, despite three roommates, his rent was higher than he had anticipated. His car insurance, books, food, and entertainment expenses seemed astronomical. At the end of his first semester, he discovered he had used most of the money he had budgeted for the entire two years.

Ricky's plan was to earn his 60 units and graduate in two years. This meant going to school full-time, taking a minimum of 12 units each semester and attending summer school. Ricky realized that the sooner he got his degree, the sooner he could get a well-paying job. At times, he toyed with the idea of transferring to a state college and getting a B.A. degree. Now, everything was in jeopardy. If he couldn't pay his rent and meet his other obligations, he obviously couldn't stay in school.

One of Ricky's roommates suggested that he talk with someone in the financial aid office. He told Ricky there were funds available for students in financial need. The next morning, Ricky called the office and told the receptionist that he was in a crisis. She offered to set up an appointment with a financial aid officer in two days and instructed him to come to the office right away and pick up a form called the FAFSA (Free Application for Federal Student Aid) and a student financial aid guide published by the Department of Education. She told him to complete the student worksheets but not the actual federal loan application. The financial aid officer with whom he would be meeting, Mrs. Carlson, would review the worksheets with him, advise him of the stipulations, and answer his questions.

When he arrived at the financial aid office, Ricky was directed to Mrs. Carlson's office. She quickly reviewed the worksheets, and Ricky filled her in on the details of his predicament. From the sympathetic expression on Mrs. Carlson's face, Ricky could tell that she had heard many similar stories.

Mrs. Carlson: From what I gather, Ricky, you're essentially out of money.

Ricky: I'm broke. I'm not sure I can even make it through this month. I don't know how I messed up. Actually, that's not true. I know I miscalculated my expenses. I didn't have enough saved, and I spent too much the first semester. Unless I do something creative, I'm going to have to drop out. Is there any financial aid money available?

Mrs. Carlson: I hate to tell you this, but it's very late to begin looking for financial aid. The semester has begun, and the SEOG (Supplemental Educational Opportunity Grant) funds have already been distributed on a first-come, first-served basis. You can apply for a Pell Grant (another federally funded student aid program), but this could take over a month to process, and the amount you're awarded usually depends on your last year's income. How much did you earn last year?

Ricky: $29,000. I worked construction in Colorado.

Mrs. Carlson: Pell Grants range from $200 to $1,150 per semester. As I said, your last year's income is used to determine eligibility and the amount awarded. You won't qualify unless we can base your application on this year's income, and I don't think we can do it. Are you currently working part-time?

Ricky: No.

Mrs. Carlson: I'll have to check with an associate about the income limitation issue. I'm relatively new in this department, but I believe that if you earned more than $8,000 the previous year, you won't qualify for a Pell Grant. I'll make certain of this. You've told me you've spent most of your savings. Is there anyone in your family who can help you financially?

Ricky: My folks are retired and have a very limited income.

Mrs. Carlson: Ricky, you have several options: Borrow money from someone you know, apply for a federally insured loan, take fewer units and find a part-time job, lower your living expenses by moving in with your parents, or apply for a state grant. I recommend that you also look at our listing of scholarships, but you must realize that it's too late to get a scholarship for this semester. The immediate priority is to make up a budget and determine how much money you'll need to get through this semester. We also have workshops that show you how to apply for a federally insured bank loan for educational expenses, and we can help you complete the application. Unfortunately, it could take from four to six weeks to process the application and get approval, and it's clear that you have to do something right away. Step one is to determine your realistic minimal expenses for the semester. I'm going to give you the Cost of Attendance: Student Budgets brochure to help you get a realistic idea of your needs. Then we can try to find a way to get you through the semester. Come back and see me on Friday with your completed budget. On your way out, tell the person at the desk that you want to sign up for the next financial aid workshop.

After the meeting, Ricky went to the library, sat down at a table, and began to examine the material Mrs. Carlson gave him. It contained a breakdown of college

FIGURE 12.1	*Model nine-month budget, 2002–2003 academic year.*		
	AT HOME– RESIDENT	AWAY FROM HOME– RESIDENT	AWAY FROM HOME [NON-RESIDENT]
Enrollment Fees	$ 286	$ 286	$ 3,666
Health Fees	$ 24	$ 24	$ 24
Books & Supplies	$ 1,206	$ 1,206	$ 1,206
Food and Housing	$ 2,988	$ 7,704	$ 7,704
Transportation	$ 864	$ 990	$ 990
Personal/Misc.	$ 2,250	$ 2,250	$ 2,250
Total:	$ 7,618	$12,460	$15,840

fees and a sample nine-month budget (see Figure 12.1). Ricky was shocked—the typical budgeted expenses were more than twice what he had planned. He now realized how badly he had miscalculated his financial needs for the two years he allocated to complete his degree.

After examining the sample, Ricky filled in the figures for his personal budget worksheet (see Figure 12.2). Fortunately he was a state resident, but not living at home added significant expenses to his monthly budget.

When Ricky looked at the total expenses he would have for the nine-month period, he became very depressed. The amount didn't even include the expenses for the six units he planned to take at summer school. From the worksheet, Ricky was able to estimate how much money he would need just to get through the current semester by multiplying his monthly expenses by four and subtracting the expenses he had already paid. He then compared what he had in the bank with what he required, and it was a shocker! It was clear that he would have to make major adjustments if he was going to get through the semester, much less through graduation.

On Friday, Ricky took his budget to Mrs. Carlson. When she looked at it, she understood immediately why he looked so discouraged.

Mrs. Carlson: It can be an eye-opening experience to see the numbers on paper. You were right when you said you miscalculated.

Ricky: I can't believe how naive I was. I thought I had saved enough. When I started school, I had over $6,500 saved. I know I wasted money, but it's clear that I only had enough for one complete semester.

Mrs. Carlson: Let's look at what can be done now. It doesn't look like you can attend full-time unless you borrow money. To get a loan, you must allow at least one month for approval. You will somehow have to borrow money in the interim until the loan is approved. One possibility would be to ask your parents for help even though they have limited resources. You must decide if you want to do this or if this is even feasible. Another option is to attend school this semester part-time and get a part-time job to help with your

Ricky's current personal budget.   **FIGURE 12.2**

MONTHLY EXPENSES:		MONTHLY INCOME:		
Rent:	$ 195.00	Part-time work:	$	0
Car:		Pell grant:	$	0
Gas:	$ 150.00	SEOG grant:	$	0
Insurance:	$ 100.00	Family:	$	0
Oil & service:	$ 7.00	State grants:	$	0
State registration:	$ 7.00	Disability:	$	0
Parking fees:	$ 50.00	Unemployment ins.:	$	0
Food:	$ 250.00	Loans:	$	0
Entertainment:	$ 100.00	Interest	$	0
Personal/misc.:	$ 50.00	Social Security:	$	0
Credit card payment:	$ 100.00			
Monthly Total:	$ 1,009.00			

9 Months Living Expenses:	$ 9,081.00
Tuition:	$ 286.00
Books/supplies:	$ 1,260.00
Health fees:	$ 24.00
Student fees:	$ 10.00
Campus vehicle registration:	$ 14.00
Total 9 months	$10,675.00 (excluding summer school)

expenses. You can work full-time during the summer or, if the loan is approved, attend summer school. You also have to cut back on your expenses wherever possible. You may have to sell your car and rely on public transportation. On the other hand, if you get a job, you may need a car to get to work. You have to weigh these options carefully.

Ricky: It's really obvious that I'm going to have to go back to work part-time and take fewer units.

Mrs. Carlson: You can begin applying for grants for the fall semester now. You will qualify for a Pell Grant because your income this year will be less than $8,000. You can also see what scholarships are available. If it looks like you also need to borrow money next fall from the bank, you can begin the process early to ensure that you have the funds in time for school. Go home and decide which courses you can afford to take this semester. You obviously have to start looking right away for a part-time job. Construction pays well, and you have experience. Save your money and reduce your expenses where possible. It may take you a semester or two longer to complete school, but if you plan carefully, you'll get your degree. Sometimes, a person's timetable has to be adjusted so that it's more realistic. Just don't lose sight of your long-term goal: to get your degree. You can do it if you think and act smart.

Ricky: Well, I can't say I'm a happy camper right now, but, at least, I know what I have to do.

When Ricky arrived home that afternoon, he began to scan the help wanted section of the newspaper. It was obvious that he needed to start earning money if he was going to get through school. Working part-time and only being able to attend school part-time were major disappointments and an inconvenience, but he was certain that he could figure out a way to get back on track and finish what he had started.

Making Astute Judgments About Finances

Not all of life's most difficult decisions involve moral or ethical issues. Many involve money and how to allocate financial resources.

Financial demands can be a major source of stress and anxiety for students with limited resources and seemingly limitless expenses. Many students must do a continuous juggling act and somehow find creative ways to pay their living and school expenses from limited savings and limited income. Even students who receive financial help from their family may face problems because many parents cannot provide all of the necessary funds. Adult students who return to school, of course, can rarely rely on their parents for help. Most must somehow figure out how to fund their education with savings, grants, loans, and part-time work.

Financial pressures combined with academic pressures can be overwhelming, and the temptation to give up and drop out may seem very appealing. The alternative is for students to use their analytical-thinking and problem-solving skills to figure out how to budget their resources.

EXAMINING YOUR FINANCES

If you are having a difficult time juggling your personal finances, you'll have to go through the same process Ricky did and write down the figures. Then, you'll have to "crunch" the numbers until you're able to come up with a budget that's realistic and practical. Use the budget form on the following page. If coming up with a workable budget seems to be an impossibility, make an appointment with a counselor in the financial aid office. The counselor can explore your options with you. (*Please note:* The figures cited in the nine-month budget are for a typical California community college. Because your fees and living expenses may be different, refer to relevant figures for your school and geographical area. If you are attending a public or private four-year college or university, the figures will obviously be very different.)

PERSONAL BUDGET

Monthly Expenses		Monthly Income	
Rent:	$ _____	Part-time work:	$ _____
Car:	$ _____	Pell grant:	$ _____
Gas:	$ _____	SEOG grant:	$ _____
Insurance:	$ _____	Family:	$ _____
Oil & service:	$ _____	State grants:	$ _____
State registration:	$ _____	Disability:	$ _____
Parking fees:	$ _____	Unemployment ins.:	$ _____
Food:	$ _____	Loans:	$ _____
Entertainment:	$ _____	Interest:	$ _____
Personal/misc.:	$ _____	Social Security:	$ _____
Credit card payment:	$ _____		
MONTHLY TOTAL:	$ _____		
9 MONTHS LIVING EXPENSES:	$ _____		
Tuition:	$ _____		
Books/supplies:	$ _____		
Health fees:	$ _____		
Student fees:	$ _____		
Campus vehicle registration:	$ _____		
TOTAL 9 MONTHS	$ _____	(excluding summer school)	

If you're not actually having financial problems or if you have already carefully budgeted your expenses, fill out the form anyway, for practice. The exercise will help you create a formal budget, and the form will provide a comprehensive overview of how you are allocating your resources. If you are struggling financially or haven't yet carefully developed a budget, the worksheet is a critically important tool to help you determine your needs.

THINKING SMART WHEN THE NUMBERS DON'T COMPUTE

It is vital that you plan strategically if you don't have adequate funds to cover your school and living expenses. Most problems can be solved if you think analytically, rationally, and logically.

Let's say that you use DIBS to get a handle on your financial problem. You defined the problem as *not having enough money.* You identified the causes as *too many expenses and too little money saved.* You're now in the brainstorming phase. Write all of the possible solutions to your problem below—list every conceivable (but legal) idea. Be creative.

1. _____

2. _____

3. _____

4. _____

5. _____

6. _____

7. _____

8. _____

9. _____

10. _____

11. _____

12. _____

If you feel overwhelmed, discuss your worksheet with a counselor in the financial aid office. He or she may have other ideas and suggestions (e.g., loans, grants, co-op jobs).

Most people can expect to have financial problems at some point in their lives. People who think strategically analyze challenging situations rationally, decide what they have to do, and then create a logical and systematic strategy for solving the problem and attaining their objective.

In Chapter 11, you completed a Personal Educational Plan. If you left the Fixed Expenses and Income section blank, go back now and plug in the numbers.

For Your Information

All students must be concerned about making a positive impression on those who can affect their future. These people may include a supervisor at work, a coach, or an instructor in college. Those who are responsible for evaluating your attitude, effort, and performance seek to identify specific traits, including:

1. honesty
2. effort
3. motivation
4. goal-directedness
5. logical, analytical-thinking skills
6. planning skills
7. ability to learn from mistakes

8. follow-through

9. attention to details

10. conscientiousness

11. ability to work and cooperate with others

12. resilience

13. respect

14. initiative

15. willingness to learn

16. desire to improve

17. enthusiasm

18. pride in accomplishments

19. confidence (but *not* arrogance and egotism)

Communicating to your instructors that you possess these qualities is unquestionably strategic. Examining a problem and soliciting advice from your instructor before a disaster occurs is also unquestionably strategic. Most instructors are willing to provide reasonable help if they believe you are serious about solving your dilemma and that you are responsible, conscientious, and willing to work. Although they certainly don't want to feel they are being manipulated into feeling sorry for you, they will usually offer assistance if they are convinced that:

- you have a genuine problem
- your request for help is reasonable and legitimate
- you are being forthright
- you are committed to prevailing over the problem.

Finding out what resources are available at your school if you run into an academic or financial problem is the first step in addressing problems strategically. Advisors and instructors are vital sources of information about these resources, and it makes sense to request their assistance and input.

When you buy a new computer, there is usually a toll-free number you can call for technical support and advice. If your computer is malfunctioning, it is foolish not to avail yourself of this service. You are equally foolish not to take advantage of the educational and financial support systems that exist at your school if you are experiencing difficulties.

13

DECISIONS, CONSEQUENCES, AND OUTCOMES

OBJECTIVES

- Avoiding problems
- Analyzing and handling moral dilemmas and hard choices
- Applying cause-and-effect principles
- Combining analytical thinking and cause-and-effect principles when making decisions
- Recognizing the decision point
- Analyzing and learning from mistakes

A Hard Choice

Things had become desperate, and Stephanie felt she was going to have a nervous breakdown. She hadn't read or taken notes on the assigned chapters in her chemistry class, and she had fallen hopelessly behind doing the experiments. She also hadn't handed in her lab notebook for the last two weeks. The lab notebook, which was supposed to be submitted after completing each experiment, would represent 40 percent of her grade in the course.

Stephanie figured she was carrying a D+ into the final. The most pressing problem, however, was her lab notebook. If she didn't hand it in by the end of the semester, she would flunk the course. If she flunked the course, she wouldn't graduate in June, and she would have to postpone looking for a better job. Her G.P.A. would be lower, and this might undermine her long-range plan of going to graduate school and becoming a social worker. Just thinking about the chain reaction of negative consequences from flunking the chemistry course was enough to drive Stephanie crazy.

There was a reasonable explanation for having fallen behind, but Stephanie didn't think her instructor would be sympathetic. Her son had fallen off his skateboard and suffered a compound fracture of his arm. There had been complications. To drain the infection, the doctor had to remove the cast. Stephanie spent almost two entire weeks taking care of Keith, who was unable to attend school. She just didn't have time to go to the lab and do the experiments.

When her best friend said she had a solution to the problem, Stephanie was eager to listen. Tameka had taken the same chemistry course the previous semester and had gotten an A–. She told Stephanie to copy her lab notebook. If she was challenged about not being in lab during the assigned times, she could claim that she did the experiments during her free time. Tameka had taken the class from a different instructor, and she assured Stephanie that her own instructor would never know she hadn't actually done the experiments. The instructor would simply look through the notebook to make sure Stephanie had followed the correct procedures and had properly recorded the experiment results.

Tameka's idea was very tempting, but Stephanie was troubled. She had never cheated before—at least, not in college. She liked her instructor, Dr. Fujita, and it seemed like a betrayal to deceive him. On the other hand, Stephanie certainly couldn't afford to flunk the course. She had invested too much time and money in getting her degree. Rationalizing that it wouldn't really matter if she copied the notebook, she tried to convince herself that the important thing was to complete the requirements without any hitches and get a good job. She had a responsibility to her family, and that took precedence over any pangs of conscience. "Copying someone's lab notebook isn't such a big deal!" she told herself. "I'll still be learning something." Convinced that her problem was solved, Stephanie breathed a sigh of relief.

Although she had spent hours wrestling with her decision and had decided to follow Tameka's suggestion, Stephanie still continued to think about this plan. One of the deciding factors was the likelihood that Dr. Fujita would want some type of verification from a lab assistant that she had actually gone to the lab and done the experiments. Stephanie, of course, would not have been able to provide this verification. As she considered both the immorality of cheating and the consequences of getting caught, her enthusiasm for the scheme evaporated. She realized she could not go through with it.

After changing her mind about copying Tameka's lab notebook, Stephanie realized that she had to develop a new strategy for passing her chemistry course. Summoning all of her courage, she made an appointment to see Dr. Fujita. As she entered his office, she took a deep breath. She had decided to tell him the truth. She fully expected him to say that he was sorry but that there was nothing he could do.

Stephanie: Dr. Fujita, I have to explain why I haven't handed in my lab notebook the last two weeks, and why I've not been in class or gone to the lab. My son had an accident on his skateboard and broke his arm. There were complications after the surgery, and he developed an infection and a fever. I'm a single parent, and I have no relatives in town to help me take care of him. I've had to stay home, and I couldn't get to the lab. Kevin is feeling a lot better now, and he should be able to go back to school on Monday.

Dr. Fujita: I'm sorry to hear that your son was so sick. I'm glad he's getting better.

Stephanie: The problem is I've fallen so far behind that I don't think I can ever catch up. My grade is now a D. I know I can get a C or even a B– if I have the time to study for the final, do my experiments, and write them up.

Dr. Fujita: Are you doing poorly in your other courses?

Stephanie: I think I can get a B– in Spanish if I study hard for the final, and I think I can get a C+ or B– in computer science. I was able to study at home while Kevin was sleeping. The class I'm really worried about is chemistry.

Dr. Fujita: I'd hate to see you get a D or an F, Stephanie. I'm glad you didn't do something dumb like copying someone else's lab notebook. We're pretty good at figuring out when someone hasn't actually done the experiments. If you get me a letter from your son's doctor confirming what you've told me, I can give you an incomplete for the semester. You can do your experiments during the first two weeks of next semester and use the semester break to study for the final. You can take the exam when you're ready. Does this plan work for you?

Stephanie: That would be great! Thank you! What a relief.

Dr. Fujita: Once you give me the note from your son's doctor, I'll fill out the paperwork for the incomplete, and I'll see you next semester.

Stephanie couldn't believe how easy it had been. Her heart had skipped a beat when Dr. Fujita brought up the subject of copying someone else's lab notebook. As she left his office, she felt euphoric. She had a new lease on life!

on the issues

Handling Temptations

As Stephanie wrestled with how to handle her problem, Tameka's solution seemed very appealing. It appeared to be an easy way for Stephanie to get out of the jam. After going through the difficult process of weighing her options and considering potential consequences, Stephanie arrived at the **decision point.** She decided to tell her instructor the truth.

How do you rate this decision?

1	2	3	4	5	6	7	8	9	10

not smart   fairly smart   very smart

Why did you evaluate her decision this way? _____

_____

_____

List the potential positive and negative consequences if Stephanie had agreed to do as Tameka suggested. After each consequence, indicate whether the outcome would have been **possible** or **probable.**

Potential Consequence #1: _____

  ○ possible   ○ probable

Potential Consequence #2: _____

  ○ possible   ○ probable

Potential Consequence #3: _____

  ○ possible   ○ probable

After Stephanie decided not to copy Tameka's lab notebook, she arrived at a second decision point. Underline this decision point in the story, write it below, and evaluate her decision.

Stephanie's second decision point: _____

_____

1	2	3	4	5	6	7	8	9	10

not smart   fairly smart   very smart

If you faced a similar situation, and explained the problem to an instructor, would you expect a supportive or nonsupportive response?

  ○ supportive   ○ non-supportive

Why did you reach this conclusion? _____

_____

_____

If Dr. Fujita had not been sympathetic, and Stephanie received an F in the course, do you believe she would have regretted being honest?

○ yes   ○ no   ○ perhaps

Do you believe she would have been able to bounce back from the setback?

○ yes   ○ no   ○ perhaps

Do you think that right and wrong are *relative* (flexible according to the situation) or *absolute* (inflexible)?

○ relative   ○ absolute

Why did you reach this conclusion? _____

_____

_____

Drawing a Conclusion from the Evidence

Having read about and carefully examined Stephanie's dilemma, what specific conclusion can you draw from the information presented in the story? Using the *inductive method*, express in a well-crafted sentence what you have concluded. *Remember:* You are summarizing the **point** of the story.

The point of Stephanie's story: _____

_____

_____

_____

_____

zooming out on the issues

Confronting Moral Dilemmas

It's impossible to go through life without making difficult decisions. Only after the decision is made can you tell whether it was right or wrong. In Stephanie's case, however, significant moral and ethical issues compounded the challenge of making the right choice. Stephanie quickly realized that because of her values, she would be tormented if she cheated. When she spoke with her instructor, she discovered that her decision had been the correct one, not only ethically but also functionally. Her instructor was willing to give her an incomplete and let her finish the course requirements after the semester ended.

Sometimes, you may *never be certain* that you made the right choice. For example, you may have two job offers after graduation, and you select the one that you believe is best. Even though you may be comfortable with your decision, you may wonder from time to time what might have happened had you chosen the other offer. Of course, if you're unhappy with your choice, you'd probably speculate a great deal about what "might have been," and you may regret your decision. This conundrum is undoubtedly the origin of the expression, "Never look back." Of course, in reality, you *should* look back if you conclude that you made the wrong call in a particular situation. Your critical and strategic analysis of what happened can help you avoid repeating the mistake if you are later confronted with a similar situation.

At times, you may find yourself tempted to run away from making tough choices. In extreme situations involving monumental decisions, stress and second-guessing may cause you to become so emotionally immobilized that you find yourself unable to make any decision at all. For example, one voice inside your head may say, "I shouldn't take a job with a start-up company because there's no job security." Another voice may say, "I should seize this opportunity and get in on the ground floor at a new and dynamic company with a great growth potential." As you struggle with your decision, you may appear indecisive and find yourself "flip-flopping." This indecisiveness is frustrating not only for you, but also for everyone around you. On Monday, you add the pros and cons and come up with one tally, and on Tuesday, you do the "math" again and come up with a totally different score.

As you wrestle with major decisions, your mind is consciously and unconsciously processing and evaluating an array of issues and considerations. You are factoring into the decision-making process not only pertinent data, but also relevant feelings. For example, a friend may ask you to tell a lie in court to help him win a lawsuit. He tries to convince you that no one would ever be able to prove that you are lying. He also tells you he would do the same favor for you. All he's asking you to do is tell a small lie. In your mind, you weigh the pros and cons. On the one hand, you realize your friend will be very upset if you refuse to help him. On the other hand, you realize that if you do as he asks, you will be committing perjury and taking a big risk. One voice tells you, "Help your friend!" Another voice tells you, "It's wrong for him to ask me to lie in court. It's not only illegal, but it is also morally wrong. Don't be a fool and take the risk!" All the while, you're probably angry at your friend for putting you in this bind—creating a moral dilemma and causing you internal conflict.

As Stephanie struggled with her own moral dilemma, she had to make a "hard" choice. Her decision could conceivably have had a major impact on her life. If she flunked, she would have to retake the course. Precious time would be wasted. Her G.P.A. would be lowered. She might not graduate on time, and this would postpone the income she was planning on earning. If she got caught, she might possibly be expelled.

At the same time, Stephanie's decision tested her morals and values. She could choose to copy the lab book and cheat, rationalizing that she had no alternative if she wanted to pass the course and get her degree. Or she could be honest and forthright with her instructor without any guarantee that he would be supportive.

Moral dilemmas are excruciating when there appear to be extenuating circumstances or compelling practical considerations that can be used as a conscious or unconscious rationale for not acting with honesty and integrity. The following inventory examines hypothetical dilemmas that highlight the potential conflict that can result when ethics appear to be pitted against pragmatic self-interests and seemingly "easy" solutions to complex issues.

Moral Dilemma Inventory

	Yes	No	Perhaps
1. Would you refuse to help a good friend if you concluded that by helping, you are placing yourself at legal risk?	○	○	○
2. Would you refuse to help a good friend if you concluded that by helping, you are placing yourself financially at risk?	○	○	○
3. Would you refuse to help a good friend even though you realize you will suffer a great deal of guilt by refusing?	○	○	○
4. If you explain that you can't help because you would be putting yourself at risk, do you believe your friend would feel betrayed?	○	○	○
5. Would you ever place the best interests of a friend or loved one ahead of your own?	○	○	○
6. Should a good friend ask you to do something dishonest?	○	○	○
7. Would you ask a good friend to do something dishonest to help you?	○	○	○
8. Would you lie, cheat, or steal to help a friend?	○	○	○
9. Would you lie, cheat, or steal to get what you want?	○	○	○
10. Would you be willing to make a highly unpopular decision if you are convinced that it's the right thing to do?	○	○	○
11. Would a good friend get over being angry at you if you refuse to do a favor (e.g., make a loan)?	○	○	○
12. Is it possible to refuse to help a friend even though the friend may not understand or appreciate that what you're doing is right?	○	○	○
13. Would you do a good deed even though no one would ever know about what you did?	○	○	○
14. If you believe a friend is making a seriously flawed or dangerous decision, would you intervene and risk losing the friendship?	○	○	○
15. Would you ask a family member to lie to protect you?	○	○	○
16. Would you be willing to sacrifice a friendship if preserving the friendship meant violating your principles, ethics, or morality?	○	○	○
17. Do you believe that you are responsible for your own decisions and behavior and for the consequences that might result from any flawed judgments?	○	○	○

18. Does an "inner voice" guide you morally and
    ethically?   ○   ○   ○

19. If you possess this inner voice, do you trust
    and follow it?   ○   ○   ○

20. Do you rationalize and justify behavior that
    you know is unethical or immoral?   ○   ○   ○

INTERPRETING THE MORAL DILEMMA INVENTORY

Responses to the questions in the inventory are likely to vary, depending on each person's personal values, ethics, principles, and beliefs. Some people view morality as flexible (e.g., "It won't really hurt anyone if I copy my lab partner's lab book") and determined by real-world considerations (e.g., "Bombing this enemy-controlled village and causing severe collateral civilian casualties is an unavoidable cost during wartime"). Others see morality as inflexible and determined by deeply felt precepts such as those encapsulated in the Ten Commandments.

Each person must struggle with life's moral dilemmas and must choose a path that is congruent with his or her personal ethics. For many, strongly held religious beliefs and imbued family values play key roles in the decision-making process. Legal consequences must also be considered because society provides sanctions and punishment for behavior it deems unacceptable. Theft and perjury are felonies that can lead to prosecution and prison. Parallel codes of acceptable and unacceptable behavior also, of course, exist in the academic arena. Cheating is a clear-cut honor code violation that can lead to expulsion, and plagiarism is all but certain to produce an F.

When a difficult choice is compounded by a difficult moral dilemma, the challenge of making the right decision increases exponentially. Under these conditions, the most effective way to handle the challenge is to think rationally, assess the pros and cons carefully, anticipate the potential consequences, consider one's personal values and beliefs, and act consistently with the conclusion that *seems or feels right*. Once you make the decision, resist any temptation to "second guess" yourself. If your decision ultimately proves to be flawed, you must be able to rebound emotionally, analyze the situation and the outcome objectively, learn from any miscalculations that were made, and do everything in your power to avoid repeating the mistake.

POWERHOUSE THINKING

Five Procedures for Handling Moral Dilemmas

- Consider the potential emotional, spiritual, and legal consequences of your choices (e.g., guilt, remorse, shame, pride, and self-esteem).
- Filter your options through your values and feelings.
- Factor conventions, rules, and laws into your decision-making process.
- Resist acting impetuously or impulsively.
- Trust what your "inner voice" tells you is right or wrong.

EXAMINING A "HARD CHOICE" IN YOUR LIFE

In life, you can expect to confront dilemmas that sorely test your mental, emotional, and moral resources. Sometimes, the right decision is obvious. In other situations, you may struggle for days or even weeks before you decide what to do. Even after making a decision you believe is right, you may have "second thoughts" and begin to doubt the wisdom of your choice. For example, you may decide to break off an engagement or get a divorce and then have grave misgivings about your decision. You may choose to accept or pass up a business opportunity. You may feel that you must "lay down the law" and punish a misbehaving child, and, in so doing, cause the child to become upset and angry, or you may choose to overlook the transgression. Depending on your decision, you may question whether you are being too harsh or too lenient.

A Hard Choice

In the space below, describe a situation in which you had to make an especially tough decision. This situation may have occurred at home, on the job, in school, or with a friend. Include how you finally handled the situation.

_____

_____

_____

_____

_____

_____

_____

_____

_____

_____

_____

_____

   In hindsight, you may now be able to identify the underlying issues with greater clarity. This ability to analyze and evaluate situations objectively is generally enhanced when you have greater distance from the actual situation. For this reason, it makes sense, whenever possible, to "sleep on" a major decision. While you sleep, your unconscious mind usually continues to process the problem and sort out the issues. In the morning, you often discover that you have a new perspective and new insights. Solutions that didn't occur to you the previous day may now be obvious.

   If you have sufficient emotional distance from the "hard choice" you described and can examine the situation objectively, _identify as many underlying issues as you can that might have created the dilemma or influenced your decision._ For example: "I believe my child misbehaved during Thanksgiving dinner because he was angry that I didn't take him to the park that morning as I had promised."

1. _____

   _____

2. _____

   _____

3. _____

   _____

4. _____

   _____

5. _____

   _____

If you were struggling with the same hard choice today, would you respond differently?

○ yes   ○ no   ○ not sure

What might you do differently? _____

_____

_____

Why would you make these changes? _____

_____

_____

_____

Using DIBS

On page 284, a hypothetical situation was given in which a friend asks you to tell a lie in court to help him win a lawsuit. He tries to convince you that no one could prove that you are lying, and he tells you he would do the same favor for you.

Some people would immediately reject this request for moral and ethical reasons. Others might refuse because of the potential legal consequences. They realize that lying in court is perjury, and that if the collusion (plot or conspiracy) is ever discovered, they would be in serious trouble. For these compelling reasons, saying "no" is a "no-brainer," and the refusal is automatic.

Let's say that you are someone who would experience inner conflict if faced with this situation. Your friend has done many favors for you in the past, and you have shared many personal problems and feelings. You realize that this person has always been loyal and supportive, and you also realize that if the tables were turned and you asked him to lie for you, he would probably agree to do so. Despite the voice in your head that tells you to help your friend, you have grave misgivings. Every instinct tells you that you would be making a mistake if you agree to the plan.

Use DIBS to handle the dilemma that your friend's request has triggered. Remember to use "I" messages.

Define: _____

Investigate: _____

_____

_____

_____

Brainstorm: _____

_____

_____

_____

Select: _____

_____

MAKING MORAL AND ETHICAL JUDGMENT CALLS

Imagine that you find a wallet on a seat in an airport waiting area. Your plane is about to leave. You wrestle with what to do. Should you give the wallet to the gate attendant? Should you take the money? No one seems to be watching. You look inside and see a picture of an elderly woman and her family, and from the other contents, you conclude that the wallet is hers. Perhaps you know without a doubt that you would turn in the wallet. Perhaps you know that you would take the money and leave the wallet on the seat. Or perhaps you're not sure what you would do.

Let's assume you are wrestling with the decision of whether or not to turn in the wallet. Describe the issues you might consider if you were faced with this situation.

1. _____

2. _____

3. _____

4. _____

5. _____

6. _____

As previously stated, some people would argue that moral issues involving honesty, loyalty, ethics, integrity, and fidelity are _absolute_ (i.e., inflexible). Most who think this way rely on ingrained family values or strongly-felt religious beliefs as a moral compass. Others might argue that moral and ethical issues are _relative_ (i.e., flexible and linked to existing conditions and extenuating circumstances). The relativists contend that each situation must be individually evaluated without preconceptions.

In the following situation, consider *how* you would respond and *why* you would choose this response.

> **Scenario:** You observe a very intoxicated man who can hardly stand up trying to unlock the driver's door to his van. Inside the van, you can see several children. You realize that once the man unlocks the door and gets inside, he will drive away.

In this situation, do you believe that you have a moral obligation to intervene and do everything you can to prevent him from driving off with the children?

○ yes   ○ no   ○ not sure

Is this obligation absolute or relative?

○ absolute   ○ relative   ○ not sure

Would you be willing to prevent the man from driving away with the children even though your intervention might precipitate an argument and even an altercation?

○ yes   ○ no   ○ not sure

When you believe something bad is "going down," do you believe you have a moral obligation to intervene actively?

○ yes   ○ no   ○ under certain circumstances   ○ not sure

Do you believe that people have a moral obligation to serve as a Good Samaritan no matter what the risks are?

○ yes   ○ no   ○ under certain circumstances   ○ not sure

Do you believe morality is:

○ absolute   ○ relative   ○ not sure

Why do you believe this?

_____

_____

Are there issues or values about which you feel so strongly that you are inflexible? In other words, do these issues fall into the category of being absolute? If so, list them below.

1. _____

2. _____

3. _____

4. _____

5. _____

6. _____

Select one of the issues or values you've listed and explain why you believe this issue is absolute.

_____

_____

_____

_____

_____

_____

Are there any moral issues that you believe are relative? For example, do you believe it's OK to cheat a "little" when you do your taxes? Do you believe that under certain circumstances it's OK to tell white lies? If you do believe some moral issues are relative, list examples below; otherwise, leave this section blank.

1. _____

2. _____

3. _____

4. _____

5. _____

6. _____

Select one of these issues or values you listed and explain why you believe this issue is relative.

_____

_____

_____

_____

_____

_____

Practice Dealing with Dilemmas

Examine the following situations and explain how you might respond.

You see someone cheating on an exam.

What action would you take?

_____

_____

Why would you respond this way?

_____

You see your neighbor forcefully slap her child on the face.

What action would you take?

_____

Why would you respond this way?

_____

You see three 13-year-olds beating up another youth in the park.

What action would you take?

_____

Why would you respond this way?

_____

You hear some coworkers telling an offensive racial joke.

What action would you take?

_____

Why would you respond this way?

_____

Your teenage daughter tells you that the son of your good friend is taking drugs.

What action would you take?

_____

Why would you respond this way?

_____

A friend tells you her husband is beating her.

What action would you take?

_____

Why would you respond this way?

_____

You see a friend psychologically abusing his child (making fun of him and calling him stupid).

What action would you take?

_____

Why would you respond this way?

_____

You see someone shoplift from a supermarket.

What action would you take? _____

_____

Why would you respond this way? _____

_____

You see your supervisor sexually harass a coworker.

What action would you take? _____

_____

Why would you respond this way? _____

_____

You see a neighbor's 13-year-old child selling drugs to other kids on your street.

What action would you take? _____

_____

Why would you respond this way? _____

_____

You suspect a coworker is embezzling money from the company where you work.

What action would you take? _____

_____

Why would you respond this way? _____

_____

CONSIDERING THE CONSEQUENCES OF CHOICES

Perhaps you have heard the expression "For every action, there is a reaction." This axiom (self-evident truth) is particularly relevant when it comes to making decisions and experiencing the positive or negative consequences or effects of those decisions.

You continually make choices that affect your life to varying degrees. Some of these choices are relatively inconsequential. For example, selecting a gray shirt or blue slacks to wear to work is not going to have a major impact on your life. Deciding on an action movie versus a romantic comedy may positively or adversely affect the quality of a particular Saturday night, but the long-term effects of this decision are obviously negligible.

Some decisions can be monumentally important and literally alter the course of your life. Examples include deciding to drop out of school, experimenting with drugs such as Ecstasy or crack cocaine, or driving a motorcycle without a helmet. A judgment error at one of life's key decision points might literally ruin your life.

That well-reasoned decisions significantly increase the likelihood of experiencing success is beyond question. For example, let's say you are assigned a research paper in a biology class, and you decide that you want to get at least a B+ on the paper. You diligently do your research, methodically take notes, painstakingly compose your first draft, carefully revise and edit your first draft before writing a second draft, and meticulously proofread the final version. The decision to make this effort is clearly directed toward attaining a specific goal; namely, to improve your chances of getting a good grade on the paper.

That unwise or thoughtless decisions significantly increase the likelihood of your experiencing negative and, in some cases, catastrophic consequences is also beyond question. For example, let's say you go to a party, drink several beers, become inebriated, and then decide to drive home. Clearly, you are at risk for getting into an accident and hurting yourself and others. You are also in serious jeopardy of being arrested for drunk driving. Your decision to drive while intoxicated would then produce a chain reaction of additional consequences: a suspended or rescinded driver's license, dramatically increased insurance rates, probable jail time, and profound lifelong remorse if you injured or killed an innocent person.

In many respects, life is a series of choices. You arrive at a crossroad, and you select a path. Someone who knows he'll be drinking at a party may make arrangements for a friend to be the designated driver. Someone else may think about having a designated driver, but not follow through. A third person may not even consider the probable consequences of driving while intoxicated. He begins to drink and gives no thought as to how he's going to get home after the party. Nor does he give any thought to the potentially disastrous repercussions of driving under the influence.

When faced with important decisions, smart people carefully analyze the situation and consider *in advance* the potential ramifications of their choices. People who aren't smart make key choices without careful deliberation or forethought. They often discover after it's too late that they've gone down the wrong path. Drifting through life in cerebral neutral and acting mindlessly, these people repeatedly miscalculate, sabotage themselves, take unnecessary risks, and significantly reduce their chances of attaining their personal goals. Because they rarely learn from their mistakes and fail to appreciate basic cause-and-effect principles, they make the same errors over and over again.

People who disregard the potential repercussions of their choices may be intelligent, but they are not particularly smart. They may possess the capacity to think logically and excel in school and in their careers, but they may manifest chronically poor judgment and appear intent on not availing themselves of their intellectual capabilities. Having never learned how to apply their intelligence functionally, they are destined to collide repeatedly with life's harsh realities. They are also at risk for becoming lifelong underachievers who consistently under-perform in school and on the job.

THE DECISION POINT

Imagine standing on a beach and gazing at a turbulent ocean. As you watch the towering waves crash down, you wrestle with the decision about whether or not to go into the water. You can tell by the drag of the water eddying around your ankles that there is a powerful undertow. You drove two hours to get to the beach, but you are hesitant to dive into the surf because you recognize that you are only an average swimmer. As you scan the ocean, you see only two people in the water. Both are wearing wetsuits and are on surfboards. You also observe that there are no lifeguards on the beach. You may not realize it, but you are facing a monumentally important decision. If you make the wrong choice, you could drown.

Not all important decisions, however, involve life-threatening situations. As the following story attests, some decisions may not be life-threatening, but they can certainly be life-altering.

Weighing the Pluses and Minuses

Jessie was worried. He was barely passing his math class, and he needed the course to earn his degree. For as long as he could remember, math had been a nightmare. He could do the basics: add, subtract, multiply, and divide, and he could usually handle problems involving fractions, percentages, and decimals. He had difficulty, however, with ratios, word problems, and especially with solving algebraic equations. Unfortunately, these were the types of problems that would be on the math final.

When Jessie added up his test grades, he realized he was carrying a D into the final. If he flunked the exam, he would get an F. To get a C in the course, he had to get at least a C+ on the exam, and getting a C+ seemed impossible. Despite the hours he had spent struggling to make sense out of the examples and problems in his textbook, he was still confused. Even when he did finally figure out how to do a challenging problem, it didn't seem to help when he confronted similar problems on a test. He'd become confused all over again—and the more confused he got, the more he would panic.

The final exam would be in three days, and Jessie was discouraged. He desperately wanted a C in the course, but he felt certain that he was going to fail the exam. Flunking the course would obviously pose a major problem.

When Collin approached Jessie with the idea of stealing a copy of the final exam, Jessie was stunned. Having a copy of the test was very tempting, especially since he might not pass the course otherwise. Collin told Jessie the instructor would leave the exam at the faculty copy center to be photocopied. Security was strict, but Collin had a friend who worked at the center. He had helped his friend out of a serious jam, and he owed Collin a favor.

Collin told Jessie that he could get a copy of the test 24 hours in advance. He would ask another friend who was a math whiz to solve the problems. All they needed to do was memorize the solutions, and they would both be able to get an A on the test. He advised Jessie to make a few mistakes so that the instructor wouldn't become suspicious.

Although Jessie and Collin knew each other from class, they weren't actually friends. Surprised that Collin had asked him to participate in the scheme, Jessie concluded that he simply wanted to involve someone else for "moral support." When he thought about it, Jessie found it ironic that Collin wanted *moral support* for stealing and cheating.

At first, Jessie didn't respond to the plan. He listened to Collin's rationalizations that the instructor was unfair and that knowing how to do word problems and algebra was totally irrelevant in the real world. They were in school to get a degree so they could get a good job and earn a lot of money. He contended that getting a decent grade in the course was the smart thing to do, and that cutting corners and "bending" the rules were simply the means to an end. "Nobody gives prizes to losers," Collin argued with great conviction. He was very persuasive, and Jessie said he would think about it.

That evening, Jessie had trouble sleeping. He was no angel, but he had never stolen a test. He certainly didn't want to flunk the course, but he also knew he wasn't a thief. He realized that despite the temptation, the risks were too great. He also realized that his conscience would bother him if he participated in the plan.

By the next morning, Jessie had made up his mind. He told Collin he would take his chances on the test and hope for the best. Collin was upset, but Jessie didn't particularly care.

Once he had made his decision, Jessie focused on doing all he could to pass the exam. He decided to go to the learning assistance lab and ask one of the tutors to help him. He planned on carefully reviewing each chapter in his textbook. He also planned to review his previous quizzes and tests so that he could identify the specific types of problems that were difficult for him. Jessie considered the worst that could happen: He would flunk the final. This would be a major setback, but he knew he could handle it. He would just have to take the course over again.

zooming in on the issues

Life-Altering Decisions

Reread the story and underline Jessie's five decisions. List each decision and predict the potential consequence. Circle **possible** or **probable** to indicate the likelihood of the consequence, and evaluate the wisdom of each choice.

Decision #1. *He would think about Collin's plan.*

Potential consequence: _____

○ possible   ○ probable

Evaluate this decision:

1	2	3	4	5	6	7	8	9	10
not smart				fairly smart					very smart

Decision #2. _____

Potential consequence: _____

○ possible   ○ probable

Evaluate this decision.

1	2	3	4	5	6	7	8	9	10
not smart				fairly smart					very smart

Decision #3.

Potential consequence:

○ possible   ○ probable

Evaluate this decision.

1	2	3	4	5	6	7	8	9	10

not smart   fairly smart   very smart

Decision #4.

Potential consequence:

○ possible   ○ probable

Evaluate this decision.

1	2	3	4	5	6	7	8	9	10

not smart   fairly smart   very smart

Decision #5.

Potential consequence:

○ possible   ○ probable

Evaluate this decision.

1	2	3	4	5	6	7	8	9	10

not smart   fairly smart   very smart

If Jessie had chosen to participate in Collin's scheme, what could have been the worst case outcome?

_____

_____

_____

Did Jessie have an honor code obligation to report Collin's plan to the instructor?

○ yes   ○ no   ○ not sure

zooming out on the issues

Making the Right Choice

Life would be much simpler if you could be absolutely certain of the outcome of every one of your decisions before you made it. Unfortunately, this isn't possible. Because you do not have a crystal ball, you cannot foretell the future with 100 percent accuracy. In many situations, however, you can significantly reduce the risk of making a flawed choice by carefully analyzing the situation, examining your options, and making reasonable predictions about the potential consequences of your actions.

You have undoubtedly made major decisions in your life, and you can expect to make more in the future. For example, you chose to go to college and continue your education. You may have also made other choices that involved changing jobs, moving to another city, or ending a relationship. Assuming you haven't already faced them, other major decisions loom in the future: getting married, having kids, and buying a house. If you haven't had to make these types of momentous choices yet, rest assured that you will one day.

When confronted with a potentially life-altering decision point, you can react in one of two ways: You can plunge ahead without careful deliberation and hope everything works out OK, or you can carefully weigh the pluses, minuses, and potential consequences of each option. The decision may involve:

- an opportunity (e.g., leaving a secure job for one at a start-up company)
- a medical risk (e.g., trying a drug offered to you at a party)
- a physical risk (e.g., climbing down a steep cliff without the necessary equipment)
- a financial risk (e.g., returning to school full-time and giving up a steady income)
- an emotional risk (e.g., ending a romantic relationship that isn't working)
- an educational risk (e.g., deciding to drop out of school)
- a career risk (e.g., refusing to accept a position in another state)

Feelings and intuition are certainly legitimate considerations, but when there are significant potential benefits or risks, reason and logic must also factor into the equation. Sometimes, you arrive at a decision point (or the "moment of truth") and it is crystal clear what your choice should be. Other times, you may struggle and experience doubts, anxiety, insecurity, and fear. Despite your best efforts to analyze the situation rationally and strategically and reduce the potential *downside risks* (benefits may be referred to as "upside"), you cannot be entirely certain of the outcome. All you can do is make your *best judgment* after careful analysis and reflection.

POWERHOUSE THINKING

Enhancing Your Decision-Making Abilities

- Identify important decision points.
- Analyze the situation and underlying issues critically and strategically.
- Carefully weigh the pluses and minuses of each option.
- Consider what you have already learned from handling similar situations.
- Predict potential positive and negative consequences.
- Do everything possible to reduce the risks of failure or damage.

A Critical Decision Point in Your Life

You can undoubtedly identify important decision points in your life. At the time, however, you may not have been consciously aware that you were at a critical decision-making juncture that could involve major potential consequences and have a profound impact on your future.

Think back and select one of the more meaningful decision points in your life and describe it below. For now, don't indicate the consequence(s) of your decision; simply describe the situation. For example, you might begin your anecdote, "When I was in the service, I had a drill instructor who . . ." Choose a real decision point that *significantly* affected your life.

A CRITICAL DECISION POINT IN MY LIFE

_____

_____

_____

_____

_____

_____

_____

_____

_____

_____

_____

_____

_____

_____

_____

_____

Underline the *decision point(s)* in your story. Sometimes, an important decision involves smaller decisions that are made along the way. If so, list each decision point below and underneath write down the consequence (if there was one). In the event that you made only one decision, leave the remaining spaces blank.

1. _____

   Consequence: _____

   _____

2. _____

   Consequence: _____

   _____

3. _____

Consequence: _____

_____

4. _____

Consequence: _____

_____

5. _____

Consequence: _____

_____

Of course, you already know the consequences of most of your past decisions. At issue is whether you could have predicted the possible or probable repercussions *before* you made these decisions, conceivably avoiding undesirable consequences.

An extreme example underscores the phenomenon of using your reasoning ability to foretell a likely outcome of a choice. The person who decides to shoplift can logically predict—if he or she is thinking clearly—the probable consequences; namely, being arrested and going to jail. Although a shoplifter may get away with stealing for a while, ultimately a hidden camera or a security officer is certain to catch the person in the act. Testing the odds in this way is the equivalent of playing Russian Roulette. Play the "game" long enough and eventually the hammer is going to fall on a chamber with a bullet in it.

People who have trained themselves to analyze the situation, underlying issues, and potential implications of their choices at critical decision points are *less likely* to make serious errors in judgment. They are also *more likely* to make astute choices that significantly increase the likelihood that they will attain their objectives.

In contrast, people who act impulsively and thoughtlessly at key decision points are more likely to experience repeated setbacks. By disregarding the potential consequences of their choices, they are, in effect, strolling mindlessly through a minefield. With every step, they risk disaster.

People who think strategically do not play Russian Roulette or walk through minefields. Acutely aware of the basic principles of cause and effect (i.e., each action triggers a reaction), they automatically consider the potential consequences of their choices, behavior, and attitudes *before* making important decisions.

Mastery: Practice Identifying Consequences

Predict the *possible* or *probable* consequences of the following decisions.

- You're having a party and decide not to invite certain friends because you do not believe they are compatible with the other people you've invited.

Consequence: _____

○ possible   ○ probable

■ A relative invites you to use his cabin by the lake. You invite six friends to join you, but you decide not to tell your relative of your plan.

Consequence: _____

○ possible   ○ probable

■ Your boss assigns you a project and wants you to work with someone you dislike. You ask your boss if you can do the project with someone else.

Consequence: _____

○ possible   ○ probable

■ You know that a good friend is having an extramarital affair. His wife has become suspicious and asks you if her suspicions are true. You tell the truth.

Consequence: _____

○ possible   ○ probable

■ You know that a good friend is having an extramarital affair. Her husband has become suspicious and asks you if his suspicions are true. To protect your friend, you lie.

Consequence: _____

○ possible   ○ probable

■ Your instructor asks you to wait in her office while she goes to a colleague's office. You can see that she's left the midterm exam on her desk. You start looking through it.

Consequence: _____

○ possible   ○ probable

■ You form a study group to prepare for a final exam, but you don't invite a friend who is taking the same course to join the group because he's not a good student.

Consequence: _____

○ possible   ○ probable

Mastery: Practice Identifying Causes

For each statement below, identify a possible cause that could create the scenario or consequence. There may actually be several possible causes for the effect. Choose one that makes sense.

■ You finally understand how to solve differential equations.

Cause: _____

■ You reduce the grammatical and spelling mistakes that you typically make on essays.

Cause: _____

▪ Your boss accuses you of having an "attitude."

Cause: _____

▪ Your grade on your history report is lowered one letter.

Cause: _____

▪ Your sociology instructor appears to get annoyed every time you ask a question in class.

Cause: _____

▪ You fail to take a course required for graduation.

Cause: _____

▪ The person interviewing you for a job gets very defensive.

Cause: _____

▪ Your English instructor tells you that you're an underachiever.

Cause: _____

▪ You don't study critically important material for your biology final.

Cause: _____

▪ Your chemistry instructor asks you to be her lab assistant next semester.

Cause: _____

Reviewing Cause and Effect

1. Define *decision point:* _____

_____

2. Evaluate the following decisions:

   ▪ Your seven-year-old child complains that an older child is teasing and hitting him. You look for the bully after school and threaten to have your child's older brother beat him up if he doesn't leave your son alone.

1	2	3	4	5	6	7	8	9	10
not smart				fairly smart					very smart

   Your reasons for making this evaluation: _____

   _____

   ▪ You bring an index card with key information from your notes with you when you take a test.

1	2	3	4	5	6	7	8	9	10
not smart				fairly smart					very smart

Your reasons for making this evaluation:

- You borrow $150 from the petty cash box at work to use over the weekend. You expect an income tax refund on Saturday, so you plan to return the money on Monday morning.

1	2	3	4	5	6	7	8	9	10

not smart   fairly smart   very smart

Your reasons for making this evaluation:

- You decide not to declare on your income tax return a bonus your boss paid you in cash.

1	2	3	4	5	6	7	8	9	10

not smart   fairly smart   very smart

Your reasons for making this evaluation:

What Would You Do?

Use your analytic and predicting skills to respond to the following hypothetical situations:

- You're driving to a ski cabin. It's snowing very hard, and the highway patrol closes the interstate because of blizzard conditions. You look at a map and discover a narrow road that snakes through the mountain and ends up near your destination. You have a four-wheel drive pickup and snow tires.

Your decision:

Consequence:

○ possible   ○ probable

- You're playing on the company basketball team. The referee calls you for a foul you feel you didn't commit, and you're angry. The referee is one of the managers in your division, and your boss answers to him.

Your decision:

Consequence:

○ possible   ○ probable

■ You're late for an important meeting. Your car starts making strange noises and a red light begins to flash on the instrument panel. The meeting is only five miles away.

Your decision: _____

_____

Consequence: _____

○ possible   ○ probable

■ You find a paper bag in the parking lot of a strip mall and discover the bag is filled with money. Inside is a deposit slip that indicates the money came from a fast-food restaurant in the mall. You don't think anyone has seen you pick up the bag.

Your decision: _____

_____

Consequence: _____

○ possible   ○ probable

■ You believe your nephew is taking drugs.

Your decision: _____

_____

Consequence: _____

○ possible   ○ probable

■ You see someone at work stealing office supplies. Only you and two other employees have access to the supply room. You're afraid that your boss may suspect you stole the supplies.

Your decision: _____

_____

Consequence: _____

○ possible   ○ probable

■ Your significant other (or best friend) wants to take a two-week vacation and rent a houseboat on a lake. You're going to school and not currently working. You have some money in savings, but you're not sure you'll be able to find a job right after you graduate.

Your decision: _____

_____

Consequence: _____

○ possible   ○ probable

- An acquaintance, who you suspect may be taking drugs, offers you $100 to hold onto a locked suitcase for a few days. He refuses to show you what's inside.

  Your decision: _____

  _____

  Consequence: _____

  ○ possible   ○ probable

- Your younger brother starts wearing gang colors and hanging out with gang members.

  Your decision: _____

  _____

  Consequence: _____

  ○ possible   ○ probable

PRESENT AND FUTURE THINKING

As you improve your "radar" for predicting the potential consequences of your decisions, you will discover that you are making fewer flawed choices. This reflex of thinking *before* you act will become an integral part of your *modus operandi.*

You may prefer to live in the *present* or the *"here and now,"* but if you think strategically, you will also deliberately factor *future* time considerations into your decision-making procedure. By automatically thinking about what could happen "down the road," you can avoid catastrophes and significantly improve your chances of success in virtually every area of your life. This capacity to connect present and future thinking is a key characteristic of thinking smart.

For Your Information

P eople who are not in the habit of thinking strategically often make important decisions without carefully analyzing the situation and their options and without considering the potential consequences of their actions. Responding impulsively, they frequently miscalculate. The consequences are predictable: marginal performance, repeated setbacks and failure, and diminished self-confidence.

People who think strategically respond very differently. They "use their head" when confronted with situations that require careful deliberation and planning. Because they consider the implications of their behavior *before* making decisions, they are generally able to avoid major setbacks. They realize that poor judgment produces *unpleasant consequences* and that strategic, analytical thinking and careful planning produce *pleasant consequences.*

When smart people do miscalculate, they assess what went wrong, make appropriate modifications in their behavior or thinking, and do everything possible to avoid repeating the mistake. Not-so-smart people have a very different *modus operandi*. Because they rarely consider potential outcomes, they may fail to allow adequate time to study for a test or write a report. They may chronically submit sloppy, illegible, incomplete, and inaccurate work. As they become habituated to making flawed decisions that result in marginal achievement, they are likely to lower their expectations and aspirations and resign themselves to minimal success in school and in life.

Analyzing and evaluating what's happening to you and around you and learning how to weigh the pluses and minuses of your options are skills that can be quickly mastered. The process is similar to mastering an athletic skill. Just as your reflexes and reactions when playing volleyball become increasingly efficient with effort and practice, so, too, will your reactions to problems and challenges become increasingly efficient with effort and practice. When faced with a key decision, you'll automatically ask, "What's going on here? What are my options? What are the potential implications of my decisions?" Once you get into the habit of thinking strategically, you will discover that you are consistently making wiser choices.

Strategic thinking will not eliminate all problems and errors, but it will reduce the frequency of serious miscalculations. Clearly, a critical distinction must be made between experiencing an *occasional* mistake, defeat, or miscalculation and experiencing a continual *pattern* of poor judgment and failure. This repetitive pattern can destroy self-confidence, cause you to abandon your goals, and result in your becoming resigned to the inevitability of failure or marginal achievement.

From time to time, *everyone* occasionally miscalculates. This is not necessarily indicative of a major problem. If, however, poor decisions are your standard operating procedure, there's reason for concern. People who are enmeshed in a self-sabotaging cycle often cannot see, or choose to disregard or deny, the obvious and predictable implications of their counterproductive choices, behaviors, and attitudes. For complex and difficult-to-identify psychological reasons, these people may have imprinted a psychological agenda that involves actually causing themselves to fail (see Figures 10.1 and 10.2 on page 235.)

People who continually sabotage themselves unconsciously feel *unworthy of success*. They then do everything they can to ensure that they don't succeed. Others make chronically poor choices for a different reason: They either have not assimilated basic cause-and-effect principles or they are intent on denying or disowning the predictable consequences of their flawed decisions and maladaptive behavior and attitudes.

Classic examples of self-sabotaging behavior include "forgetting" to study for exams and not allowing adequate time to proofread one's work for careless errors. Students who develop these counterproductive behaviors are on a collision course with the academic grading system and are likely to manifest the same maladaptive behavior and judgment patterns on the job. They may arrive late for work, fail to complete projects on time, appear unmotivated and lazy, display a negative attitude, and become actively or passively resistant to direction. By so doing, they cannot help but alienate their bosses and all but guarantee that they will be denied promotion or be fired.

By deliberately training yourself to be aware of your own pivotal role in determining the effects of your choices and behavior, you'll discover that life will throw you fewer "curve balls." You'll be able to anticipate the trajectory, time your swing, and slam the ball over the center field fence. This is one of the major payoffs for thinking and acting smart.

BEING SMART

OBJECTIVES

- Making certain that you are using strategic thinking and study skills
- Reviewing the principles taught in this program

Having a Master Plan

he semester would be over in one week, and Tamara couldn't wait for the summer vacation to begin. She felt exhausted, and she needed a nine-week break to recharge her batteries.

As she waited in line for dinner in the school cafeteria, Tamara reviewed what had happened during her first year in college. She had gotten off to a very shaky start, but all in all, it had been a good year. She had gotten all Cs her first semester and her G.P.A. was a 2.0. Although she hadn't yet received her grades for this semester, she was optimistic that she would get a B– in English, a B in math, a B in computer science, and an A– in world history. This would improve her G.P.A. to 2.7. If she continued to earn A's and B's next year, she had an excellent chance of graduating with a 3.3 or 3.4 G.P.A.

Tamara still felt confident she could complete her A.A. program in four more semesters. Because she was working 20 hours per week at the department store, this represented a major accomplishment, and she was proud of herself.

Tamara's plan was to continue working part-time and transfer into a four-year state college. Because the college was only 20 miles from her parents' home, she could save money by living at home and using public transportation to commute to school. She could get by without a car to cut down her expenses. On the weekends, she could borrow one of her parents' cars. If she did graduate with a 3.3 or 3.4 G.P.A., she was hoping to get a partial scholarship to help cover tuition and other living expenses.

Tamara's parents vividly remembered her struggles in high school, and they were ecstatic about the improvement in her schoolwork. She had barely graduated with a 2.1 G.P.A. Even her dad, who rarely gave compliments, had told her he was pleased with her effort. If she received the grades she wanted this semester, she and her boyfriend were going to celebrate by going to dinner at a good restaurant and buying concert tickets.

When Tamara returned home that evening after taking her last final, she looked at the sheet on which she had written her goals at the beginning of the school year. She was curious to see which goals she had attained and which goals had changed during the last nine months. Here is what it said:

MY LONG-TERM GOALS

1. Complete my A.A. degree with a minimum G.P.A. of 3.4.
2. Get accepted at the State University and receive a scholarship.
3. Earn a B.A. in marketing.
4. Get a promotion and a raise at work.
5. Save $1,000 for next year's school expenses.
6. Become an account executive at a top-notch advertising agency.
7. Get married and have two kids.
8. Own a red Italian sports car.
9. Own a big house near a lake.

MY SHORT-TERM GOALS

1. Get A's and B's in all my classes.
2. Save $750 for a summer vacation on Nantucket.
3. Paint my room.
4. Work out every day so I can get in shape for the beach this summer.
5. Read a book each month for pleasure.
6. Get along better with my younger sister.

Tamara had already achieved one of her long-term goals—she got the promotion and raise she wanted. She had also partially achieved another important goal: She now had more than $900 in the bank to cover next year's school expenses. She was certain she could stash away the remaining money if she was frugal during the summer.

As she scanned her list of goals, Tamara realized that she still wanted all of her other long-term goals, with one exception. She now wanted a silver German sports car. That goal, of course, would have to be put on the "back burner" for now. Getting married, having kids, and buying a big house by the lake would also have to wait. Knowing it would take time to attain these long-range goals did not bother her. She was, after all, only 20 years old. If she was patient, she was confident she would ultimately get what she wanted. Her priorities were to become an account executive, make a huge salary, settle down, marry Matthew, and have children when she was 30. She figured they would be able to afford the big house by the lake by the time she was 35, assuming she and Matthew carefully saved and invested their money after they married.

To see how well she had done, Tamara checked off her short-term goals. She was impressed. She had painted her room. The study skills program had paid off—she was now getting at least B's on tests. Unfortunately, she still had a ways to go as far as getting in shape. Because of her packed schedule, she wasn't getting to the gym as often as she wanted. She was also disappointed that she hadn't put money aside for her vacation. It was clear that she had to save virtually all of her money during the next two months to afford the trip to Nantucket that she and her best friend were planning for the end of August. As far as getting along with her 14-year-old sister was concerned, that was easier said than done. Samantha could be very inconsiderate and selfish. All Tamara could do was hope that the situation would improve and that Sam would become more tolerable. "Miracles can always happen," she assured herself.

Her plan to read one book for fun each month was a bust. She had only read two books during the entire year. There never seemed to be enough time to get everything done. She hoped she would have time during the summer to read more.

When Tamara objectively assessed all that she had achieved, she felt proud. She was already thinking about her goals for next year. A master's degree in business administration sounded nice. That would certainly speed up the timetable for buying the silver sports car and the house. Not bad for someone who had graduated high school with a 2.1 G.P.A.

on the issues

Taking Stock

Despite her shaky start in college, Tamara had begun to do much better academically. Evaluate Tamara's overall strategy for attaining her objectives.

1	2	3	4	5	6	7	8	9	10
not smart				fairly smart					very smart

Why did you reach this conclusion?

_____

_____

Evaluate Tamara's goal-setting procedure.

1	2	3	4	5	6	7	8	9	10
not smart				fairly smart					very smart

Why did you reach this conclusion?

_____

_____

Predict the likelihood of Tamara earning her B.A. degree.

1	2	3	4	5	6	7	8	9	10
poor				fair					excellent

Why did you reach this conclusion?

_____

_____

Predict the likelihood of Tamara attaining her professional goals.

1	2	3	4	5	6	7	8	9	10
poor				fair					excellent

Why did you reach this conclusion?

_____

_____

Predict the likelihood of Tamara attaining her personal goals.

1	2	3	4	5	6	7	8	9	10
poor				fair					excellent

Why did you reach this conclusion?

_____

_____

Do you have any ideas that might improve her chances of achieving her objectives?

1. _____

2. _____

3. _____

4. _____

5. _____

Drawing a Conclusion from the Evidence

Having read about Tamara's assessment of her first year in college, what specific conclusion can you draw from the information in the story? Using the _inductive method_, express in a well-crafted sentence what you have concluded. _Remember:_ You are summarizing the **point** of the story.

The point of Tamara's story: _____

_____

_____

_____

_____

Reviewing the Principles

t's time to review what you've learned about studying and thinking smart. The following inventory lists the skills you've practiced. Evaluate yourself by putting the appropriate number after each statement.

Final Study Wise Checklist

CODE: 0 = Never   1 = Sometimes   2 = Usually   3 = Always

_____   I use DIBS or the goal-setting method to analyze and solve problems.

_____   I establish goals.

_____   I set priorities.

_____   I develop logical strategies for achieving my goals.

_____   I consider the potential consequences of my attitudes and behavior.

_____   I think about how to avoid predictable problems.

_____   I analyze and learn from my mistakes and miscalculations.

_____ I am able to bounce back from setbacks.

_____ I create a study plan each semester.

_____ I develop and maintain my study schedule.

_____ I record my assignments.

_____ I make certain that I submit my completed assignments on time.

_____ I organize my materials.

_____ I create a good study environment that is conducive to concentration.

_____ I use power reading techniques, including mind-mapping when appropriate.

_____ I take effective notes from textbooks and lectures.

_____ I use the chewing-up information method.

_____ I carefully proofread my work to avoid careless errors.

_____ I make up practice tests.

_____ I identify important details and concepts in my textbook and lecture notes.

_____ I capitalize on my learning strengths and preferences.

_____ I use an individualized memorization method to help recall key information.

_____ I gear my studying to the types of questions my instructor typically asks.

_____ I study and review for tests with classmates who are serious students.

_____ I use relaxation techniques if I experience anxiety when taking a test.

_____ Total Points

If your total is *61 or better*, you deserve to be proud of yourself! You've clearly learned how to study and think smart. If your score is *below 61*, you should concentrate on improving your skills in the areas where you marked "0" or "1." A *perfect score of 75* indicates your brain is operating at peak efficiency, and your study procedures are excellent.

Handling Temptations

Life can throw many temptations at you. Some can be quite tantalizing: "Should I send a Valentine's card to that cute guy (or gal) I went out with last week?" Some can be exciting but potentially dangerous: "Should I skip the intermediate run and ski the advanced run with my friend even though I've only been skiing 10 times?"

Being able to think smart, effectively analyze situations, and anticipate potential consequences are powerful resources when you find yourself at one of life's crossroads. For example, imagine you have an important math exam on Friday. You plan ahead and schedule time to review the math formulas and the previous tests your instructor has given. Your strategy is to do a final intensive review on Thursday night. On the way home after school on

Thursday, your best friend tells you that a group of your friends are getting together that evening. You want to be with them, but you had planned on studying, and you want to do well on the exam. How should you handle the situation? Well, one option is to use DIBS.

Define: *I want to go to my friend's house after dinner, but I had planned to use this time to review for the math exam.*

Investigate: *I've had a rough day, and I deserve some rest and relaxation time. I promised myself I would make a final all-out effort to study for the exam.*

Brainstorm: *I could visit for a while and then come home early and study. I could keep to my original plan. I could get together with my friends another time.*

Select: *I will keep to my original plan and try to set something up with my friends tomorrow or over the weekend.*

Some temptations can be very difficult to resist and can pose a major dilemma. In many cases, the solution to the dilemma becomes evident when you review your goals and priorities and determine what is ultimately in your best interests. You could decide to socialize with your friends, or you could improve your chances of getting a good grade on the exam by adhering to your study plan and study schedule. The choice is yours, and the pivotal issue is what is most important to you. Dealing with temptations is certainly easier when you are clear about what you want, when you carefully analyze the situation, and when you consider the potential implications. If you think strategically, more often than not you will make the right decision.

Feeling Powerful and Confident

One of life's most satisfying pleasures is to attain an important personal goal after working conscientiously. The thrill can be as exhilarating as that experienced by an athlete who wins a medal at the Olympics. The athlete pits himself or herself and his or her abilities against the challenge and despite the intense competition, prevails.

Well, you, too, have pitted yourself against the challenge of learning how to think and study more productively, and ideally you have prevailed. You have worked hard, and you deserve the payoffs. You recognize the value of establishing goals and priorities and planning ahead. You know how to use your time efficiently. You consider in advance the potential consequences of your decisions, attitudes, and actions. You know how to solve complex problems by carefully defining the problem, analyzing the underlying issues, brainstorming, and selecting a possible solution to try (DIBS). You know how to study efficiently, take first-rate lecture and textbook notes, and prepare effectively for tests. You have every right to feel powerful, confident, and proud.

Although you have finished the *Study Wise* program, the process does not stop here. To derive the full benefit from the program, you must continue to use the skills you've learned and apply them whenever you confront a challenge, problem, or barrier. Unless you practice and apply the skills, you will forget them, and you may slip back into old, counterproductive habits.

You now possess powerful resources that are available whenever you need them. *These resources are your mind and your capacity to think and study effectively.* These capabilities will serve you throughout your life. Don't waste them. *Use your mind!* Think about what you're doing, consider what you want from life, and analyze your options. Weigh the pluses and minuses of your decisions. If you do so, you'll discover you can solve most of the difficult problems you encounter, attain your personal goals, and learn more efficiently. *You'll also discover you're on a track leading to achievement and a rewarding career.*

On Being Successful

The nuts and bolts of academic success are not mysterious. Students who think strategically figure out how they learn most efficiently. They capitalize on their natural learning strengths, develop their own personalized study system, organize themselves, carefully plan the necessary steps to do a first-rate job, budget their time, identify key information when studying, and devise effective and ingenious methods for understanding and remembering this information. They delight in their achievements and take pride in their work. Their success motivates them to continue achieving.

If you are determined to do well in school, you must intentionally and consistently apply the strategic thinking and studying methods you have learned in this program. You must:

1. establish personal goals (e.g., "I will become an attorney.")

2. set priorities (e.g., "I must do this before proceeding further.")

3. develop a practical plan for getting from point A to point B (e.g., "I better start studying for the midterm now!")

4. learn from mistakes (e.g., "I already tried this, and it didn't work. I need to use another approach.")

5. calculate the odds (e.g., "My chances of failing are greater if I choose this option.")

6. apply basic cause-and-effect principles (e.g., "If I follow this course of action, then I can predict the following probable consequences.")

7. bounce back from setbacks (e.g., "I'm going to have to start over, only this time I'll get it right!")

8. overcome obstacles (e.g., "Learning all of these formulas is a pain. I've got to figure out an effective way to get the job done.")

9. survive and prevail in a competitive world (e.g., "I have to impress this instructor because I am counting on her giving me a good letter of recommendation.")

THE A LIST: DISTINCTIVE TRAITS OF SMART STUDENTS

Smart students:

- select their targets (e.g., "I want an A on my science report.")
- identify the challenges and barriers that stand between them and their objectives (e.g., "I need at least a B+ on this essay to get a B in the course. I'm going to proofread it carefully so that I can avoid the spelling and syntax errors I made on the last essay.")
- examine and assess their options (e.g., "If I want to get a good grade in chemistry, I'll have to budget extra time for rewriting my lab reports.")
- do what has to be done to reach their goal (e.g., "I'll make sure I have the English paper finished by Tuesday so that I can begin to study for the algebra midterm.")

THE D AND F LIST: DISTINCTIVE TRAITS OF NOT-SO-SMART STUDENTS

Not-so-smart students:

- have little sense of purpose or direction
- are poorly motivated
- spend inadequate time studying
- study and learn passively
- fail to attend to the details
- do not take pride in their work
- repeat the same mistakes
- are disorganized
- forget to do assignments or submit them late
- do not pay attention in class

Rest assured that you now possess all of the thinking and studying tools you need to make the A list!

Some Final Words

Over the last several months, you've practiced and applied a wide range of thinking and study skills. You now possess a comprehensive assortment of powerful tools for handling specific challenges and for achieving success in school and in life.

It's easy to lose perspective about how much progress you have made and how many new skills you've acquired since you first began this program. The process of periodically "taking stock" and evaluating your attitudes and your actions will help you acquire greater self-awareness, self-discipline, and appreciation for your talents and insights.

This final chapter underscores once again the vital cause-and-effect link between strategic studying and thinking and academic achievement. In many respects, connecting the components of this program is similar to connecting the components of a new stereo system. Unless you hook up the wires and turn on the power, there will be no music.

This final chapter also reviewed the problem-solving, analytical thinking, and strategic study skills you've learned. The review has been a final tune-up designed to ensure mastery of the methods.

Like ice cream, achievement is habit-forming. Students who experience repeated success in school and in life feel powerful and productive. Convinced that they can attain their personal goals, prevail over challenges, and handle life's problems and setbacks, they recognize that they have control over their own destiny. These students are on a winning track, and their success cannot help but generate self-appreciation and self-confidence—two of the most potent personal resources people can possess.

If provided with effective instruction, sufficient practice, and productive study methods, virtually all motivated students can achieve at a level commensurate with their true potential. The objective of this program has been to provide you with the resources you need to prevail in a highly competitive world and to help you make effective study and thinking skills an integral part of your daily life. Your personal heat-seeking missiles are now armed, fully operational, and ready to fire. Simply select your target and pull the trigger.

REFERENCES

Dworetzky, Jeremy P. (1992). *Psychology*, 5th ed. Belmont, CA: Wadsworth/Thompson Learning.

Encyclopedia Americana (1995). Danbury, IL: Grollier.

Encyclopedia Britannica (1998). Chicago: Micropedia.

Gardner, Howard E. (1993). *Frames of Mind*. New York: Basic Books.

Greene, Lawrence J. (2001). *Guide to the Tutoring Process: Desk Reference to Learning Problems*. Chicago: World Book/TutorLink.

Greene, Lawrence J. (2002). *Roadblocks to Learning*. New York: Warner Books.

Hart, Lianne, and Weinstein, Henry. (Nov. 7, 2002). The Nation: Execution of Schizophrenic Killer Stayed, *Los Angeles Times*.

Vancouver Island Invisible Disability Association. (2003). *Learning Styles and Multiple Intelligences*, at www.ldpride.net/. Victoria, Canada: Author.

World Book Encyclopedia. (2001). Chicago: World Book.

Zametkin, A.J. et al. (Nov. 15, 1990). Cerebral Glucose Metabolism in Adults with Hyperactivity of Childhood, *New England Journal of Medicine*.

INDEX